THE BOOK OF
ESSEX CRICKETERS

THE BOOK OF
ESSEX
CRICKETERS

by David Lemmon

Breedon Books
Publishing Company
Derby

First published in Great Britain by
The Breedon Books Publishing Company Limited
44 Friar Gate, Derby, DE1 1DA.
1994

ISBN 1 873626 77 0

Printed and bound by Hillman Printers, Frome, Somerset.
Covers printed by BDC Printing Services Limited of Derby

Ridley's, The Essex Brewer, has much in common with the County Cricket Club: a great love of the County; representation of its wares throughout Britain; friends in many and widespread areas; and a dedication to quality in its product and its presentation.

Ridleys has over 150 years' history as a brewer in the heart of Essex, and so it is perhaps appropriate that we sponsor this cricket volume which itself portrays so much of the cricketing history of the Club.

Our links with Essex cricket are growing year by year; and just as we hope the players of years gone by enjoyed a Ridleys beer, we regard today's County players and staff as good friends and people in whose company we like to share a chat and a pint of ale.

We are delighted to be associated with this publication, and we hope it becomes a treasured reminder of heritage and tradition, two elements which are so important in our own sphere of activity, and fosters our excellent relationship with Essex County Cricket Club.

Nicholas Ridley
September 1994

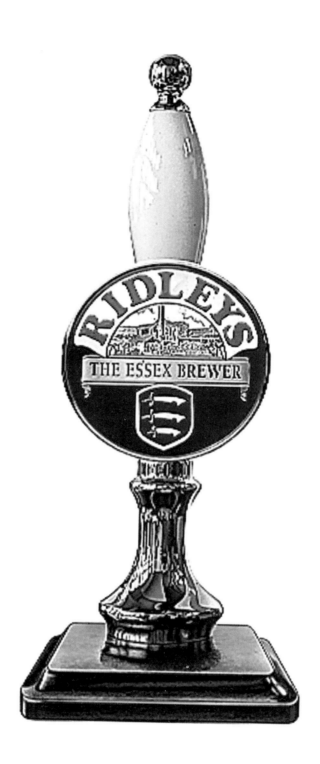

Author's Introduction

THIS book aims to celebrate one hundred years of Essex County Cricket Club in first-class cricket and in the County Championship. It is an attempt to give information about every cricketer who played a first-team game for the county and to provide the statistics of his career with Essex. It will be obvious that while the lives of men like Ken Farnes and Peter Smith have been fully documented there were several amateurs who made single appearances for Essex in the 1920s and early 1930s of whom little is known.

Through the assistance and kindness of friends, many gaps have been filled, but some remain, and, hopefully, this publication could prompt a response which would fill more gaps.

With regard to the statistics, the number of balls in an over has changed in the past one hundred years, from five to six to eight to six. In the bowlers' records, this is noted, and the number of five and eight-ball overs is listed *in addition to* the six-ball overs bowled.

This has been an absorbing study, bringing the joy of lives fulfilled and the sadness of lives blighted. The work would not have been possible without the many people who have been unstinting with their aid, and it would be most ungenerous not to thank them for their kindnesses.

Firstly, I must grant the debt that I owe to the late Leslie Newnham. It was he who compiled the list of first-class cricketers of Essex and their statistics for the official history of the county published in 1987. The statistics in this volume are based on those figures, and without his work my task would have been enormous, almost impossible. Anyone who studies or writes on Essex cricket will ever be in debt to Leslie Newnham.

Coupled with his name should go those of Philip Bailey, Philip Thorn and Peter Wynne-Thomas of the Association of Cricket Statisticians who compiled *Who's Who of Cricketers* (1993) which seems to me to be the single most important cricket reference ever to have been published. The research that went into this book in clarifying dates and places of birth and death was as meticulous as it must have been exhausting, and their work has lifted a great burden from my shoulders in the writing of this book.

As mentioned earlier, some questions still remain unanswered. No deaths have been recorded for three or four former Essex cricketers who, if still alive, would be among the oldest in the land. There are some who remain total enigmas, and any information would be gratefully received.

The work of the Association of Cricket Statisticians in so many fields is a constant source of wonder, and the publication of *First-Class Matches*, now complete until 1899, is a mighty contribution to the game and its history. With regard to more recent cricket, Les Hatton's *Sunday League Record Book, 1969 to 1992* has been an invaluable source of information and I am deeply grateful to Les for all his work in this field.

To Caroline Byatt and all at Essex County Cricket Club I owe much for information, patience and constant encouragement. There are many others who have been plagued by telephone calls at unusual hours bringing unusual requests. They have all responded with warmth and willingness. Among those who have been particularly helpful are Geoffrey Copinger, Trevor Bailey, the late Tom Pearce, Ron Lynch, Jack Leiper, Felsted School, C.Puckett, Mrs P.Jackson and John Polson.

Finally, I must single out my friend Brian Croudy of the Association of Cricket Statisticians who has been untiring in answering the numerous queries with which I have pestered him. My deepest thanks are due to him and to all those mentioned above.

David Lemmon
Leigh-on-Sea, Essex, 1994

Apart from the publications mentioned above, main reference has been made to *Cricket, A Weekly Record of the Game; The Cricketer; Wisden; Wisden Book of Cricket Records* (Bill Frindall) and to *Essex* (Charles Bray).

David Laurence ACFIELD

Born: Chelmsford, 24 July 1947.

David Acfield, like Ray East, was most unlucky not to win representative honours in the 1980s. Like all good off-spinners, he matured with age, and it was this maturity that eventually helped Essex to gather trophies. He turned the ball sufficiently to defeat the batsman, and he had an excellent command of length and flight.

Educated at Brentwood School, he made his county debut during his first year at Cambridge, 1966. He took 28 wickets for the university in that first season, but he did not get his blue until the following year. He did not get a bowl in his first match for Essex, against Kent at Westcliff, but he was ever-present for the rest of the season, finished with 25 wickets and created a most favourable impression.

David Acfield was a double blue at Cambridge, for he represented the university at fencing. He later became British sabre champion, and represented Great Britain at the Olympic Games in Mexico in 1968, and in Munich in 1972. He won a team Gold Medal at the Commonwealth Games in 1970.

Certainly, David Acfield's early days in the

Essex side were not easy ones, for these were the times of economic problems and a very small playing staff under the captaincy of Brian Taylor. This provided a challenging and productive atmosphere in which a young spinner could develop his art, and those years gave much of the substance on which later successes were built.

David Acfield was capped in 1970, toured East Africa with MCC 1973-74, and enjoyed his best season statistically, in 1981 when he captured 76 wickets. It was in this season that he returned his best bowling figures, 8 for 55 against Kent at Canterbury. He retired at the end of the 1986 season.

When playing cricket David Acfield had often spent the winter months teaching history in local comprehensive schools, but he later took up an appointment with Save and Prosper where he works alongside the former Kent cricketer Graham Johnson. For a period, he was a BBC cricket commentator, and his perception, wit and intelligence made him an outstanding observer of the game. Sadly, in a 'pop' era, the BBC probably considered him *caviar to the general* , and he is a grievous loss in this area.

He has maintained a range of interests outside cricket, notably a passion for Western films and for bird watching, and his dry humour and breadth of knowledge make him the best of companions.

Succeeding Doug Insole as chairman of the Essex Committee, he will continue to play a major role in the future of the club.

M	Inns	NOs	Runs	HS	Avge	Ct
378	353	191	1259	38	7.77	120

Overs	Mds	Runs	Wkts	Avge	Best	10/m	5/inn
9908.1	2790	23509	855	27.49	8/55	4	30

Sunday League

M	Inns	NOs	Runs	HS	Avge	Ct
125	48	32	81	9*	5.06	19

Overs	Mds	Runs	Wkts	Avge	Best	5/inn
815.2	74	3284	127	25.85	5/14	2

Benson and Hedges Cup

M	Inns	NOs	Runs	HS	Avge	Ct
22	4	3	15	6*	15.00	3

Over	Mds	Runs	Wkts	Avge	Best
142	18	502	14	35.85	2/14

Gillette Cup/NatWest Trophy

M	Inns	NOs	Runs	HS	Avge	Ct
12	8	7	8	4*	8.00	5

Overs	Mds	Runs	Wkts	Avge	Best
112.3	22	357	11	32.45	3/9

Stephen John Walter ANDREW

Born: Marylebone, London, 27 January, 1966.
A tall fast medium pace bowler, Stephen Andrew, in the words of his two county captains, Mark Nicholas and Graham Gooch, has the capacity for bowling the *wicket ball*. Brought up in Dorset, Andrew attended Milton Abbey School and Portchester Boys School, and it was at Milton Abbey that he first got his enthusiasm for cricket.

He made his debut for Hampshire in 1984 and played for them until 1989, joining Essex for the 1990 season. He made his debut for his new county against Middlesex at Lord's and captured the wickets of Roseberry, Gatting and Emburey. He finished the season with 43 Championship wickets, but at a rather high cost. He showed considerable improvement in 1991, but fell away in 1992, having injured his shoulder in a pre-season domestic accident.

At Old Trafford in 1993, he returned the best bowling figures of his career, 7 for 47 against Lancashire. In the winter of 1993-94, he played in South Africa. A moderate batsman, he caused a sensation by hitting a century in a 2nd XI match early in 1994.

M	Inns	NOs	Runs	HS	Avge	Ct
70	59	18	299	35	7.29	9

Overs	Mds	Runs	Wkts	Avge	Best	5/inn
1599.4	282	5457	150	36.38	7/47	3

Sunday League

M	Inns	NOs	Runs	HS	Avge
21	10	3	45	14	6.42

Overs	Mds	Runs	Wkts	Avge	Best
135.3	8	727	19	38.26	3/25

Nat/West Trophy

M	Inns	NOs	Runs	HS	Avge
3	1	1	1	1*	-

Overs	Mds	Runs	Wkts	Avge	Best
21	4	71	4	17.75	2/34

Francis APPLEYARD

Born: Clifton, Yorkshire, 26 September, 1905.
Died: Stevenage, Hertfordshire, 11 October 1971.
A farmer from Yorkshire who moved south in 1932, Francis Appleyard was bred in the tough school of northern cricket and won an immediate place in the Hertfordshire side when he moved to the county. He was a fast-

medium pace bowler who maintained an impeccable length, and he made over 60 appearances in the Minor Counties Championship, taking 193 wickets. He was an active member of the National Union of Farmers from the time of his arrival in Hertfordshire and made a significant contribution to the industry. During the last ten years of his life, he developed important agricultural interests in Western Australia.

In World War Two, he appeared regularly for the British Empire XI who toured the country playing matches to raise money for war charities. He took 165 wickets at under 11 runs each in these games.

He played ten games for Essex in 1946, and four in 1947. He took five wickets against Glamorgan at Chelmsford in his first season, but he was an amateur, unable to play regularly, and already past 40.

He joined the Forty Club in 1959, played for them regularly and was later chairman and president.

M	Inns	NOs	Runs	HS	Avge	Ct
14	19	11	55	15*	6.87	6

Overs	Mds	Runs	Wkts	Avge	Best	10/m	5/inn
334	86	817	19	43.00	5/14		1

Harold Arthur ARKWRIGHT

Born: Oswestry, Shropshire, 10 November 1872.
Died: Virginia Water, Surrey, 10 December, 1942.

A right-arm medium pace bowler and lower order right-handed batsman, Arkwright was in the Eton XI before going up to Magdalen College, Oxford, in the autumn of 1892. He played for Essex during his first year at university, 1893, but the county did not have first-class status at that time.

Of his 24 first-class matches, only three were for Essex, against Yorkshire in 1894, and against Hampshire and Derbyshire, when he took 3 for 25, in 1895. That was the year that he got his blue at Oxford and went with Mitchell's side to North America.

M	Inns	NOs	Runs	HS	Avge	Ct
3	6	-	35	19	5.83	2

Overs	Mds	Runs	Wkts	Avge	Best
38	9	109	4	27.25	3/25

(five-ball)

Claude Thesiger ASHTON

Born: Calcutta, India, 19 February, 1901.
Died: Caernarfon, Wales, 31 October, 1942.

The youngest of four sporting brothers, Claude Ashton captained Winchester at cricket, football, racquets and fives. An attacking middle-order batsman and a medium pace bowler, he won his blue as a freshman and succeeded his brothers Gilbert and Hubert as captain of Cambridge in 1923. Caught on a damp wicket, the light blues were bowled out twice in a day in the Varsity match, with Claude Ashton the only one to reach double figures in the first innings, but the university had enjoyed a good season under his leadership.

He made his debut for Essex during his first year at Cambridge, 1921, qualifying through residence at the family home in Wanstead. Towards the end of that season he played alongside his brothers, Gilbert and Hubert, in A.C.Mac-Laren's side which beat Warwick Armstrong's Australians, but his contribution to that famous victory was minimal.

In 1922, he played a Jessop-like innings of 110 not out for Essex against Middlesex at Leyton. He straight-drove the fast bowler Jack Durston for six and hit 24 fours. The following season he proved his worth as a bowler, taking 7 for 51 against Gloucestershire at Cheltenham. Six of his victims were clean bowled. The problem thereafter was that he was seldom available for county cricket although his appearances for Essex were spread over a period of 18 years.

The Ashtons' father had played soccer for Darwen, was an all-round sportsman and president of Essex in the 1930s. His sons outshone him in their versatility. Claude was a triple blue at Cambridge, hockey and soccer, at which he excelled, being his other sports.

He was a member of the famous Corinthians soccer side of the 1920s, playing at half-back or at forward. For the Amateurs against the Professionals in a match at Tottenham, he scored four times, and, more significantly, he hit a hat-trick for the Corinthians when the amateurs won 5-0 at Norwich City in the FA Cup of 1929. Claude Ashton played in 13 amateur internationals for England and won a full cap when he played centre-forward against Northern Ireland in October, 1925.

It was his work as a chartered accountant, however, which kept him away from the more time-consuming game of cricket for long periods. He did not play for Essex for five seasons, reappearing when modern county cricket was introduced to Brentwood at the end of May, 1934. Ashdown made a triple century, Ames 202 not out, and Kent declared at 803 for 4. Essex scored 408 and 203, and in the second innings Claude Ashton was unbeaten on 71. Later the same week, he hit 118 as Surrey were beaten by an innings. He ended the season at the top of the Essex batting averages, and he had not played for five years!

He last played in 1938, appearing against Lancashire at Ilford in May, scoring nine and 33 and taking a catch.

He joined the RAF at the outbreak of war and was commissioned, rising to the rank of Squadron Leader. He was killed on active service, and another noted cricketer, Roger Winlaw, Surrey and Cambridge, perished in the same plane.

M	Inns	NOs	Runs	HS	Avge	100s	Ct
89	146	10	3193	118	23.47	3	72

Overs	Mds	Runs	Wkts	Avge	Best	5/inn
888.5	149	2923	97	30.13	7/51	3

Sir Hubert ASHTON

Born: Calcutta, India, 13 February, 1898.
Died: South Weald, 17 June, 1979.
The third of four cricketing brothers, Hubert Ashton was in the Winchester XI for two years and captained the side in his second year, 1916. He went straight from school into the Royal Field Artillery and served until August, 1919. He won the Military Cross.

Going up to Trinity College, Cambridge,he hit 32 and 62 in his first match, against Essex, but he did not get another chance in the side for a month. When he was brought back into the team he scored 236 not out against Free Foresters, which, at the time, was a record both for Fenner's and for Cambridge. He was to win his blue in each of his three years at university, and, in each of those seasons he

was to head the batting averages and to play for the Gentlemen at Lord's. Like his brothers Gilbert and Claude, he captained Cambridge in his last season.

He won blues for soccer and hockey at Cambridge, and he was also to play soccer for Clapton Orient and Bristol Rovers. In spite of his achievements on the sports field at Cambridge, Hubert Ashton is best remembered as a member of A.C.MacLaren's England XI which beat Warwick Armstrong's Australians at Eastbourne in 1921. He and Aubrey Faulkner added 154 for the fifth wicket in MacLaren's side's second innings, and the all amateur XI went on to win a famous victory. The match passed into cricket folk lore, and, although at this distance its importance would seem to have been greatly exaggerated, those who played in MacLaren's side became gods of

the game for the rest of their lives. That match was, in fact, the high point of Hubert Ashton's career although he had hit a century in the Varsity match earlier in the summer and was to declare the Cambridge innings closed the following year when he was on 90. He first played for Essex in 1921, but, although he assisted the county until 1939, he appeared in only 21 matches.

In 1922, he went to Burma and worked for eight years on the staff of the Burmah Oil Company. During that time, he played for the Europeans in India, but he returned to England in 1930 to take up a senior executive position with Burmah Oil before becoming an underwriter at Lloyd's in 1936. He was able to play cricket only infrequently, and his form was never to reach the heights of his university days, but there are those close to the game who insist that he was asked to lead England in Australia, 1932-33, and that when he declined Jardine was given the task. He was president of MCC in 1960, and chairman of Essex, 1946 to 1951. He was also president of Essex from 1949 to 1970.

An unsuccessful candidate in the General Election of 1945, he won Chelmsford for the Conservatives in 1950 and held the seat until 1964. He served as Parliamentary Private Secretary to R.A.Butler. Ironically, he was married to Margaret Gaitskell, sister of the Labour leader.

A county councillor for a period, Hubert Ashton farmed at Ingatestone, was a church commissioner and served Essex well.

M	Inns	NOs	Runs	HS	Avge	Ct
21	35	1	819	90	24.08	21

Captain Percy ASHTON, MC

Born: Calcutta, India, 27 February, 1895.
Died: Bigsbury-on-Sea, Devon, 18 September, 1934.

One of the famous Ashton brotherhood, Percy was educated at Winchester, but, although he found a place in the soccer side, he did not win a spot in the cricket XI. He went straight from school into the Army, rose to the rank of captain, lost an eye and was awarded the Military Cross.

A fast medium pace bowler and a useful batsman, he played in one first-class match, for Essex against Middlesex, at Leyton, in 1924. In spite of his handicap, he played two useful innings at number eight and captured the wicket of 'Patsy' Hendren.

M	Inns	NOs	Runs	HS	Avge
1	2	-	52	31	26.00

Overs	Mds	Runs	Wkts	Avge	Best
12	1	55	1	55.00	1/55

Alfred Victor AVERY

Born: New Beckton, 19 December, 1914.

'Sonny' Avery was one of the most solid and reliable of opening batsmen and a smart fielder. When he joined Essex he was looked upon primarily as a slow left-arm bowler, yet he did not bowl on the occasion of his debut, against Surrey at The Oval, June, 1935. He batted number nine and scored 28 not out and 0. Within four years he was opening the innings and topping the county batting averages.

In the years immediately after World War Two, his right-handed batting provided an admirable foil for the more flamboyant approach of 'Dickie' Dodds. They were a most successful opening pair, and their partnership of 270 against Surrey at The Oval in 1946 remains a county record.

Avery enjoyed his best season in 1948 when  he scored 1,890 runs, but he was handicapped by injury and retired after the 1954 season. His final appearance was against Gloucestershire in June of that year, and he made 20 and 0. By coincidence, he was to become the Gloucestershire coach in 1957 and 1958.

It was as a coach that he spent his years after leaving Essex. Initially, he worked at the Ilford Indoor Cricket School and at Forest School. In 1960, he was appointed groundsman and coach at Monmouth School. He played occasionally for Monmouth Town CC, and later concentrated on coaching and on general administration until his retirement in 1979.

A fine soccer player, he played centre-forward for Leyton in the FA Amateur Cup Final, 1936-37, and he went on a world tour with Islington Corinthians the following winter.

M	Inns	NOs	Runs	HS	Avge	100s	Ct
268	453	35	14045	224	33.60	25	119

Overs	Mds	Runs	Wkts	Avge	Best
203.5	41	627	9	69.66	1/11

7 (eight-ball)

George White AYRES

Born: Thames Ditton, Surrey, 5 July 1871.
Died: Riverside Park, Feltham, Surrey, 28 August 1934.

George Ayres graduated from the Thames Ditton village side and the Kingston club to play for Surrey. He carried his bat for 53 not out against Hampshire on the occasion of his debut, but he was unable to command a regular place in a very strong side although he did go to South Africa with W.W.Read's side in 1891-92. A right-handed batsman and occasional bowler, Ayres was a brilliant fielder. His first-class career for Surrey was from 1892, two years after his debut against Hampshire, until 1896. He played one season for Essex in 1899, but he was a cricketer who never really fulfilled his promise.

M	Inns	NOs	Runs	HS	Avge	Ct
12	17	1	263	83	16.43	12

Overs	Mds	Runs	Wkts	Avge	Best
55.4	19	139	5	27.80	1/2
(five-ball)					

Jack Arthur BAILEY

Born: Brixton, London, 22 June 1930.
Jack Bailey was educated at Christ's Hospital School and played club cricket for Buckhurst Hill and for The Grange in Edinburgh where he was studying and teaching. An all-round sportsman, he played rugby, he bowled right-arm fast medium pace and used his height to very good advantage.

Jack Bailey first appeared for Essex in 1953. A teacher, he played against Nottinghamshire at Southend in the August holiday. Six overs in the first innings brought him no reward, but in the second, he took 7 for 32, capturing his last four wickets for one run. It was an astonishing debut, and he maintained his form impressively, finishing the season with 25 wicket at 13.04 runs each from only four matches.

The following season, he took 69 wickets in 27 Championship matches and was awarded his county cap. His form lapsed in 1955, but he went up to Oxford that autumn and won his blue as a freshman the following summer. He was in the university side against Cambridge in each of his three years at Oxford and led the team in 1958 when he also played for the Gentlemen against the Players at Scarborough.

At the end of the season, he made three appearances for Essex and took 6 for 49 in the victory over Somerset at Taunton. He did not appear for Essex again although he did play in occasional first-class matches until 1968.

By that time, he had become Assistant Secretary of MCC, having previously worked as a journalist. He became Secretary of MCC in June 1974, and held the post until January 1987, when he retired in rather controversial circumstances.

He reverted to journalism, working for *The Times*, and he wrote his autobiography as well as a most interesting study of his former county colleague Trevor Bailey.

M	Inns	NOs	Runs	HS	Avge	Ct
71	88	24	295	27*	4.60	49

Overs	Mds	Runs	Wkts	Avge	Best	5/inn
1782.4	385	4553	198	22.99	7/32	11

Trevor Edward BAILEY

Born: Westcliff-on-Sea, 3 December 1923.
Trevor Bailey was one of the great all-rounders of English cricket. He played a mighty role in England's rise from the immediate post-war depths to the recapturing of the Ashes in 1953 and the subsequent eminence in world cricket. For Essex, only Morris Nichols and Peter Smith took more wickets, but he scored over 5,000 runs more than than either of them. First he was Assistant Secretary, than Secretary of the County, 1955 to 1965, and he captained the side from 1961 to 1966.

He learned his early cricket from Denys Wilcox at Alleyn Court School, and, like Wilcox, he went to Dulwich. His exceptional talent as a batsman was soon recognised, and he was in the XI at the age of 14. Later he was accepted as an all-rounder as his pace bowling became more controlled, and in his second season as captain, his last at school, 1942, he scored 635 runs and took 66 wickets at 6.16 runs each, topping both the batting and the bowling averages. It was the fourth season in succession that he had topped the batting averages, and he was already becoming well known to the public who watched war-time matches at Lord's.

Bailey joined the Royal Marines as soon as he left school. Service abroad kept him out of the Victory Test series in 1945, but he made his first-class debut at Lord's before the end of that season, playing for Under-33 against Over-33. He was demobilised in 1946, and he first played for Essex in May of that year, opening both the batting and the bowling against Derbyshire at Ilford. He had taken up a teaching post at Alleyn Court and was available only in the school holidays.

He went up to Cambridge, got his blue as a freshman in 1947, topped the bowling averages and hit centuries against Yorkshire and Gloucestershire, both good sides at that time. For Essex, in the vacation, he scored 630 runs and took 25 wickets. He was top of the batting averages and hit 205 in 260 minutes against Sussex at Eastbourne.

He was less successful in 1948 , but with England being routed by Bradman's Australians, Trevor Bailey was now spoken of as the fast bowler who would lead his country on the road to recovery. He began to answer the call in 1949, bowling quickly in the series against New Zealand, the first four of his 61 Tests, taking more wickets than anyone else and hitting 93 in the Second Test. He fielded brilliantly close to the wicket, and he was the first man to reach the 'double'. In all, he was to complete this feat on eight occasions. On three occasions, he did the 'double' in Essex matches alone. In 1959, he took 100 wickets and scored 2000 runs, the only cricketer to have achieved this record in post-war cricket.

In August 1949, at Clacton, Bailey took all ten Lancashire wickets at a personal cost of 90 runs. He became only the second Essex bowler to take all ten wickets in an innings, but his side still lost by an innings. He had something of a reputation initially of being an angry young man, reacting strongly to dropped catches and lapses in the field. He says that Tom Pearce's geniality and constant good humour cured him of this, but he never lost his competitive edge.

Strains and niggling injuries marred his 1950 season, but he performed the hat-trick when he ended Glamorgan's innings at Newport in August. Essex still lost by an innings. That winter he went on his first tour of Australia, and he was one of the few successes of Freddie Brown's team.

Len Hutton took over the England captaincy, and Trevor Bailey became an integral part of the plan to wrest back the Ashes from Australia. At Lord's, in 1953, he batted 257 minutes for 71 and added 163 with Willie Watson. This was one of the classic rearguard actions of Test cricket. The partnership saved the match and Bailey was a national hero. He played another fine rearguard innings at Headingley and then bowled six overs of leg theory for nine runs to thwart Australia just as they seemed set for victory. An innings of 64 in the victorious final Test completed a memorable series.

Trevor Bailey went to West Indies in 1953-54 as Hutton's vice-captain. Captain and vice-captain were instrumental in drawing the series and bringing England's first victory at Kingston, Jamaica. Hutton hit a double century, and Bailey had the remarkable first innings figures of 7 for 34. The England captaincy should have been his after Hutton retired, but he was not forgiven for his ventures as a journalist and the loss was England's. Years later, a computer was fed information and statistics for an imaginary Test match, and the computer named Bailey as England's captain.

There was success in Australia with Hutton's side in 1954-55, success at home to West Indies and an outstanding Test career of 2290 runs and 132 wickets which lasted until Melbourne in February 1959. Ironically, he was to enjoy the best season of his career the following summer, and he was to play for Essex until 1967.

Born in Westcliff, he played for Westcliff CC, and he has never lived out of the area. His devotion to Essex cricket has been unwavering. The 'Barnacle' of Test cricket was rarely seen in the county game where he could bat with flair, characteristically going down on one knee and hoisting the ball over square-leg. He was never a selfish cricketer. He batted and bowled as the occasion demanded. He appeared in 682 first-class matches, and 482 of them were for Essex. He was a colossus for the county.

Wickets, Catches and The Odd Run, the title of his delightful autobiography, reveals only part of his contribution to the county club, for it was he who was responsible for borrowing the money from Warwickshire interest free which enabled Essex to buy the Chelmsford headquarters; and it was he who discovered an unknown cricketer named Keith Boyce. It was he who led Essex through a difficult period and who brought men like Jim Laker to Essex to encourage youngsters and bring interest in the county. He was one of the first to organise coaching courses, and courses for coaches; and he was a founder director of the Ilford Cricket School from which Essex cricket has benefited enormously.

He relinquished the captaincy in 1966, but played a few games under Brian Taylor in

1967. His last appearance was against Middlesex at Lord's in August that year.

An all-round sportsman, he got his blue for soccer at Cambridge and played in an FA Amateur Cup Final for Walthamstow Avenue. He also played for Leytonstone and was a director of Southend United for whose reserve team he appeared. After retiring from first-class cricket he continued to play for Westcliff and has remained active in the local tennis club.

He has had many business ventures. He ran a wholesale toy business, had an interest in sports shops, was employed by a large public relations company, runs his own smaller public relations company, masterminded the Wrigley's Soft Ball Cricket tournament, and is a director of Essex Radio. Most importantly, he has worked consistently in the media.

For 20 years he wrote on cricket and soccer in the *Financial Times*, and he has been a regular contributor to *The Daily Telegraph* and *The Cricketer*. He is the author of several books and he is the longest serving member of the *Test Match Special* team. As an after dinner speaker he is much in demand.

His strength as a commentator and a journalist is that he is forthright. He has never been afraid to give a judgement nor offer an opinion.

A devoted family man, he has retained a zest for life and a generosity of spirit which make him the most amiable of companions. His place in the history of cricket is secure. In 1994 he was awarded the CBE in the Queen's Birthday Honours.

M	Inns	NOs	Runs	HS	Avge	100s	Ct
482	774	152	21460	205	34.50	22	320

Overs	Mds	Runs	Wkts	Avge	Best	10/m	5/inn
14415.5	3599	35042	1593	21.99	10/90	10	91

Gillette Cup

M	Inns	NOs	Runs	HS	Avge	Ct
7	7	1	93	38	15.50	3

Overs	Mds	Runs	Wkts	Avge	Best
84	12	290	11	26.36	4/37

Richard Kenneth BAKER

Born: Gidea Park, 28 April 1952.
Educated at Brentwood School, Richard Baker was the regular second team wicket-keeper when he was called upon to deputise for Brian

Taylor against Kent at Maidstone in July 1972. He performed admirably in a match ruined by rain.

He got his blue at Cambridge the following season and again in 1974. He also won a blue for soccer.

M	Inns	NOs	Runs	HS	Avge	Ct
1	1	1	14	14*	-	2

Arthur Ernest BANFIELD

Born: Hackney, London, 28 January 1897.
Died: Raynes Park, Surrey, 3 January 1972.
One of many amateurs who assisted Essex in the years after World War One, Banfield played as a bowler in the match against Surrey at Leyton in 1921. He took the wickets of Bill Hitch and William Abel.

M	Inns	NOs	Runs	HS	Avge
1	2	1	0	0*	0.00

Overs	Mds	Runs	Wkts	Avge	Best
17	3	62	2	31.00	2/62

Arthur Norman BARBER

Born: West Ham, 23 November 1898.
Arthur Barber was on the Essex staff as a professional, a medium pace bowler and lower order batsman. In June 1925, he appeared against Oxford University at Chelmsford, and against Sussex at Colchester, but he had little success.

M	Inns	NOs	Runs	HS	Avge	Ct
2	4	-	46	31	11.50	2

Overs	Mds	Runs	Wkts	Avge	Best
25	4	76	1	76.00	1/42

Gordon BARKER

Born: Bramley, Yorkshire, 6 July 1931.
Once described in the press as 'the sad looking man with the happy disposition', Gordon Barker had played cricket in the Bradford League and was recommended to Essex while completing his national service. Insole and Bailey were impressed with what they saw of the young batsman in an Army game at Richmond in Yorkshire and invited him to play for Essex against the Canadians at Clacton in August 1954.

Opening the innings with Dodds, Barker

was caught behind off the West Indian pace bowler Padmore for 0, but in the second innings, he hit 107 not out and shared a second wicket stand of 166 with Paul Gibb. Qualified to play in the Championship in 1955, he scored 1000 runs in his first full season, and he was to reach four figures in each of his first ten seasons with the county.

Initially a carefree batsman with some lavish strokes, he formed a most exciting opening partnership with 'Dickie' Dodds. As he matured, he eliminated some of his more exotic shots, but he never lost his entertainment value. His play was built on a sound defensive technique, and his cutting and hooking were particularly strong.

Short and slight of build, neat in appearance, he was nimble, eager and quick in all he did and he excelled in the field, notably at cover point. He hit a century before lunch against Kent in 1962, but Doug Insole considers that the finest innings he ever saw Barker play was against Derbyshire at Derby in 1964. Essex were set to make 237 in two and three quarter hours to win the match, and they reached their target with 15 minutes to spare thanks mainly to Barker's 121 not out. He hit 18 fours in 'an innings which defied description in terms of its brilliant execution.'

Vice-captain to Trevor Bailey for a period, Gordon Barker played for Essex from 1954 until 1971, scoring 82 in his last innings, against Hampshire.

A fine all-round sportsman, he played soccer for Bishop Auckland and made 57 appearances as a creative forward for Southend United between 1954 and 1958. He scored nine times.

He became coach and groundsman at Felsted School and helped to bring on many good players like Pringle and Knight. A man of happy temperament, he is often to be seen at Essex matches. Had he had a little more confidence in his own ability, he must surely have won representative honours. As it was, he played for MCC on several occasions.

M	Inns	NOs	Runs	HS	Avge	100s	Ct
444	797	46	21895	181*	29.15	30	232

Overs	Mds	Runs	Wkts	Avge	Best
73.1	19	200	5	40.00	2/34

Sunday League

M	Inns	NOs	Runs	HS	Avge	Ct
42	42	8	1127	87*	34.15	12

Gillette Cup

M	Inns	NOs	Runs	HS	Avge	Ct
14	14	-	309	46	22.07	2

Overs	Mds	Runs	Wkts	Avge	Best
11	-	64	-	-	

James David BARNFARTHER

Born: Leicester, 22 July 1896.
Died: Grays, 21 August 1957.

James Barnfarther learned most of his cricket at Southampton Grammar School where he once bowled C.B.Fry. The great all-rounder was not amused. Barnfather served in the last years of World War One and was decorated. Like so many of his generation he found himself jobless, but he determined to study for the building industry. It was while he was studying building and engineering in order to qualify as a surveyor that he played as a professional for Essex.

A right-arm fast-medium pace bowler compared in later years to Alec Bedser, he had the ability to swing the ball both ways, and although he batted in the lower order, he was a competent batsman. In 1924, he appeared in five matches for Essex, and, in the last game of the season, he took the last six wickets of the Leicestershire first innings for 32 runs.

He was offered a contract by the county club which he declined, preferring to follow his career in the building trade. It is interesting to note that had Barnfather accepted the contract, Essex would have almost certainly released Morris Nichols whose bowling only showed signs of flourishing late the following season.

Barnfather played senior amateur soccer. He was a left back who anticipated modern trends by moving forward when his side was in search of a goal. He was offered professional terms by Arsenal, but again he declined. His father, a lay preacher, was opposed to his son being a professional sportsman, seeing such a career as both ill-paid and precarious.

James Barnfather enjoyed a successful career and during World War Two, working for Lovatt's, was in charge of building the ICI extension at Huddersfield. During this period, he played for North Leeds in the Leeds League, and he appeared in many of the charity matches organised by Jack Appleyard. His duels with John Lawrence who played for Bingley and later went to Somerset became legendary.

M	Inns	NOs	Runs	HS	Avge	Ct
5	5	3	50	28*	25.00	1

Overs	Mds	Runs	Wkts	Avge	Best	5/inn
110.5	18	355	13	27.30	6/32	1

Patrick Lindsay BARROW

Born: Plaistow, Bromley, Kent, 22 January 1893.
Died: Adstock, Buckinghamshire, 7 May 1974.
Educated at Wellington, Patrick Barrow played for Dorset from 1914 to 1920, and made his one appearance for Essex in 1922. He played in the first match of the season, against Combined Services and took the wicket of Captain Jameson. In Minor Counties cricket, Barrow was a useful left-handed batsman.

A man of many talents, he played ice hockey for England, and he was a composer of some repute.

M	Inns	NOs	Runs	HS	Avge
1	1	-	0	0	0.00

Overs	Mds	Runs	Wkts	Avge	Best
12	2	43	1	43.00	1/21

John Francis BAWTREE

Born: Witham, 26 November 1873.
Died: Great Totham, 25 March 1938.
A good, all-round club cricketer, John Bawtree was in the Haileybury XI of 1891, and he first played for Essex when they entered the county championship in 1895. He hit 47 on the occasion of his debut, against Somerset at Taunton, and he also appeared against Derbyshire and Hampshire. He found it hard to force his way into a side that was strong in

batting and had Kortright, Pickett, Mead and Bull to do the bowling, and he did not play after two more matches in 1896.

M	Inns	NOs	Runs	HS	Avge	Ct
5	9	1	96	47	12.00	5

Overs	Mds	Runs	Wkts	Avge	Best
21	4	66	2	33.00	1/16
(five-ball)					

Michael John BEAR

Born: Brentwood, 23 February 1934.
Michael Bear joined Essex in 1949, but he did not make his first-class debut until 1954 when he made one against Derbyshire at Chesterfield. He did not establish a regular place in the side until 1957 when he hit his first century, and the following year he was

awarded his county cap.

A left-handed batsman of cultured style, he had an abundance of strokes and was a delight to watch. He quite frequently opened the innings, and he was one of the first batsmen in first-class cricket to play in contact lenses. Mike Bear played soccer for Romford, and his fleetness of foot was much in evidence on the cricket field. In spite of the quality of his batting, he will be remembered most for his outstanding fielding. He was the finest outfielder of his generation, and it is doubtful that the game has seen a better man running around the boundary, gathering the ball and throwing in one movement. Bear's fielding had a beauty of its own.

He coached in Argentina in the winter of 1958-59, and in 1960-61, he coached Canterbury in New Zealand and played some non-first-class cricket for the MCC touring side. A confident and integrated batsman himself, he was an encouraging coach, a man always full of laughter and fun.

He scored 1000 runs in a season on four occasions and had an outstanding year in 1968 when he hit 1833 runs. His highest score came against Glamorgan at Cardiff the following season, but, troubled by injury, he was forced to retire at the end of the 1968 season. His last game was against Lancashire at Leyton. In a match ruined by rain he made four.

He took up an appointment as a sales and public relations officer for a firm which imported timber and plastic, and in 1973, he bought and ran a hotel in Paignton, Devon. He was forced to sell the hotel in 1979 when he became ill. First treated for intrinsic asthma, and then, more seriously, he underwent open heart surgery because of a condition brought about by the use and misuse of powerful drugs in an attempt to cure his asthma. Restored to health, he and his wife ran a small supermarket.

Mike Bear assisted the Lord's Taverners and the Rothman's Cavaliers until he moved to Devon.

M	Inns	NOs	Runs	HS	Avge	100s	Ct
322	562	44	12564	137	24.25	9	113

Overs	Mds	Runs	Wkts	Avge
16.2	2	53	-	-

Gillette Cup

M	Inns	NOs	Runs	HS	Avge	Ct
8	8	-	177	71	22.12	2

Brian Henry BELLE

Born: Woodford Green, 7 April 1914.
A product of Forest School, Brian Belle made his debut for Essex as a right-handed middle order batsman while up at Oxford in 1935. He scored 33 and ten against Middlesex at Ilford, and he went with the side for their next match

against Yorkshire at Huddersfield. This was the occasion of the famous innings victory by Essex when Yorkshire were bowled out by Read and Nichols for 31 and 99. Belle played a most important part in the victory, scoring 63 and sharing a partnership of 174 in three hours with Nichols after Essex had lost their first five wickets for 65 runs.

He got his blue in 1936 and assisted Essex in the summer holidays in that year and again in 1937. He went with the Oxford and Cambridge side to Jamaica in 1938-39, and he did not play for Essex after 1937. He ran a preparatory school in Ipswich and played for Suffolk from 1939 until 1957.

Belle was an Army officer during World War Two.

M	Inns	NOs	Runs	HS	Avge	Ct
26	42	3	776	63	19.89	20

Charles Edward BENHAM

Born: East Ham, 24 June 1880.
Died: Broxburn, West Lothian, Scotland, 13 December 1961.

Seen as a useful recruit to the county side in 1904, Charles Benham was a right-handed batsman and a right-arm fast bowler. In 1908, he took 30 wickets and scored 404 runs in first-class cricket, but the high expectations were never realised. He left Essex and took up a professional appointment in Scotland for whom he played in 1912. His son also played for Scotland, in 1949.

M	Inns	NOs	Runs	HS	Avge	Ct
57	80	11	985	65*	14.27	31

Overs	Mds	Runs	Wkts	Avge	Best	5/inn
717.4	133	2176	65	33.47	7/60	4

Reverend Maurice Berkley

Born: Navestock, 6 September 1872.
Died: Bangor, Caernarvonshire, 9 August 1947.

Educated at Fettes, Maurice Berkley appeared in the trial matches at Oxford, but he did not appear in a first-class match. A slow right-arm bowler, he appeared twice for Essex during his last season at university, 1894. On the occasion of his first-class debut, against Yorkshire at Halifax, he took 6 for 50, dismissing Wainwright and Mounsey with his first two deliveries. He accounted for Charlesworth in the second innings of a match attended by very few people, and he later played against Leicestershire. Son of the Vicar of Navestock, he took Holy Orders and was lost to cricket.

M	Inns	NOs	Runs	HS	Avge	Ct
2	3	1	6	5	3.00	2

Overs	Mds	Runs	Wkts	Avge	Best	5/inn
27.3	3	103	7	14.71	6/50	1

(five-ball)

Frank Denis BILLHAM

Born: Georgetown, British Guiana, 27 September 1896.
Died: Sudbury, Suffolk, 16 November 1980.
Frank Billham was a noted club cricketer with Ilford for many years. He was a slow left-arm bowler and played for Essex against Nottinghamshire and Sussex in 1924, but failed to take a wicket. Very active in club cricket, he was on the Council of the Club Cricket Conference and was an honorary vice president.

M	Inns	NOs	Runs	HS	Avge
2	3	1	12	12*	6.00

Overs	Mds	Runs	Wkts	Avge
23	1	72	-	-

David Jonathan Peter BODEN

Born: Eccleshall, Staffordshire, 26 November 1970.
Having taken a diploma in Business Studies at Stafford College of Further Education and learned his cricket with Stone in the North

Staffordshire and South Cheshire League, David Boden made his first-class debut for Middlesex against Oxford University in 1989. A fast-medium pace bowler, he enjoyed an excellent baptism, taking 4 for 11.

He joined Essex in 1990. In 1992, he played against Cambridge University at Fenner's, and in 1993, he played against both Kent and Middlesex as well as appearing in four Sunday League games.

M	Inns	NOs	Runs	HS	Avge	Ct
3	3	-	10	5	3.33	1

Overs	Mds	Runs	Wkts	Avge	Best
56	9	258	3	86.00	2/118

Sunday League

M	Inns	NOs	Runs	HS	Avge	Ct
4	2	-	13	7	6.50	2

Overs	Mds	Runs	Wkts	Avge	Best
34	2	162	4	40.50	2/48

John Wardell BONNER

Born: Mile End, London 3 April, 1869.
Died: East Cliff, Bournemouth, 26 November, 1936.
Business commitments prevented John Bonner from giving much time to cricket, and he played as an amateur during the first three years of Essex's entry into the County Championship. Educated at Forest School, he was very consistent in his first season and scored 59 against Derbyshire at Derby in August. A reliable right-handed batsman in a strong side, he showed immense promise, but he played little after that first season, 1896.

M	Inns	NOs	Runs	HS	Avge	Ct
16	27	1	339	59	13.03	5

Allan Robert BORDER

Born: Cremorne, Sydney, Australia, 27 July, 1955.

Allan Border was captain of Australia and established as one of the finest left-handed batsmen the game had known when he joined Essex in 1986. He scored more than 1000 runs for Essex in his first season although he could not complete the Championship programme because of international calls. International calls also robbed Essex of his services in 1987 when he was able to appear in only one NatWest Trophy match. He returned in 1988 and again batted in masterly fashion. His slow left-arm bowling was also of considerable value.

Border's qualities as a player were well known long before he joined Essex, but what was not known was what a fine club man he would be. He adopted Essex wholeheartedly, willingly attending functions and meeting supporters. Nothing was too much trouble for him, and he became a great favourite.

He played some outstanding innings, the highest being his 169 not out against Derbyshire at Chesterfield in 1988, and he excelled as a close to the wicket fieldsman. He took 27 catches in 1988 and 16 in his shortened first season. His 1393 runs in 1988 was the higher of his two aggregates.

Allan Border's stay with Essex was brief,

but he is remembered with great affection in the county, and he has constantly alluded to the joy that his two seasons in Essex gave him. In 1994 he announced that he was standing down as captain of Australia.

M	Inns	NOs	Runs	HS	Avge	100s	Ct
40	64	12	2778	169*	53.42	10	44

Overs	Mds	Runs	Wkts	Avge	Best
63	12	233	2	116.50	1/8

Sunday League

M	Inns	NOs	Runs	HS	Avge	Ct
24	24	4	674	77	33.70	16

Overs	Mds	Runs	Wkts	Avge	Best
16.4	1	65	4	16.25	2/21

Benson and Hedges Cup

M	Inns	NOs	Runs	HS	Avge	Ct
11	10	2	254	75*	31.75	5

Overs	Mds	Runs	Wkts	Avge
11	-	70	-	-

NatWest Trophy

M	Inns	NOs	Runs	HS	Avge	Ct
5	5	3	111	46*	55.50	2

Overs	Mds	Runs	Wkts	Avge	Best
2.4	-	12	1	12.00	1/1

Oswell Robert BORRADAILE

Born: Westminster, London, 9 May, 1859.

Died: Bexhill, Sussex, 11 May, 1955.

O.R.Borradaile was secretary of Essex County Cricket Club from 1890 until 1921 when ill-health forced him to step down. He managed the affairs of the club through the most difficult period of its history with unbounding energy, efficiency and courtesy. He was a most popular man, and evidence of this came in the generous testimonial he received on his retirement. He was elected a life-member of the club.

Educated at Westminster School, though leaving too soon to win a place in the XI, he was a good club cricketer. He captained Stoics for ten years and also played for Wanstead. His one appearance for Essex was against Surrey, at Leyton, in 1894, the last match of the county's first season in first-class cricket.

M	Inns	NOs	Runs	HS	Avge	Ct
1	2	-	7	5	3.50	1

Norman Francis BORRETT

Born: Wanstead, 1 October, 1917.
Educated at Framlingham, Norman Borrett went up to Cambridge and got his blue for racquets as a freshman. In 1939, he played in the Seniors' Match and, a slow left-arm bowler and right-handed batsman, he performed the hat-trick. One of his victims was Sam Silkin, the future Labour MP and peer. In spite of this achievement, Borrett did not appear in a first-class match at Cambridge.

He played for Essex against Cambridge University in 1937 and 1938 and reappeared against Nottinghamshire at Clacton in 1946. He played for Devon in 1949 and 1950.

M	Inns	NOs	Runs	HS	Avge	Ct
3	4	2	33	15*	16.50	2

Overs	Mds	Runs	Wkts	Avge
16	3	43	-	-

Cecil Stanley Reginald BOSWELL

Born: Edmonton, Middlesex, 19 January, 1910.
Died: Brundall, Norfolk, 15 August 1985.
A professional on the Essex staff in the early 1930s, Boswell was a leg-break and googly bowler, and a useful right-handed batsman. With Peter Smith and Lawrie Eastman available, his opportunities were restricted, and his 30 matches were played between 1932 and 1936. He left the staff after the 1937 season and moved to Norfolk for whom he played with considerable success from 1939 until 1955.

He was commissioned in the Army in World War Two.

M	Inns	NOs	Runs	HS	Avge	Ct
30	46	8	406	69	10.68	12

Overs	Mds	Runs	Wkts	Avge	Best
432.5		64	1345	36	37.36	4/22

Keith David BOYCE

Born: Castle St Peter, Barbados, 11 October, 1943.
For 11 years, all too short a time, Keith Boyce was the most exciting player in county cricket, and it would be true to say that Essex have never had a more thrilling all-rounder. For two or three years he bowled quickly, and his pace was only reduced by wear and tear and injury. His batting could be violent. His lithe athletic frame would be coiled into a spring which would release in one explosive movement. In the field, he was electric. He picked up and threw in one rapid gesture, and he held on to any catch, close to the wicket or in the deep. He loved every moment of every match, and his commitment to Essex was total. He was not always easy to manage, but he was a morale-booster on and off the field.

A natural sportsman, he kept goal for Barbados against Chelsea, Boyce was educated at Coleridge and Parry School and played for the Empire Club alongside Everton Weekes, Charlie Griffith and Seymour Nurse. He also appeared for Barbados 'B', but he was, at this time, a defensive batsman and a leg-spin bowler. Under the influence of the School groundsman, Osman Best, and the games master, Ernest Rochford, he was to change to offence as both batsman and pace bowler.

In February, 1965, he made his first-class debut, playing for Barbados against the touring Cavaliers. He won a place in the side only because Hall and Griffith were needed in preparation for a Test series against Australia. On the strength of what he saw of Boyce in that match, Trevor Bailey engaged him for Essex, and he arrived in England a few weeks later to begin a two-year qualifying period.

He responded enthusiastically to the coaching of Frank Rist and practised avidly. In club cricket, he often reverted to leg-spin when his pace became too devastating for the opposition. His second first-class match did not come until June, 1966, when he made his debut for Essex against Cambridge University, at Brentford. He was out for 0, but, in the university's first innings, he took an

excitement, but he could turn the course of any game whether it be as batsman, bowler or fielder. There were times when his enthusiasm, his commitment to Essex and his team-mates, cost him dearly. He would injure himself diving to complete impossible singles, but he believed there could be a run every ball. To see him running between the wickets with a batsman like Stuart Turner was a thrill in itself.

He enjoyed a fine Test record for West Indies, and he played a major part in West Indies winning the World Cup in 1975, but he never forgot that before Essex signed him he had played in only one first-class match, and that something of a 'friendly'.

Keith Boyce learned the game, and he loved it. He was knowledgeable and understanding, and he was vice-captain to Keith Fletcher in 1976. He arrived at Essex at a time when they were losing two outstanding all-rounders, Bailey and Knight, and he reached a standard of which both those fine players would have been proud. In the end, injury took its toll of him.

astonishing 9 for 61, bowling at great pace. He followed this with 4 for 47 in the second innings, and a star was born.

Qualified for Essex in 1967, he scored 910 runs and took 81 wickets. That winter he went to Pakistan with the Commonwealth side and benefited greatly from the advice given to him by Richie Benaud. His maiden first-class century came in February, 1969, for Barbados against Guyana, and he won the first of his 21 Test caps for West Indies in 1971. In 1972, he won the Cricket Society's Wetherell Award as the outstanding all-rounder in English cricket.

The advent of the one-day game had made Boyce an even greater asset to Essex than he had been. In 1972, in his 56th Sunday League game, he became the first player to complete 1000 runs and take 100 wickets in the competition.

He was unpredictable, which was part of his

In his benefit year, 1977, he was able to play in only seven first-class matches, six John Player League matches and the four zonal matches in the Benson and Hedges Cup. He played his last match against the Australians at Chelmsford in mid-June and bowled Robinson and Sergeant without a run on the board. He finished with 4 for 90, and in the second innings he took the wicket of McCosker at a personal cost of 19 runs. It was not known at the time that that was the end of Boyce's career, but the recurrence of a serious knee injury meant that he was unable to play again. He continued to follow the fortunes of the side, and he asked to maintain his registration in the hope that he could play again, but he said his farewell in a deeply moving television interview during a Sunday League game late in the season.

At the time of his departure, the glories of Essex lay two years ahead, but surely he was part of them in the spirit, the passion and the joy that he brought to the county and to the game.

He returned to Barbados and coached young cricketers from his old school and for the president's youth group, but his main occupation has been to become responsible for the Barbados Cricket Association lottery. He is in charge of the administration of the lottery which provides vital funds for cricket on the island.

M	Inns	NOs	Runs	HS	Avge	100s	Ct
211	319	18	6484	147*	22.75	3	181

Overs	Mds	Runs	Wkts	Avge	Best	10/m	5/inn
5578.3	1080	15704	662	23.72	9/61	6	30

Sunday League

M	Inns	NOs	Runs	HS	Avge	Ct
108	100	6	1677	98	17.84	30

Overs	Mds	Runs	Wkts	Avge	Best	5/inn
780.1	109	2720	179	15.19	8/26	2

Benson and Hedges Cup

M	Inns	NOs	Runs	HS	Avge	100s	Ct
27	20	-	341	123	17.05	1	7

Overs	Mds	Runs	Wkts	Avge	Best
260.2	43	738	38	19.42	4/18

Gillette Cup

M	Inns	NOs	Runs	HS	Avge	Ct
13	11	-	185	47	16.81	4

Overs	Mds	Runs	Wkts	Avge	Best	5/inn
129	29	316	26	12.15	5/22	1

Michael John Herbert BOYERS

Born: Plaistow, 16 April 1948.

A fast-medium pace bowler and right-handed batsman, Michael Boyers was educated at Sir George Monoux Grammar School and opened the bowling for MCC Schools against both the Indian Schools and the Combined Services in 1968. Interestingly, the Indian side included the Amarnath brothers and Syed Kirmani.

An all-round sportsman, he was a fine rugby player as well as a cricketer, he went up to Loughborough College and, at the end of his first year, he appeared for Essex against Middlesex at Westcliff. Thereafter his time was taken up by his work as a schoolmaster, and he played club cricket for South

Woodford. Later he became chairman of the Essex League.

M	Inns	NOs	Runs	HS	Avge
1	2	-	2	2	1.00

Arthur BRADFIELD

Born: Box, Wiltshire, 5 January 1892.
Died: Mochdre, Colwyn Bay, Denbighshire, 25 December, 1978.

One of the several wicket-keepers that Essex employed in the 1920s in an effort to solve a problem, Arthur Bradfield was engaged from the Hornchurch club and was on the staff in 1922 when he played five games as a professional.

M	Inns	NOs	Runs	HS	Avge	Ct	/st
5	7	3	7	4*	1.75	2	/3

Charles BRAY

Born: Portslade, Sussex, 6 April 1898.
Died: Bedford, 12 September 1993.

Late in his life, Charles Bray wrote that he regretted that he had not been able to play cricket more regularly. He was a journalist,

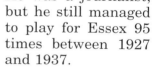

but he still managed to play for Essex 95 times between 1927 and 1937.

Charlie, for recent research by the Association of Cricket Statisticians suggests that this is how he was christened, was educated at Luton Modern School and learned his craft as a journalist in Bradford and Belfast. At the age of 24, he became London editor and lobby correspondent of the Belfast paper, *Northern Whig*. He lived in Hornchurch, but he played his club cricket for Southend, and for the North and South of the Thames Licensed Victuallers.

He enjoyed a phenomenal season for

Southend in 1927, and it was suggested to him by a committee member that he should play for the county in Southend week as a *local boy* would help to bolster the attendance. Douglas refused to have him, saying that if Bray were good enough, he should play in two away matches *after* the Southend Festival. This he did, and he impressed Douglas enough to be invited to return at the beginning of the following season. The two matches in which he appeared were at Leicester and Leyton.

Bray was in the side for the first match of the 1928 season, against the West Indians, and, in all, he appeared in ten matches. When he seemed to be losing form and heart Douglas made him open, and Bray responded with 108 against Middlesex at Leyton.

Charles Bray was a slim man with a sallow complexion. It was said that his motto in batting was 'get set and hold', which made him a useful opener. He batted with his shirt buttoned at the wrists, and such was his appearance that he was affectionately known among his press colleagues as 'the Ranji of Leyton'.

The 1928 season was the last in which Johnny Douglas was captain of Essex, and two years later, the great man was drowned. Bray had the greatest possible admiration for Douglas and was shocked at his sacking. In 1959, he wrote a memorable essay on Douglas in *Cricket Heroes*, a book published by the Cricket Writers' Club, an organisation of which he was an early chairman.

One of the reasons for Bray opposing the dismissal of Douglas was that, like Douglas, he felt that the new captain, H.M.Morris, did not have and could not have total commitment to the job. It transpired that this belief was correct. When Essex were due to play the Australians at Leyton in May 1930, Bray was told shortly before the start that he would have to captain the side as Morris was not available. Bray had never captained a side before, but he was to captain Essex on several occasions thereafter.

One of the matches in which Bray was captain was the one against Yorkshire at Leyton in 1932 when Holmes and Sutcliffe scored 555 for the first wicket.

Charles Bray's last match for Essex was against Middlesex at Lord's in May 1937. He scored 23 and 32, top scorer in the second innings, and he caught Jim Sims.

He had become cricket correspondent for *The Daily Herald,* and he also wrote on rugby and golf. During World War Two, he served in the RAF and, attaining the rank of Wing Commander, he acted as Public Relations Officer successively to Sir Arthur Longmore and Sir Arthur Tedder in the Middle East. Later, he returned to *The Daily Herald* as war correspondent, covering the Normandy landings and events up to the fall of Berlin.

Reverting to his work as a sports correspondent, he contributed to *The Sun*, in its original format at Odhams Press, and to *The Times* as a freelance after the closure of *The Daily Herald*. He covered several tours abroad and was most popular among the players as a knowledgeable, honest and perceptive journalist.

In 1950, he published a short, but delightful history of Essex CCC, the first ever written. A man of good humour and dry wit, he retired to Spain, but, after many years, ill health and increasing devaluation of currency, forced him to return to England where he died at the age of 95.

M	Inns	NOs	Runs	HS	Avge	100s	Ct
95	154	14	3474	129	24.81	5	54

Overs	Mds	Runs	Wkts	Avge	Best
32.5	5	104	2	52.00	1/1

Orme Cheshyre BRISTOWE

Born: Watford, Hertfordshire, 12 April 1895.
Died: Frieston Shore, Lincolnshire, 27 December 1938.

A hard-hitting batsman and a leg-break and googly bowler, Orme Bristowe played for Essex in 1913 after leaving Eton and before going up to Christ Church College, Oxford. He performed only moderately in his five matches for Essex in 1913, but he was outstandingly successful at Oxford the following year, scoring useful runs and taking 46 wickets, including 8 for 100 in the Varsity match which played a significant part in his side's victory.

Later in the season, he played six matches for Essex, and although he did not have quite the success with the ball that he had had at Oxford, he hit 81 against Leicestershire at Leyton and generally performed well in an all-round capacity.

After World War One, he played occasionally for Cheshire, but he concentrated on golf at which he had won a blue at Oxford. Even here his activities were restricted by a weak heart, and he died of heart failure while out shooting.

M	Inns	NOs	Runs	HS	Avge	Ct
11	16	1	249	81	16.60	2

Overs	Mds	Runs	Wkts	Avge	Best
221.2	30	901	22	40.95	4/74

Victor Charles George BROOKS

Born: East Ham, 29 June 1948.
An outstanding club cricketer with Walthamstow, where he was a wicket-keeper as well as a left-handed batsman, Vic Brooks was educated at East Ham Grammar School and at the University of Manchester where he had an excellent record.

He played for Essex in two Sunday League matches in 1969, and the following year, he appeared in their rain-ruined match against the Jamaica XI at Leyton in which Keith Pont made his debut. Matches against Warwickshire and Kent in 1971 and one Sunday League game marked the end of his career with the county. He declined the offer of a contract and now successfully runs his own computer firm which centres on aids to industry and commerce.

Vic Brooks has assisted Loughton in the later stages of his career and helps to coach young cricketers.

M	Inns	NOs	Runs	HS	Avge	Ct
3	5	-	53	22	10.60	1

Sunday League

M	Inns	NOs	Runs	HS	Avge	Ct
3	3	-	6	6	2.00	1

Adrian Desmond BROWN

Born: Clacton-on-Sea, 18 May 1962.
Adrian Brown was educated at Clacton County High School and was ever-present in the Cambridge University side of 1986 when his wicket-keeping won high praise, 'his skills when standing up to the seam bowlers made so much difference to the attack.' He held four

catches in the Varsity match which his side won in thrilling fashion. In the same season,

he also kept wicket for Combined Universities of Oxford and Cambridge in all four Benson and Hedges Cup matches. He had already established himself as the Suffolk wicket-keeper by that time, having played for them since 1984.

When Burns moved to Somerset Brown kept wicket regularly for the 2nd XI in 1987, and the following year, he kept in four Championship matches in June when David East was injured, the first being against Yorkshire at Sheffield.

A teacher by profession, he plays club cricket in Suffolk, and it was thought that his first-class days were behind him until, in August 1991, with Garnham injured in the NatWest Trophy semi-final and Rollins playing for England under-19, he was called up to play in the vital Championship match against Nottinghamshire at Colchester. He held four catches and made a brilliant leg-side stumping as Essex won with ease and went on to take the title.

M	Inns	NOs	Runs	HS	Avge	Ct	/St
5	5	3	13	6*	6.50	13	/3

Sunday League

M	Inns	NOs	Runs	HS	Avge	Ct	/St
3	1	1	1	1*	-	2	/-

NatWest Trophy

M	Inns	NOs	Runs	HS	Avge	Ct
1	-	-	-	-	-	1

George Rainy Reynolds BROWN

Born: Maldon, 8 December 1905.
A slow left-arm bowler, Rainy Brown first played for Essex at the end of July 1924, just

after leaving Felsted. His debut match was against Lancashire at Leyton, and he claimed the formidable wicket of Ernest Tyldesley, bowled.

The following summer, he was up at Emmanuel College, Cambridge, and performed creditably in the freshmen's match. He played against Free Foresters, but he was unable to force his way into a strong Cambridge side and did not get his blue.

He did, however, continue to assist Essex until 1932, although his appearances after his days at university were very limited. He was employed by ICI in India, and he continued his cricket, playing for Europeans from 1936 until the outbreak of war, and then again in 1945-46.

Rainy Brown served as a lieutenant-commander in the RNVR during World War Two. He now lives in retirement in Storrington, West Sussex.

M	Inns	NOs	Runs	HS	Avge	Ct
23	35	10	302	38*	12.08	14

Overs	Mds	Runs	Wkts	Avge	Best	5/inn
321.4	64	834	30	27.80	5/55	1

Herbert Jack BRUNWIN

Born: Layer-de-la-Haye, 28 April 1912.
Died: Colchester, 17 January 1990.
A right-arm fast-medium pace bowler from the Colchester and East Essex club, Brunwin played for Essex against Northamptonshire in Colchester Week, July 1937. He took the wicket of Grimshaw, the Northamptonshire opener.

M	Inns	NOs	Runs	HS	Avge	Ct
1	1	1	2	2*	-	-

Overs	Mds	Runs	Wkts	Avge	Best
4	1	5	1	5.00	1/5

Claude Percival BUCKENHAM

Born: Herne Hill, Surrey, 16 January 1876.
Died: Dundee, Angus, Scotland, 23 February 1937.
'When Buckenham was in his prime the weakness of the Essex slip fielding was notorious, and it is significant that when he was chosen for representative matches . . .he

invariably did well.' So said *The Cricketer* when Buckenham died, surprisingly, after a short illness in 1937.

That he was one of the outstanding fast bowlers of his time is unquestionable. He played in four Test matches in South Africa, 1910-11, and captured 21 wickets. In 1909, he was in the party for The Oval Test against Australia, and when he was omitted on the morning of the match Pardon, the editor of *Wisden*, called it an act 'touching the confines of lunacy'.

Tall and slim, with a fine nose and a little dark moustache, he was genuinely quick. He had a good, high action, could make the ball rear uncomfortably and could bring it back venomously. He was a smart, efficient player, and there was a unanimous verdict that had he played for a side that could field to his bowling, he might well have taken more than 2000 wickets in his career.

It was possibly his frustration that would cause him to change his style on occasions. One observer commented that when Buckenham performed great deeds for the South against the North in E.G.Hayes' benefit match at The Oval in 1908 he discarded off theory and 'aimed straight and true for the sticks, hitting them on five occasions, in two instances sending a stump flying into the air.'

Educated at Alleyn's School, Dulwich, he became associated with cricket at Leyton. He made his debut against Surrey at Leyton in 1899. The pitch had been badly overwatered, and the game was over in two days. Buckenham did not establish anything approaching a regular place in the Essex side until 1902, and thereafter he progressed rapidly. In 1906, he took 100 wickets in matches for Essex alone. In all games, he captured 100 or more wickets in six seasons.

By the outbreak of World War One, his form had declined a little and he appeared in only a handful of matches. He became professional to Forfarshire in Scotland, and then served in the Royal Garrison Artillery.

After the war he became coach at Repton, and he was still coaching young cricketers at the time of his death.

As well as being one of the deadliest pace bowlers in England for a period of six years, he was also a very useful batsman, one with the knack of scoring runs when they were most needed.

M	Inns	NOs	Runs	HS	Avge	100s	Ct
258	394	63	4882	124	14.74	2	143

Overs	Mds	Runs	Wkts	Avge	Best	10/m	5/inn
7224.5	1093	24629	934	26.36	8/33	16	72

59.3 (five-ball)

Frederick George BULL

Born: Hackney, London, 2 April 1875.
Died: St Annes-on-Sea, Lancashire, 16 September 1910.
Frederick George Bull is one of the tragic figures of Essex cricket. An off-break bowler in whom Kent had shown a mild interest, he joined Essex as an amateur in 1895, their first season in the county Championship. He retained his amateur status throughout his short career, being appointed assistant secretary to O.R.Borradaile.

He took only 15 first-class wickets in 1895, but the author of *Lillywhite's Cricketers' Annual* recognised a talent -

'In Mr F.G.Bull Essex found a young player of considerable promise. It was not the season for slow bowlers, but on wickets which help the ball he is sure to be of use, and with more experience ought to develop into a very useful all-round cricketer.'

These were prophetic words, for Bull enjoyed outstanding success in the seasons that followed. The off-break was his stock delivery, but he would vary his deliveries in pace and would occasionally send down a straight ball and a genuine leg-break. He was an intelligent bowler with a mastery of length. Warner considered him to be the best spinner of the day and took him to the United States in 1897, but others felt that there was a peculiarity in his action.

In 1896, at the age of 21, he took 85 wickets in first-class cricket, and they cost him only 16 runs each. Chosen for the Gentlemen against the Players at The Oval, he took 8 for 94, and 2 for 59, and for Essex against Yorkshire at Bradford, he had 8 for 44.

The following season, he took 120 wickets, and this included his career best 9 for 93 against Surrey at The Oval. This was also the season in which he was involved in a controversy.

It was the law of the day that a side had to follow-on if they were 100 runs or more in arrears on the first innings. Essex were playing Lancashire at Leyton, and Lancashire's ninth wicket fell at 132 in reply

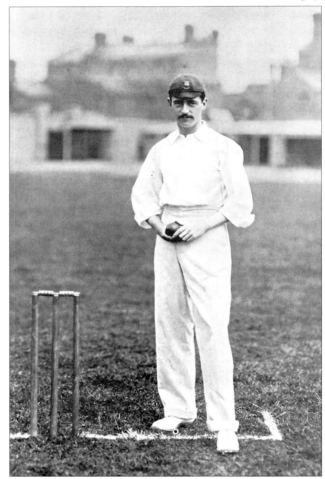

to Essex's 290. Essex were not anxious to bat last on a crumbling wicket and Bull deliberately bowled a fast wide ball to the boundary. Mold, the Lancashire number 11, out-manoeuvred Bull by knocking his own wicket down. There was acrimony on both sides, and the Essex Committee denied any complicity in the affair. All ended well. Bull finished with match figures of 14 for 176, and Essex went on to win by six wickets and to go top of the Championship table for the first time in their history.

Bull was one of *Wisden's* Five Cricketers of the Year in 1898, and a brilliant future was predicted for he was still very young, but, in fact, he had only two good seasons left. There was general concern about *suspect* bowling actions, and in 1900 county captains drew up a list of those whom they would not bowl and a second list of those who would be warned. Bull's name was on this second list. He attempted to change his style, but he took only five wickets in 1900, and Essex terminated his contract as assistant secretary.

There was talk that he would join Surrey, and then there was the idea that he would join the Stock Exchange. Eventually, he went to Blackburn to sell insurance. He played for East Lancashire and took 91 wickets. Then he turned professional and had two successful seasons with Perthshire, and he represented Scotland. He returned to East Lancashire as professional, and then moved to Rishton.

At the end of the 1910 season, he went to Blackpool in search of winter employment. On 16 September 1910, his body was washed up on the beach at St Anne's. His pockets had been weighed down with stones and a large stone was tied in a handkerchief around his neck. Disappointed and disillusioned at the age of 35, he had walked into the Irish Sea and taken his own life.

M	Inns	NOs	Runs	HS	Avge	Ct
88	125	31	117	41*	12.45	41

Overs	Mds	Runs	Wkts	Avge	Best	10/m	5/inn
77	952	7923	365	21.70	9/93	5	29

3246.4 (five-ball)

James BURNS

Born: Liverpool, Lancashire, 20 June 1866.
Died: Hampstead, London, 11 September 1957.
Charles Green had always been opposed to the importation of cricketers, but when he was guiding Essex towards first-class status he realised the need to strengthen the club if Essex was to compete on equal terms with other counties. Accordingly, James Burns joined Essex in 1887.

Burns was a right-handed batsman who generally opened, and a slow left-arm bowler. He played non-first-class cricket for Lancashire between 1884 and 1886, and he was an excellent soccer player with West Bromwich Albion and Notts County.

He made his first-class debut for MCC in 1890, and he was in the Essex side that took the field against Leicestershire at Leyton in May 1894, for the county's first first-class

match. The following season he made history, for when Essex made their Championship debut, against Warwickshire at Edgbaston in May he batted number five and shared a stand of 205 with George Higgins for the fourth wicket. Both men made centuries. Burns scored 114.

He played one more season for Essex, and then continued on the MCC groundstaff, playing his last first-class game for the famous club in 1901.

M	Inns	NOs	Runs	HS	Avge	100s	Ct
26	47	1	713	114	15.50	1	11

Overs	Mds	Runs	Wkts	Avge	Best
125.3	25	310	6	51.66	3/24

Neil David BURNS

Born: Chelmsford, 19 September 1965.
A stylish wicket-keeper and most able left-handed batsman, Neil Burns graduated from the Cricket School at Chelmsford and Essex Schools' sides onto

the Essex staff. He represented Young England, but the consistency of David East gave him little opportunity and after a few first team appearances in 1986 when East was injured he moved to Somerset where he has enjoyed a highly successful career.

He has coached and played in Western Province, South Africa, and he runs his own business.

M	Inns	NOs	Runs	HS	Avge	Ct	/St
2	3	-	54	29	18.00	2	/2

Sunday League

M	Inns	NOs	Runs	HS	Avge
1	-	-	-	-	-

Reverend Herbert John Edwin BURRELL

Born: Kirtling, Cambridgeshire, 15 November 1866.
Died: Trumpington, Cambridge, 23 May 1949.
Most of Herbert Burrell's cricket was for non-first-class counties, including Essex whom he first assisted in 1888. At Oxford, he played Lawn Tennis Doubles against Cambridge in 1886 and 1887, but he did not get his blue at cricket, appearing for the university only in the match against MCC in 1889.

His two first-class matches for Essex came at the end of June 1895, when he appeared against Warwickshire and Hampshire at Leyton.

A right-handed batsman and medium pace bowler, he played for Hertfordshire from 1901 until 1904. He became Honorary Canon of Ely Cathedral.

M	Inns	NOs	Runs	HS	Avge
2	4	-	15	10	3.75

Overs	Mds	Runs	Wkts	Avge
1	1	0	-	-

(five-ball)

Reginald John BURRELL

Born: Kirtling, Cambridgeshire, 26 August 1870.
Died: Risby Place, Suffolk, 16 March 1948.
The younger brother of Herbert Burrell, Reginald, like his brother, was educated at Charterhouse. A middle-order batsman, he made an excellent impression when he scored 31 out of an innings of 72 against Surrey at

The Oval on the occasion of his debut in 1894. He was the only Essex batsman to withstand the great fast bowler Tom Richardson who took all ten wickets.

Burrell was one of the Essex XI who played in the county's first Championship match, at Edgbaston in 1895. He did not play for the county again after that season but appeared for Suffolk in 1904.

M.	Inns	NOs	Runs	HS	Avge	Ct
6	9	-	127	40	14.11	1

Keith Andrew BUTLER

Born: Camden Town, London, 20 January 1971.

Although born in Camden Town, Keith Butler has lived in Dagenham from an early age. Coached at Ilford Cricket School, Butler developed through Essex Schools' cricket and Ilford CC. A right-handed batsman, he played for England Under 19 side and joined Essex in 1988. Having played grade cricket in Australia, he appeared for the county against Cambridge University at the beginning of the 1989 season.

Butler was desperately unlucky in that while fighting to establish himself he suffered a back injury which caused him to miss most of the 1991 season, and he was not re-engaged at the end of the 1992 season. He works in the security business.

M	Inns	NOs	Runs	HS	Avge
1	1	1	10	10*	-

Sunday League

M	Inns	NOs	Runs	HS	Avge	Ct
4	2	1	6	5*	6.00	1

Overs	Mds	Runs	Wkts	Avge
1	-	5	-	-

Clement Noel CALNAN

Born: Mile End, London, 25 December 1888.
Died: Southend: 30 January 1974.
A middle-order batsman, Clem Calman was one of many amateurs who made occasional appearances for Essex in the years after World War One. He first played in 1919, and his last appearance was in 1929.

M	Inns	NOs	Runs	HS	Avge	Ct
4	8	-	49	24	6.12	1

Overs	Mds	Runs	Wkts	Avge
3	-	25	-	-

Percivale CAMPBELL

Born: West Ham, 26 December 1887.
Died: South Woodford, 18 March 1960.
A middle-order batsman, Percivale Campbell, registered *Percival* at his death, was educated at Eastbourne and played in four matches for Essex in 1911, scoring 35 against Yorkshire at Sheffield. He appeared occasionally until the outbreak of World War One, and reappeared in one match in 1919.

M	Inns	NOs	Runs	HS	Avge	Ct
13	21	2	270	35	14.21	6

Overs	Mds	Runs	Wkts	Avge
3	-	26	-	-

George Nigel CAPEL-CURE

Born: Kensington, London, 28 September 1908.
An Old Etonian who batted left-handed and bowled leg-breaks, Nigel Capel-Cure played for Essex against Cambridge University where he was in residence at Trinity College in May 1930. Formerly of Blake Hall, Ongar, he is a member of a family that dates back to Thomas Cure, MP for East Grinstead and saddler to Edward VI.

High Sheriff of Essex, 1951-52, and Vice Lord-Lieutenant, 1958-78, Nigel Capel-Cure remains a keen follower of cricket and is a member of MCC. Now retired, he was an insurance broker, landowner and farmer.

M	Inns	NOs	Runs	HS	Avge
1	2	-	6	6	3.00

Overs	Mds	Runs	Wkts	Avge	Best
11	1	58	2	29.00	2/58

Major Noel John Obelin CARBUTT

Born: Gingindhlovu, Zululand, 25 December 1895.
Died: Durban, South Africa, 31 October 1964.
One of several Regular Army officers who made fleeting appearances for Essex in the 1920s, Noel Carbutt was a leg-break and googly bowler who made his first-class debut for Combined Services in 1920. He played cricket in various parts of the globe, including first-class matches for Madras, 1926-27.

Carbutt's career for Essex was restricted to two matches in the last week of July 1923. In the first game, against Middlesex at Leyton, he encountered 'Patsy' Hendren at his best. With Freddie Mann, Hendren added 256 in 140 minutes, and Carbutt had 0 for 127 in 19 overs. He did get two wickets in the second innings, but in his next match, at Northampton, he bowled just 11 overs and did not bat.

M	Inns	NOs	Runs	HS	Avge
2	1	1	12	12*	-

Overs	Mds	Runs	Wkts	Avge	Best
36	1	202	2	101.00	2/23

Herbert Arthur CARPENTER

Born: Cambridge, 12 July 1869.
Died: Whipps Cross, 12 December 1933.
Son of Robert Carpenter who, in the mid-19th century, was considered the finest batsman in England, Herbert Carpenter emulated his father in style, correct and strong with excellent back play. He also bowled off-breaks. He first played for Essex in 1888, and his batting was a major factor in the county attaining first-class status in 1894. He opened the innings in the first first-class match in which the county appeared, against Leicestershire, and was the only batsman to reach double figures.

Although he was to be selected for the Players on three occasions, he was to win the reputation of being one of the very best batsmen never to play for England. He scored 1000 runs in a season for Essex on six occasions, and his best year was in 1901 when he hit a century in each innings against Kent

M	Inns	NOs	Runs	HS	Avge	100s	Ct
262	466	24	13403	199	29.50	22	220

Overs	Mds	Runs	Wkts	Avge	Best
411.3	122	2163	46	47.02	4/57
256.1 (five-ball)					

Ronald Bernard CARR

Born: Johannesburg, South Africa, 24 June 1933.

Ronald Carr came to England from South Africa in 1960 and spent a year on the Essex staff in an attempt to establish himself as a leg-break and googly bowler. He appeared in the match against Oxford University in June, but he failed to win a place in the county side on a regular basis and returned to South Africa at the end of the season.

He went into business and later followed a highly successful career as a wholesale meat trader.

Carr played club cricket for Old Maristonians, and, in October 1964, he played for Transvaal against the MCC touring side led by M.J.K.Smith. He failed to take a wicket, and he did not appear in first-class cricket again.

M	Inns	NOs	Runs	HS	Avge
1	1	1	7	7*	-

Overs	Mds	Runs	Wkts	Avge
16	1	62	-	-

at Leyton. 'Bob' Carpenter was never blessed with good health, and illness restricted his appearances in 1902, and he did not play at all in 1903 although there is debate as to whether his non-appearance was due to illness or due to a dispute with the committee which had first taken place the previous season. He was back in 1904 when he shared a third wicket stand of 328 with Charlie McGahey against Surrey at The Oval. Carpenter hit 199 which was his highest score in first-class cricket.

In 1907, he appeared against Gloucestershire at Leyton early in the season, but was absent hurt in the second innings. He was not seen again in the season, and it was believed that his career was over, but he made a surprising reappearance in 1909. It proved to be a false dawn, and, in 1913, he assisted his father's old county, Cambridgeshire.

His days in first-class cricket were not quite done, for he played for Essex in the last two matches of the 1920 season, against Lancashire and Somerset. He was 51 years old. Sadly, his career ended with a 'duck'.

An uncle of Jack O'Connor, he was a fine judge of the game and did excellent work as a coach both for Essex and in Melbourne, Australia.

George CARTER

Born: Stoke Newington, London, 10 May 1901.

A right-handed batsman and medium pace bowler, George Carter assisted Essex as an amateur between 1921 and 1923. He played in five matches in 1921, scored 144 runs and made 44 against Northamptonshire at Northampton, and 44 not out against them at Leyton. His last match was against the West Indians two years later.

Business took him to Canada where he played cricket, and he retired to Florida.

M	Inns	NOs	Runs	HS	Avge	Ct
7	11	1	163	44*	16.30	3

Overs	Mds	Runs	Wkts	Avge
4	-	18	-	-

George Rodney CASS

Born: Overton, Yorkshire, 23 April 1940.

A capable left-handed batsman and wicket-keeper, Rodney Cass joined the Essex staff in 1963 and made his debut the following year. By 1966, he was appearing in the side with some regularity, and, in 1967, he often kept wicket in the early part of the season with Taylor concentrating on the captaincy. He was later used as an opening batsman and surrendered the gloves to Taylor. At the beginning of July, he hit a century against Warwickshire at Edgbaston. A few weeks later his contract was cancelled.

Cass joined Worcestershire and played for them until 1975. He then assisted Shropshire from 1976 to 1981. He often played and coached in Australia and appeared for Tasmania from 1970 to 1973.

M	Inns	NOs	Runs	HS	Avge	100s	Ct/st
45	77	11	1447	104*	21.92	1	27/5

Gillette Cup

M	Inns	NOs	Runs	HS	Avge	Ct
2	2	1	34	33*	34.00	2

Brian Kenneth CASTOR

Born: Mahaica, British Guiana, 21 October 1889.
Died: Maida Hill, London, 2 October 1979.

One of the outstanding administrators of the game, Brian Castor was appointed permanent secretary of Essex in 1930. When H.M.Morris resigned the captaincy in 1932 it was originally proposed that Castor should succeed him provided that there were no objections from other counties as to his qualifications. Not all counties were happy about the appointment and the idea was

dropped although Castor did captain the 2nd XI on a number of occasions.

He played for Essex against Sir Julien Cahn's XI in 1930, a match not recognised as first-class, and he appeared against Cambridge University at Cambridge in May 1932. As a reserve officer, he was called to Aldershot as soon as hostilities looked certain in September 1939. A lieutenant-colonel, he was taken prisoner at Singapore. In 1947, he became secretary of Surrey, a post he held for ten years.

M	Inns	NOs	Runs	HS	Avge
1	1	-	13	13	13.00

Ivan CHAPMAN

Born: Pudsey, Yorkshire, 12 October 1906.
Died: Hamilton, New Zealand, February 1976.

A right-handed middle order batsman and right-arm medium pace bowler, Ivan Chapman appeared as an amateur for Essex against Surrey at Leyton in June 1929.

M	Inns	NOs	Runs	HS	Avge
1	1	-	9	9	9.00

Overs	Mds	Runs	Wkts	Avge
7	2	18	-	-

John Henry CHILDS

Born: Lipson, Plymouth, Devon, 15 August 1951.

Born in Plymouth, John Childs and his family moved to a village near Newton Abbot when he was very young. He went to school in Torquay, enjoyed all sports and found his way into the Devon Under-15 and Under-19 cricket sides. Soon he was in the Devon Minor Counties' team.

Unsuccessful in his attempt to get into art college, he became an apprentice signwriter. His club cricket was for South Devon and Exeter, and he was in the Devon side on a regular basis.

Graham Wiltshire, the Gloucestershire

coach, came to watch a game between Devon and Cornwall as his county was interested in one of the Cornish players. But Wiltshire's eye was taken by the slow left-arm bowling of John Childs. Childs was asked to play a couple of matches for Gloucestershire as a trial. He did well, and in 1975, he joined the county.

He played under Procter, and very often Gloucestershire played two left-arm spinners, Graveney and Childs, in their side. Childs took 421 wickets for Gloucestershire and was with them until 1984 when, after two leaner seasons, it was decided to release him. Counties were told that he was available, and he himself was astonished that Essex, the reigning county Champions, approached him.

His first season with Essex, 1985, was a disaster. He took five wickets and they cost him 105.60 runs each. He thought that this was the end of his career, but Essex told him that they still believed that he could bowl, and he was given another year's contract. In 1986, he took 89 wickets at 16.28 runs each, and he was the leading English-qualified bowler by a considerable margin. Two years later, he appeared in two Test matches for England against West Indies.

A kind and gentle man, one of the most popular on the county circuit, John Childs has been a vital part of three Championship-winning sides, and he was 35 years old when Essex claimed the first of them.

Charlie took Essex to his heart, and the county embraced him in return. He has shown total commitment with bat and ball, and few will forget his innings against Hampshire in the final home Championship match of 1992, nor his last wicket stand with Mike Garnham in the NatWest Trophy the same season.

His bowling successes have tumbled one upon another, and he has turned the course of many matches, like the one at Folkestone in 1986, and the one against Nottinghamshire at Colchester in 1992. His partnership with Peter Such became as good a spin partnership

as any in the country. Tall, dark, neat, fresh, ever smiling, he has been a wonderful ambassador for Essex on and off the field where the county has utilised his talents in the Marketing Department in the winter months.

M	Inns	NOs	Runs	HS	Avge	Ct
191	171	83	1039	43	11.80	45

Overs	Mds	Runs	Wkts	Avge	Best	10/m	5/inn
5824.5	1856	14427	517	27.90	8/58	6	29

Sunday League

M	Inns	NOs	Runs	HS	Avge	Ct
33	14	8	43	10	7.17	7

Overs	Mds	Runs	Wkts	Avge	Best
229	12	1050	25	42.00	4/38

Benson and Hedges Cup

M	Inns	NOs	Runs	HS	Avge	Ct
1	-	-	-	-	-	1

Overs	Mds	Runs	Wkts	Avge	Best
11	-	46	2	23.00	2/46

NatWest Trophy

M	Inns	NOs	Runs	HS	Avge
4	1	1	13	13*	-

Overs	Mds	Runs	Wkts	Avge	Best
47.4	4	198	3	66.00	2/43

Horace George CLARK

Born: West Ham, 23 January 1889.
Died: Epping Plain, 28 February 1967.
A committee member and vice-president of the club for many years, Horace Clark acted as honorary secretary and treasurer from 1950 to 1954, a time when Essex's finances were at a low ebb. He was made an honorary life member of the club in recognition of his great services to Essex cricket.

A man of dry and infectious humour, Clark appeared twice for Essex as an amateur in 1923.

M	Inns	NOs	Runs	HS	Avge
2	3	-	13	11	4.33

Leonard Stanley CLARK

Born: Manor Park, 6 March 1914.
A highly successful right-handed batsman

with Southend, Len Clark assisted Essex as an amateur in the first two seasons after World War Two. He began the 1947 season in particularly good form, hitting 51 against Cambridge University in the opening match and 64 against Northamptonshire in the first Championship game.

M	Inns	NOs	Runs	HS	Avge	Ct
24	44	3	745	64	18.17	11

Overs	Mds	Runs	Wkts	Avge
5	1	15	-	-

Ronald Disston CLARK

Born: Romford, 22 February 1895.
Died: East Wittering, Sussex, 20 February 1983.
Lacking a regular professional wicket-keeper for many years, Essex called upon a number of amateurs either side of World War One. Among them was Ronald Clark who made his debut, against Lancashire at Leyton in July, 1912. He was only 17 and a half, had just finished at Christ's Hospital School and created a very favourable impression. Unfortunately, two matches the following season and one match in 1919 was to be the extent of his career. Business claimed him and he disappeared into club cricket in London.

His father was a famous amateur footballer with Clapton.

M	Inns	NOs	Runs	HS	Avge	Ct	/st
7	11	1	61	14	6.10	10	/1

Dr Carlos Bertram CLARKE

Born: Lakes Folly, Catts Castle, St Michael, Barbados, 7 April 1918.
Died: Putney, London, 14 October 1993.
C.B.Clarke was an unexpected selection for West Indies tour of England in 1939. A leg-break and googly bowler, he had had two seasons with Barbados and was recommended to the selectors by George Headley. Tall and gangly, he took 87 first-class wickets on the tour, but he had little success in the three Tests.

Impressed by all that London had to offer, he resolved to stay in England and enrolled as a student at Guy's Hospital, later qualifying as a doctor. During the war, he became one of the most familiar figures in the charity matches played up and down the country. He captained the British Empire XI on numerous occasions, and he is said to have taken 746 wickets in wartime cricket.

In the years immediately after World War Two, 'Bertie' Clarke was a tremendous power in London club cricket with the BBC club. He played occasionally for Northamptonshire between 1946 and 1949, but his work as a National Health Doctor restricted his appearances.

Steadfastly overcoming personal problems, he continued to excel in club cricket, and, in 1959, at the age of 41, he played for Essex with success. He played again the following year and then retired.

He played club cricket until he was in his 60s, still maintaining his high delivery, his pronounced loop and well disguised googly.

'Bertie' Clarke continued in his London practice until two years before his death at the age of 75. He wrote for *West Indian Digest*, and, in 1983, he was appointed OBE for his voluntary social work within the West Indian community.

M	Inns	NOs	Runs	HS	Avge	Ct
18	27	14	177	39	13.61	6

Overs	Mds	Runs	Wkts	Avge	Best	5/inn
439.4	88	1353	58	23.52	7/130	3

David Frederick COCK

Born: Great Dunmow, 22 October 1914.
Died: Great Dunmow, 26 September 1992.
David Cock was a farmer, a most capable batsman and a useful wicket-keeper who assisted Essex occasionally in 1939 and 1946.

Educated at Bishop's Stortford School, he played his club cricket for Bishop's Stortford and the Gentlemen of Essex. In 1936, he played for Hertfordshire, and in 1951, he returned to Minor Counties cricket for Cambridgeshire.

M	Inns	NOs	Runs	HS	Avge	Ct
14	20	2	355	98	19.72	5

Edward Charles COLEMAN

Born: Southend, 5 September 1891.
Died: Salonika, Greece, 2 April 1917.
A left-handed batsman and very good wicket-keeper, Coleman was in the Dulwich XI for four seasons, 1907-10. He went up to Pembroke College, Cambridge, and although he did not get his blue, he played for Oxford and Cambridge against Army and Navy at Portsmouth, 1911. The universities' wicket-keeper in this match was Walter Monckton, later to be a famous politician and barrister, and here making his one first-class appearance.

Coleman kept wicket for Essex in two matches in 1912. A lieutenant in the Royal Fleet Auxiliary, he was killed in action in Salonika.

M	Inns	NOs	Runs	HS	Avge	Ct	/st
2	3	-	10	6	3.33	1	/1

Edward James CONNOR

Born: Folkestone, Kent, 9 November 1872.
Died: Enfield, Middlesex, 11 January 1947.
A member of the Leyton groundstaff, Connor was a right-arm medium pace bowler who appeared twice for the county in 1905.

M	Inns	NOs	Runs	HS	Avge
2	4	-	43	26	10.75

Overs	Mds	Runs	Wkts	Avge	Best
42	9	131	2	65.50	2/21

Robert Michael Oliver COOKE

Born: Adlington, Cheshire, 3 September 1943.
Bob Cooke joined Essex in 1973 along with

Neil Smith and Brian Hardie. All three men were experienced in first-class cricket. A left-handed batsman and an occasional leg-break bowler, Cooke was educated at Rossall where he was a highly successful all-rounder.

He played league cricket for Stockport and Fleetwood and appeared for Lancashire 2nd XI in 1967 and 1968. He was Cheshire's leading batsman from 1969 to 1972 and established a county record with an innings of 192 against Yorkshire 2nd XI. He represented the Minor Counties (North) in the Benson and Hedges Cup, and he played for the Minor Counties against the Australians in 1972. Later the same season, he made his debut for the Essex 2nd XI, and the following season he joined the staff.

An aggressive bespectacled batsman, he began well and hit 139 against Sussex, at Ilford, in June, and, in 1974, he hit 718 runs. By 1975, however, the development of such batsmen as Gooch and Pont gave Cooke very limited opportunities. He played in only four matches, and his contract was not renewed at the end of the season. He returned to Cheshire where he has always run a most successful and profitable sports business.

M	Inns	NOs	Runs	HS	Avge	100s	Ct
40	66	5	1373	139	22.50	2	24

Overs	Mds	Runs	Wkts	Avge	Best
34	3	149	3	49.66	2/55

Sunday League

M	Inns	NOs	Runs	HS	Avge	Ct
25	24	-	318	83	13.25	7

Benson and Hedges Cup

M	Inns	NOs	Runs	HS	Avge	Ct
8	7	2	101	50*	20.20	2

Gillette Cup

M	Inns	NOs	Runs	HS	Avge	Ct
1	1	1	29	29*	-	1

Albert Vincent COOPER

Born: Stoke Newington, London, 3 December 1893.
Died: Stoke Newington, London, 3 May 1977.
A.V.Cooper did well as an all-rounder at Bancroft's School and had a trial for Essex as an amateur batsman against the West Indies in 1923. He batted right-handed and, at school, turned the ball both ways.

M	Inns	NOs	Runs	HS	Avge
1	1	-	14	12	7.00

Frederick Joseph COOPER

Born: Wetherby, Yorkshire, 16 March 1888.
Died: York, 27 June 1958.
A right-arm medium pace bowler and lower middle-order batsman, Fred Cooper appeared as an amateur for Essex between 1921 and 1923. He played cricket and golf for Shropshire and soccer for Bradford Park Avenue.

In 1921, Mr A.Brown is recorded as having played against Gloucestershire at home, and against Middlesex away. There are no other records of this player, and it is now believed that *A.Brown* was Fred Cooper appearing under an assumed name. *Wisden,* while listing *Brown* in the score-cards of the matches against Gloucestershire and Middlesex, makes no mention of him in the county averages and includes his statistics as part of Cooper's final figures, including the 52 against Gloucestershire at Leyton.

M	Inns	NOs	Runs	HS	Avge	Ct
10	18	1	170	52	10.00	3

Overs	Mds	Runs	Wkts	Avge	Best	5/71
109.4	9	385	8	48.12	5/71	1

Walter COOPER

No records have yet been unearthed as to the place and date of birth of Walter Cooper who was on the Essex groundstaff at the start of the century. He was a left-handed batsman and a slow left-arm bowler who played three matches for the county between 1905 and 1910. In 1928, he was a first-class umpire.

M	Inns	NOs	Runs	HS	Avge	Ct
3	6	-	32	18	5.33	1

Overs	Mds	Runs	Wkts	Avge
19	1	69	-	-

Francis William COTTAM

Born: Redhill, Surrey, 6 June 1900.
Died: Redhill, Surrey, 19 May 1987.
A slow left-arm bowler, Cottam was one of the many amateurs who assisted Essex in the 1920s. He played in the match against Dublin University at Brentwood in 1922.

M	Inns	NOs	Runs	HS	Avge
1	-	-	-	-	-

Overs	Mds	Runs	Wkts	Avge
10	3	25	-	-

Peter COUSENS

Born: Durban, South Africa, 15 May 1932.
A slow left-arm bowler and right-handed batsman from the Epping club, Peter Cousens  made his debut in 1950, playing in three matches. The first was at Old Trafford; and the second was against Surrey at Chelmsford. Surrey, joint Champions with Lancashire, won by an innings, but Cousens bowled Peter May for 91, and then trapped Clark leg before. In his third match, he performed the hat-trick. His third victim was Brian Close whom he bowled.

The young South African spinner excited much interest, but, because of national service, nothing was seen of him again until the second half of the 1953 season when he held a regular place in the side, but met with very little success.

He took 27 wickets in 1954, including 4 for 63 against Yorkshire at Romford, but he played little the following season, and he was not re-engaged for 1956.

M	Inns	NOs	Runs	HS	Avge	Ct
39	50	26	72	13	3.00	3

Overs	Mds	Runs	Wkts	Avge	Best
663.2	193	1707	44	38.79	4/63

Darren Mark COUSINS

Born: Cambridge, 24 September 1971.
A tall, right-arm fast medium pace bowler, Darren Cousins joined the Essex staff in 1992. Educated at Impington Village College, he represented Cambridgeshire at all levels in soccer, swimming and cricket. He played for Milton CC and followed his father into the Cambridgeshire side.

Cousins impressed with Essex 2nd XI as a trialist, and he also played for the 2nd XIs of Northamptonshire, Worcestershire and Leicestershire.

He made his first-class debut against Kent at Maidstone in 1993 when he also appeared in the Sunday League.

M	Inns	NOs	Runs	HS	Avge	Ct
5	7	1	24	11	4.00	2

Overs	Mds	Runs	Wkts	Avge	Best	5/inn
139	25	446	14	31.85	6/35	1

Sunday League

M	Inns	NOs	Runs	HS	Avge	Ct
12	6	1	10	6	2.00	1

Overs	Mds	Runs	Wkts	Avge	Best
80.3	5	382	19	20.10	3/18

NatWest Trophy

M.	Inns	NOs	Runs	HS	Avge
2	1	1	1	1*	-

Overs	Mds	Runs	Wkts	Avge	Best
10	1	57	1	57.00	1/33

Harry Pollard CRABTREE

Born: Barnoldswick, Yorkshire, 30 April 1906.
Died: Great Baddow, 28 May 1982.

If Harry Crabtree had been readily available for cricket, he would have opened the Essex innings for the best part of 15 seasons. As it was, his scholastic duties restricted his appearances to the tail end of the season. He was a Yorkshireman with a zest for living and a passion for cricket and rugby.

Educated at Ernysteds Grammar School, Skipton, he trained at the International College of Physical Education, Silkeborg, Denmark, and became Games and P.E.Master at Westcliff County High School in the late

1920s. He first played for Essex in 1931, and he last played for them in 1947, but he made only 24 appearances in all that time. During World War Two, he appeared regularly for the British Empire XI, and he scored 2908 runs in those years. Only Joe Hulme and Frank Lee scored more.

In 1946, he hit 793 runs, with centuries against Nottinghamshire, Worcestershire and the Indians, averaged just under 50 and finished tenth in the national averages. There was a century against the South Africans the following season, but his form fell away and he retired.

Captain of Westcliff, he prospered in club cricket, but it is as a coach and an administrator that he will be best remembered. As PE adviser for Essex, he exerted great influence, and he, Denys Wilcox and Trevor Bailey set up the first residential course for cricket coaches in this country. He became MCC youth coaching adviser in 1951 and was awarded the MBE for services to cricket in 1957.

A sound batsman of impeccable technique, he was a man of great friendliness and enthusiasm. He died some hours after attending the Old Brentwoods' annual dinner.

M	Inns	NOs	Runs	HS	Avge	100s	Ct
24	41	1	1281	146	32.02	4	12

Overs	Mds	Runs	Wkts	Avge
15	1	63	-	-

Charles Lambert CRAWLEY

Born: Brandon Park, Suffolk, 1 May 1908.
Died: Sunderland, Co.Durham, 24 July 1935.
Younger brother of Leonard Crawley, Charles played for Essex against Leicestershire at Leicester in August, 1929. He opened the innings with his brother but was twice bowled by Shipman.

M	Inns	NOs	Runs	HS	Avge	Ct
1	2	-	3	3	1.50	1

Leonard George CRAWLEY

Born: Nacton, Suffolk, 26 July 1903.
Died: Worthington, Suffolk, 9 July 1981.
Tom Pearce believed that if Leonard Crawley had been able to play regularly, Essex would have won the Championship in the 1930s. He was a batsman in the mould of the amateurs of the golden age, upright, moustached, a magnificent driver of the ball and ever on the attack. His batting was shot with romance, but the demands of teaching and later of journalism restricted him to 56 matches for Essex between 1926 and 1936, rarely more than half a dozen a season in July and August.

A member of a notable games-playing family of whom the most famous was probably his cousin Aidan, Leonard Crawley scored a memorable 103 for Harrow against Eton in 1921. The following season, still a schoolboy, he topped the Worcestershire batting averages and also played for Durham City. He won his blue in his first year at Cambridge, 1923, and again topped the Worcestershire averages, but his qualification for that county was challenged by Lord Harris. A famous quarrel ensued in the Long Room at Lord's between Harris and the Worcestershire president, Lord Deerhurst, and Crawley did not play county cricket again until 1926 by which time he was qualified for Essex.

In his last Varsity match, 1925, he was 98 not out at lunch and so within two runs of equalling the record of his uncle, Eustace Crawley, the only man to have scored centuries in both the Eton and Harrow game and the Varsity match. Unfortunately, Leonard was out to the first ball after lunch.

He went with MCC to West Indies, 1925-26, but this was the only tour he was able to make during his career. Had he played regularly, he would surely have played for England, and, in spite of his restricted appearances, he was asked if he were available to tour Australia, 1932-33.

At Leyton, in 1927, he played one of the most spectacular innings ever seen on the famous old ground. Sussex had set Essex the task of scoring 276 in under three and a half hours to win the match. Crawley hit 176 not out in 185 minutes and Essex won by seven wickets with 25 minutes to spare. Twice he hit Maurice Tate on to the pavilion roof, and there were 18 fours in his innings. At the end, he was carried from the field shoulder high.

The following season, he made 222 in four and a half hours against Glamorgan at Swansea. His innings included six sixes and 21 fours. Sadly, there were all too few opportunities to see him at the crease. In his last season, 1936, he was able to play in only five matches. The first of them was against Glamorgan at Pontypridd. He arrived at Paddington Station wearing his cricket flannels and carrying a brown paper parcel containing his night requirements. No play was possible until the Monday, and then he scored 118, an innings which included five sixes, two of them out of the ground, and nine fours. He was physically unprepared for the match and was so stiff after his knock that he could take no further part in the proceedings. That year, he became Headmaster of Warriston School, Moffat, in Scotland, and he was lost to Essex cricket thereafter.

In truth, he had too many talents to restrict himself to cricket. He won his blue for racquets at Cambridge, and he won the North Lawn Tennis Doubles Championship with his uncle. He took a gold medal for ice skating, and he was an outstanding shot. He appeared for England in 97 golf internationals, and he was a member of four Walker Cup sides, notching Great Britain's only win in the 1932 contest. The previous year, he had won the

English Amateur Championship at Hunstanton. For 25 years, he was golf correspondent of *The Daily Telegraph*.

Most importantly, he was, in the words of his cousin, 'a truly lovable man'.

M	Inns	NOs	Runs	HS	Avge	100s	Ct
56	91	4	2949	222	33.89	6	17

Overs	Mds	Runs	Wkts	Avge
12	-	39	-	-

Stanley James CRAY

Born: Stratford, 29 May 1921.
'Chick' Cray spent a year on the Surrey staff before joining Essex and making his debut in 1938, playing in one match. He had an extended run in the side in 1939 but with little success. His was a

career mutilated by World War Two although he did play cricket in India between 1943 and 1945, appearing in first-class matches for the Europeans.

He was not demobilised from the Army until early in 1947, but as a right-handed opening batsman, he made an immediate impact in that year with 1339 runs, including three centuries. He was very much in the mould of 'Sonny' Avery and had all the shots, but he had a loss of form in 1948, and with Dodds and Avery establishing themselves as the regular opening pair, he left the staff after the 1950 season. Ironically, that was the season when, batting at number three, he made his highest score, 163 against Nottinghamshire at Ilford.

After moving to Devon he assisted that county between 1954 and 1957 although he played very infrequently.

M	Inns	NOs	Runs	HS	Avge	100s	Ct
99	172	6	4062	163	24.46	7	22

Overs	Mds	Runs	Wkts	Avge	Best
7	1	40	1	40.00	1/0

James Albert CUTMORE

Born: Walthamstow, 28 December 1898.
Died: Brentwood, 30 November 1985.
Jim Cutmore was educated at Clark's College and studied accountancy. He served in the navy and made his first century while in South Africa. In 1924, he joined Essex as a professional and established a regular place in the side the following season when he scored over 1000 runs, a feat he was to accomplish on ten more occasions.

He was an aggressive batsman who came to open the innings, and his career was dotted with some spectacular knocks. In 1927, he hit 238 not out against Gloucestershire at Bristol, but perhaps two of his most memorable innings were his 77 in 75 minutes out of an Essex total of 111 against Lancashire, at Blackpool, 1930, and 31 not out in an Essex total of 64 against Yorkshire at Dewsbury in 1933.

Cutmore contributed to several big

partnerships and, in 1934, he hit 1876 runs, average 40.78, but within two years his career was over. He made his 1000 runs in 1935, but, in spite of an innings of 137 against the Indian tourists at Brentwood at the end of May the following season, he showed a loss of form, was dropped from the side in mid-June and was not retained at the end of the season. After such wonderful service he at least had the right to expect a benefit, but those were less understanding days.

Perhaps uniquely among Essex cricketers, Jim Cutmore also earned a living as a music hall entertainer. He had a fine tenor voice, and he appeared on the stage of the Walthamstow Palace in 1930 with a cricket bat in his hand and dressed as though he had just come from the wicket. He also appeared in pantomime at the Dominion, Tottenham Court Road, and made a record of *The Things We Want Most are Hard to Get* and *Those Smiling Irish Eyes*.

When Essex jettisoned him in 1936, however, there was no opportunity for him to follow a full time career in the entertainment world, and he spent two years selling newspaper advertising space. He played for Crompton in the Central Lancashire League and he coached and played for Forfarshire in Scotland. In 1938, he became a sales representative for Horlicks, a position he held for 27 years.

He settled in Brentwood after World War Two, played for Brentwood, Shenfield and Navestock and was an active agent in the early years of the Essex Supporters' Association Pool. He appeared in a benefit match at Chelmsford when he was in his 70s and defended his wicket resolutely. He was still playing some rugged hockey at this time, and he remained very fit until his death from a heart attack at the age of 86.

M	Inns	NOs	Runs	HS	Avge	100s	Ct
342	593	36	15937	238*	28.61	15	121

Overs	Mds	Runs	Wkts	Avge	Best
160.1	13	687	11	62.45	2/31

Arthur George DAER

Born: Bishopsgate, London, 22 November 1905.
Died: Torquay, Devon, 16 July 1980.
The elder of two brothers who played for the county, A.G.Daer appeared as an amateur between 1925 and 1935. *Wisden* described him

as *rather fast* when he took 34 wickets in 1929, and, able to play in 21 Championship matches in 1930, he took 51 wickets and scored 429 runs to suggest that he had all-round potential.

Troubled by a knee injury, he fell away in 1931, and the following winter he underwent an operation. He was never as effective, nor as quick a bowler after this operation as he had been previously, and he developed what the *News Chronicle* described as a 'liberal physique'. He played only twice in his last season, 1935, against Kent and Lancashire, and claimed Eddie Paynter as his final victim.

Remarkably, the deaths of both he and his brother went unnoticed by *Wisden* and the cricketing press.

M	Inns	NOs	Runs	HS	Avge	Ct
100	141	42	1469	59	14.83	48

Overs	Mds	Runs	Wkts	Avge	Best	5/inn
2311.2	495	6183	195	31.70	6/38	3

Harry Bruce DAER

Born: Hammersmith, London, 10 December 1918.
Died: Plymouth, Devon, 19 December 1980.
Unlike his brother, Harry Daer played as a professional, but he appeared in only nine matches in 1938 and 1939. All his bowling was done in his eight matches in 1938. Like his brother, he was of fast-medium pace, and in club

cricket with Gidea Park, they were both renowned as hitters. Harry served as a lieutenant in the war.

M	Inns	NOs	Runs	HS	Avge	Ct
9	12	3	60	17	6.66	4

Overs	Mds	Runs	Wkts	Avge	Best
95	16	387	11	35.18	3/21

Geoffrey Boisselier DAVIES

Born: Poplar, Londn, 26 October 1892.
Died: Hulluch, France, 26 September 1915.
An all-round cricketer of considerable talent, Geoffrey Davies was a right-handed batsman who often opened the innings and a right-arm slow-medium bowler. He was a member of the Rossall School XI for four years and captained the side in 1912 when he made his debut for Essex.

Young as he was, he gave early evidence of exceptional ability, and he claimed the great George Brown of Hampshire as his first wicket in first-class cricket. He went up to Oxford and won his blue as a freshman. Later that season, 1913, he took 29 wickets in the matches for Essex and finished second in the bowling averages to Louden.

In 1914, he again failed to do himself justice in the Varsity match, but by the end of the season he had scored 852 runs and taken 83 wickets. 38 of his wickets came in 16 Championship matches for Essex, and he hit centuries for the county against Somerset and Northamptonshire.

His 100 in 81 minutes against Northamptonshire at Leyton came three weeks after the outbreak of World War One. A week later, at Weston-super-Mare, he took 4 for 18 and hit 118 out of 155 as Essex won their last game of the season. It was the last first-class cricket match of Davies' career. Commissioned in the Essex Regiment, he rose to the rank of captain, but was killed in action on the Western Front little more than a year

after that game at Weston. 'There can be little doubt,' wrote *Wisden*, 'that he would have developed into an England player.' He was 22.

M	Inns	NOs	Runs	HS	Avge	100s	Ct
32	51	8	757	118	17.60	2	27

Overs	Mds	Runs	Wkts	Avge	Best	5/inn
512.3	73	1769	68	26.01	6/51	2

W. DAVIS

Davis has so far defied research and remains an enigmatic figure. A professional who was a lower order batsman and a change bowler, he played four matches for Essex in 1920. He captured the wicket of Mr C.P.Johnstone of Kent in the match at Dover, and, apparently injured while fielding, he was unable to bat in the second innings of the match against Lancashire at Leyton at the end of August. This proved to be his last match, and we have no idea as to how serious was his injury.

M	Inns	NOs	Runs	HS	Avge	Ct
4	6	-	26	13	4.33	2

Overs	Mds	Runs	Wkts	Avge	Best
14	1	69	1	69.00	1/67

Michael Henry DENNESS

Born: Bellshill, Lanarkshire, Scotland, 1 December 1940.
Capped for Scotland while still a schoolboy,

Mike Denness played for Kent from 1962 to 1976 and captained the side for the last four years of his time with the county. He appeared in 28 Test matches and captained England in 19.

He joined Essex in 1977 and played for the county for four seasons. A right-handed opening batsman, he brought a wealth of experience to the Essex side, not least the experience of winning trophies, and he was a prominent member of the side which won the Championship and the Benson and Hedges Cup in 1979. His contribution to the rise of Essex cricket was immense, and he remained with Essex for a time as 2nd XI captain and fund-raiser.

Denness returned to Kent as a committee member, and he has long been concerned with insurance and finance as well as running his own public relations firm which has contacts with cricket through its association with Britannic Assurance and National Grid. He was marketing manager for Kerry Packer's World Series Cricket.

M	Inns	NOs	Runs	HS	Avge	100s	Ct
83	137	9	4050	195	31.64	6	38

Overs	Mds	Runs	Wkts	Avge
1	1	0	-	-

Sunday League

M	Inns	NOs	Runs	HS	Avge	100s	Ct
34	32	1	569	102	18.35	1	9

Benson and Hedges Cup

M	Inns	NOs	Runs	HS	Avge	Ct
15	14	1	337	66	25.92	5

Gillette Cup

M	Inns	NOs	Runs	HS	Avge	Ct
7	6	-	114	71	19.00	2

John Newman DENNIS

Born: Leytonstone, 4 January 1913.

A middle-order right-handed batsman who was educated at Forest School, John Dennis first played for Essex in 1934, and, in 1937, when he appeared in seven Championship matches he was awarded his county cap. An amateur, he captained the county in the match against Glamorgan at Westcliff in that season.

Unfortunately, his

work as a solicitor prevented him from playing much after the 1937 season, and although he was expected to play in 1946, his career, in fact, ended in 1939.

After the war Jack Dennis captained Loughton for some years. Technically correct, he was described as a charming man with a disarming smile.

M	Inns	NOs	Runs	HS	Avge	Ct
22	33	3	530	53	17.66	13

Herman Walter DE ZOETE

Born: Bromley Common, Kent, 13 February 1877.
Died: Ipswich, Suffolk, 26 March 1957.

Brother-in-law of C.J.Round and therefore son-in-law of the great founder of Essex County Cricket Club, James Round, De Zoete was a left-arm medium pace bowler, who also bowled spin on occasions, and a very useful lower order right-handed batsman. He was in the Eton XI and played for Cambridge against Oxford in 1897 and 1898. In the first match, he enjoyed considerable success, sharing in an

important eighth wicket stand and then taking 4 for 26 to bowl Cambridge to victory after they had trailed on the first innings. F.L.Fane was in the Oxford side.

De Zoete, an excellent golfer who represented Cambridge for three years, played for Essex against Surrey and Hampshire in 1897 and claimed the great Tom Hayward as his first wicket, but thereafter business claimed him.

M	Inns	NOs	Runs	HS	Avge
2	2	2	2	2*	-

Overs	Mds	Runs	Wkts	Avge	Best
32	8	91	3	30.33	2/44

(five-ball)

William James DINES

Born: Colchester, 14 September 1916.
Died: Gidea Park, 16 June 1992.

It is quite strange to realise that Bill Dines played only 20 matches for Essex, for his name seemed to be part of the county and the club for many years. Although he was born in Colchester, he was educated at Victoria School in Chelmsford, and it was in Chelmsford that he worked and played for Crompton Parkinson whose managing director, T.H. Windibank, contributed much in hospitality to the cricket world. Dines played for this 'works team' for many seasons before Essex gave him a contract in January 1946.

He made his debut for Essex against Cambridge University in May 1947, and he played in 14 Championship matches that season, generally batting low in the order and bowling medium pace off-breaks. He had a sensational start to his Championship career, dismissing Walker and Barron of Northamptonshire with only one run on the board. He later captured the wicket of Timms, but his 3 for 35 in that tied match was to remain the best performance of his career. He appeared in only five matches in 1948, and only against Cambridge University in 1949 after which he left the Essex staff.

He became the groundsman at Ind Coope and played for Romford Brewery, Essex Wanderers and many other sides. When the Brewery Ground was built upon he gave up cricket and turned to bowls at which he became so proficient that he played at county level and was invited for an international trial.

He was essentially an Essex man, resolute in his demand for high standards and an ever courteous colleague and opponent.

M	Inns	NOs	Runs	HS	Avge	Ct
20	30	7	431	69*	13.85	7

Overs	Mds	Runs	Wkts	Avge	Best
325.2	71	980	15	65.33	3/35

Stephen Charles DINSDALE

Born: Buckhurst Hill, 30 December 1948.

A left-handed batsman and a left-arm medium pace bowler, Stephen Dinsdale was educated at Sir George Monoux School, Walthamstow and played for Essex, London and for South of England Schools. He also played basketball for England Schools.

His first-class debut in cricket came for Rhodesia in the 1969-70 South African season, and, in 1970, he played five times for Essex. He returned to South Africa, played soccer for Natal 'A' and worked as a Computer Operations Supervisor. He played two seasons for Transvaal, 1974-75, and 1975-76.

M	Inns	NOs	Runs	HS	Avge	Ct
5	7	-	97	29	13.85	4

Muneeb DIWAN

Born: St Stephen's, Canada, 20 March 1972.

A right-handed batsman, Muneeb Diwan was

born in Canada of Pakistani parents but moved to England at the age of three. He was educated at Sir George Monoux School, Walthamstow, represented Essex Schools and attended the Haringey Cricket College (now the London Cricket College) in Tottenham where he obtained a coaching qualification. Having scored over 700 runs in the 2nd XI, he was signed by Essex in 1993. He scored prolifically in 2nd XI games at the beginning of the 1994 season, and injuries and Test calls brought his opportunities in the first team in Sunday League matches, and in the Championship side at Leicester, where, unfortunately, he began his first-class career with a 'pair'. He was released at the end of 1994.

M	Inns	NOs	Runs	HS	Avge
1	2	-	0	0	0.00

Sunday League

M	Inns	NOs	Runs	HS	Avge
4	4	-	31	14	7.75

Joseph Gilbert DIXON

Born: Chelmsford, 3 September 1895.
Died: Great Baddow, 19 November, 1954.
Educated at Felsted where he was in the XI for three years, Joseph Dixon was a very tall amateur with 'pretention to pace'. He was also a very hard hitter of the ball, a particularly strong driver.

He first played for Essex in 1914, his last year at school, appearing in four matches. He played more regularly in 1919 but was used mainly as a batsman, hitting 108 against Gloucestershire at Leyton and sharing a brisk partnership with Johnny Douglas of 141. His batting fell away the following season when he played regularly and often opened the innings. He

took 46 wickets at 28.71 runs each, which *Wisden* considered very expensive.

He was quick, but he was erratic and when he enjoyed his best all-round season, 1921, his 67 wickets cost him 34.47 apiece, *terribly expensive.* He hit a century against Hampshire at Colchester that year and finished with 810 runs.

Dixon continued in much the same vein in 1922, taking 51 wickets at 31.68 – only Douglas took more wickets – and enjoying days of success. He played a spectacular innings of 173 against Worcestershire at Leyton. He opened and 'hitting at almost everything and putting plenty of power into his strokes, he scored his 173 out of 296 in two and a half hours, his figures including one six and 24 fours'. That proved to be his swan song. Business claimed him after 1922, and his cricket was restricted to club cricket for Chelmsford.

M	Inns	NOs	Runs	HS	Avge	100s	Ct
93	148	12	2214	173	16.27	3	48

Overs	Mds	Runs	Wkts	Avge	Best	10/m	5/inn
1870.4	257	6484	206	31.47	7/61	2	9

Thomas Carter DODDS

Born: Bedford, 29 May 1919.
For 13 seasons the white hair of 'Dickie' Dodds was a prominent feature in Essex cricket, and Dodds himself was a much loved personality in the game. This is not surprising, for throughout his career as an opening batsman, he averaged something like 44 runs an hour.

The son of a clergyman, he was educated at Wellingborough and Warwick Schools, and left school when he was 17. A weak chest prevented him from going into insurance and caused him to be confined to bed for six months. He worked for his uncle's building firm and played for North Oxford CC.

Success brought him to the attention of Warwickshire, and he assisted the 2nd XI before moving to London to work for the Amateur Football Alliance and later for Barclay's Bank for whom he played primarily as a leg-break bowler. In 1939, he appeared for Middlesex 2nd XI and joined the Somerset Light Infantry shortly after the outbreak of war. He served in France and India, and it was in India that he made his first-class debut, playing for the Services against an Indian XI. The Services were led by Douglas Jardine. Dodds scored 14 and took the wicket of Modi.

With help from his former Barclay's Bank captain 'Nobby' Hunt, Dodds was given a trial for Essex in 1946 and was immediately recognised as a batsman good enough to open the innings. He made his debut against Sussex at Ilford at the end of May, scoring 18 and 63, an innings which occupied two and a half hours. He played as an amateur in 1946 and became a professional the following year.

He hit two centuries in his first season and reached 1000 runs and, in 1947, he scored more than 2000 runs in all matches, although he made only one century. A deeply religious man, Dodds became a member of the Moral Re-armament movement, and, in his own account, he asked God how he should bat. He said that God had told him to 'Hit hard and enjoy it!' This attitude made him a most entertaining batsman to watch, but it also meant that he was frequently dismissed for scores between 50 and 100 when a century looked to be his for the taking.

Dodds reached 1000 runs in each of his 13 seasons with Essex, a remarkable record, but he was not re-engaged after 1959. He had struck a bad patch, and he was then past 40. He gave all his benefit money to the Moral Re-Armament movement, and he has continued to work for them since leaving county cricket in his efforts to help build a new and better world.

He has also done some coaching and is the author of a coaching manual as well as an autobiography, written at the request of Sir Neville Cardus and entitled, appropriately, *Hit Hard and Enjoy It*.

M	Inns	NOs	Runs	HS	Avge	100s	Ct
380	663	17	18565	157	28.73	17	176

Overs	Mds	Runs	Wkts	Avge	Best
293.1	54	1053	35	30.08	4/34

Cecil Herbert DOUGLAS

Born: Clapton, London, 28 June 1886.
Died: Frinton-on-Sea, 30 September 1954.
The younger brother of the great Johnny Douglas, 'Pickles' Douglas was more noted as a boxing referee than as a cricketer. J.H.Douglas, the father, was president of the ABA for 18 years, and both Johnny and 'Pickles' served on the council and acted as judges. 'Pickles' refereed the George Cook v Joe Beckett fight as early as 1922, and in the 1930s he was the leading British referee. He had the reputation of being a bit of a martinet, but he controlled with fairness and humour. He had charge of the contests which involved Carnera, Len Harvey, Petersen and Neusel so that it can be seen that he was indeed the top referee.

His cricket career was shorter and less distinguished. He was in the XI at Felsted and played for Essex against Northamptonshire at Northampton in 1912. He was run out for 0, and caught for 1. Nothing was seen of him in 1913, but he played six times in 1914, and then returned in 1919.

This was the season that saw the unsuccessful experiment of two-day matches, and C.H.Douglas appeared in 14 of Essex's 20 fixtures. Generally, he batted at number seven or eight, and in June, he took the last three Kent wickets to fall at a personal cost of 46 runs. He bowled spin. When the side went up to Manchester in July he was at number five

and scored 78. In the next match, against Somerset, he was back at number seven, and when Essex went down to Weston-super-Mare in August he was at number ten. He confronted his brother, asserted that he should be higher, and was told that the captain determined the order.

When 'Pickles' joined Johnny in that match, Essex were more than 50 runs short of saving the follow-on, but the pair stayed together for two hours, saved the day, and C.H. made 45. He felt he had proved his point, but when the side went to Bournemouth for the next game he was told that he would again be at number ten. He said something rather impolite to his brother, packed his bags and went home.

In fact, he did appear in one more match, at the end of August, but thereafter he concentrated on his first love, boxing.

With his father and brother, he ran J.H.Douglas & Company, a firm that made the staves, the wooden tubs, in which cement was stored. In the 1930s, the cement manufacturers decided to store their product in paper sacks, which were lighter and cheaper. 'Pickles' struggled to keep the Douglas firm going until the outbreak of World War Two when it finally closed.

He spent his last days in Frinton-on-Sea, working for the Clacton District Council. He did jobs like sweeping and cleaning, and he remained defiantly cheerful to the end. Like his brother, he had an air of indestructibility about him

M	Inns	NOs	Runs	HS	Avge	Ct
21	27	-	326	78	12.07	4

Overs	Mds	Runs	Wkts	Avge	Best
74.1	2	350	6	58.33	3/46

John William Henry Tyler DOUGLAS

Born: Clapton, London, 3 September 1882.
Died: Laesoe, Denmark, 19 December 1930.

'If the Essex County Cricket Club ever decided to have a Roll of Honour and were foolish enough to place the names in order of merit, there would be much heart-burning, much discussion and, no doubt, much dispute over the one chosen for the top position. It would be a most unenviable task, indeed almost impossible to single out one of the many giants of Essex cricket and say that he was greater than any other. Yet I should be prepared to advance and support the claims of John William Henry Tyler Douglas.' So wrote Charles Bray in 1950, and if much has happened in Essex cricket since then, one would still find it difficult to dislodge Johnny Douglas from this pedestal. It is likely that, but for him and his father, there would be no Essex County Cricket Club today.

Old Douglas, J.H., was a sportsman of note, a boxing champion and administrator, a good club cricketer and chairman of the Club Cricket Conference. He ran a successful firm in Bishopsgate which imported timber from which the tubs which housed cement were made. He was a brusque man of controlled passion who wanted his own way and got it, and in all the walks of life into which he strode he wielded power.

The Douglas family lived in Clapton, the Middlesex side of the Middlesex/Essex border, and old Douglas captained a strong Clapton Cricket Club. He lodged in his son Johnny a passion to succeed at sport, and Johnny responded with a dedication that has rarely been equalled.

Educated first at Moulton Grammar School, near Spalding, deliberately so because the headmaster was a fine cricketer, and then at Felsted, J.W.H.T.Douglas was not a natural sportsman. He had little innate ability, but through will and determination he excelled at school in soccer, fives, athletics (at which he beat a future Olympic runner), boxing, hockey, gymnastics and cricket. He took only one

academic prize, a junior one in mathematics, but in sport he was supreme. In later life, he was to win an Olympic Gold Medal as a middle-weight boxer, and he was to play for England in an amateur international soccer match against Bohemia.

He left Felsted in July 1901, his school career having been dedicated to sport, and the discipline and application which he and his father saw as integral to sport. At Felsted, he was nicknamed 'Pro', not entirely complimentary, but a grudging admiration of his ruthless determination to be first in games.

The Douglas family moved to Wanstead at the turn of the century, and a long association with the Wanstead Club began. Johnny Douglas enjoyed quick success with Wanstead, did well for Essex 2nd XI and, in 1901, he made his first-class debut, for Essex against the county Champions Yorkshire at Leyton. He was twice bowled by George Hirst for 0. He also failed to score at Clifton, but he hit 61 not out against Derbyshire at Chesterfield. He did not bowl in any of the three matches.

It was apparent that Douglas' skills needed to be honed, and he played with W.G.Grace's London County XI in 1903 and 1904, and he learned much. He returned to the Essex side at the end of June 1903, and he bowled Joe Vine of Sussex to claim his first wicket for the county. His development was slow, and it was not until 1905, the year that he won the amateur middle-weight Championship of Great Britain, that he made his first real advance.

He took 35 wickets and topped the Essex bowling averages, and he became the first Essex bowler to perform the hat-trick. This was against Yorkshire at Leyton when he took five wickets in eight balls. He always did well against Yorkshire. They understood his type of cricket, hard and fair.

In 1906, Essex faced one of their innumerable crises. Walter Mead had not played for two seasons, support was poor, and extinction was by no means improbable. Happily, the differences with Mead were resolved, the county was more successful, support increased, and Douglas played his first full season, reached 1000 runs and took 93 wickets. In the first county match played at Southchurch Park, Southend, he took eight Leicestershire wickets for 33 runs. That winter he went on his first overseas tour, with MCC to New Zealand.

He enjoyed another successful all-round season in 1907, and he hit his maiden first-class century, 102 not out against Sussex at Leyton, the following season. It was in 1908 that he also won his Olympic Gold Medal.

Back at Essex in 1909, however, times were bad. On the playing side and financially, the county was sliding into an abyss. There was some slight improvement in 1910, but at the end of the season Charlie McGahey resigned as captain. To the surprise of many, and to the anger of some, Douglas succeeded him.

The truth of why Douglas, and not Perrin, succeeded McGahey will never be known, but it is generally accepted that his appointment was made because old Douglas had taken up one of the mortgages on the Leyton ground in 1907-08 and so saved the club from extinction. In 1911, he named his price for that salvation.

Whatever the politics or the reasoning, J.W.H.T.Douglas led Essex for 18 years, and only Hawke and Grace have captained a county side longer. He was a strong disciplinarian, and he could be a hard man to deal with, but Essex was his life. He had compassion and concern for his side, but he wanted the best out of them. He was untiring and unrelenting on himself, and he could never understand why others could not emulate his stamina and resolve. He lived hard and he played hard. To the slacker or the under-achiever, he could be merciless. He was not, perhaps, the greatest of tacticians, but he was a great leader of men. In a medieval war, he would have been first up the ladder and onto the ramparts.

Douglas never wore a cap, and he would polish the ball on his bare forearm. In hot or cold, he defied the elements. In return, he tested people, and if they passed, they had the most reliable of allies for the rest of their lives. There were few who played under him or against him who did not have the greatest admiration and respect for him.

As a bowler, he had the ability to move the ball both ways, and to obtain that mythical nip from the pitch. In his early days, he was quick, and Jack Hobbs was one of those who considered him to be one of the best bowlers he ever encountered.

As a batsman, he shed the hard-hitting of his early youth to become notably obdurate. He was correct, playing within the confines of what he considered his limitations. In Australia, they nicknamed him 'Johnny Won't Hit To-day', but his rate of scoring would still put many of to-day's cricketers to shame. He was by nature and instinct a bowler; he was a batsman by hard work and application.

He first played for the Gentlemen against the Players in 1906, and in the 1911 match, at Lord's, recognised as a Test trial, he hit 72 and 22 not out, and had figures of 5 for 53 and 2 for 38, bowling 'with unremitting endeavour and outstanding skill'. He was chosen to go with Warner's side to Australia.

Warner fell ill. There were only two other amateurs in the party, Douglas and F.R.Foster, the captain of the Warwickshire side that had just won the Championship. Warner handed the captaincy on to Douglas who thereby led England on the occasion of his Test debut. That match was lost, but the next four were won. Douglas was a hero. Two years later, after others had declined invitations, he led England in South Africa, and his side won by four Tests to nil. Had his Test career ended there, at the age of 32, he would have been remembered as one of the most successful captains in Test history, but there was to be a post-war period.

In 1914, Douglas performed the 'double' for the first time, and the feat was accomplished in Essex matches alone so he became the first Essex player to do the 'double' for the county. In all, he was to perform five 'doubles', reach 1000 runs in ten seasons and take 100 wickets in seven. He led Essex well, and the county's fortunes took a turn for the better. He and J.R.Freeman established an Essex seventh wicket record, 261 against Lancashire at Leyton. World War One ended cricket for four years. Douglas was commissioned in the Bedfordshire Regiment and rose to the rank of lieutenant-colonel.

In 1919, he returned to cricket and did the 'double' in all matches. The following year, he took 147 wickets, and in 1921, he scored 1547 runs, including 210 not out against Derbyshire at Leyton. It was in this match that he took a career best 9 for 47 and added a record 251 for the ninth wicket with Hare. Two years later, with Jack O'Connor, he claimed the sixth wicket record, since equalled, of 206 against Gloucestershire at Cheltenham.

While he thrived for Essex he had his problems with England. He led the side to Australia, 1920-21, and suffered five defeats in the Tests. Australia came to England and won three more. Douglas was replaced as captain although he was retained in the side. He accepted his dismissal with dignity.

He was to tour Australia once more, 1924-25, as vice-captain and to lead England in one more unsuccessful Test Match.

In 1924, Douglas limped through most of the season, took 100 wickets, but Essex floundered. The following year, Essex improved, but Douglas showed a decline. His speed and stamina seemed to have left him, and, typically, he refused to say that he was in considerable pain. At the end of the season, he was operated upon for appendicitis, and he could not take his place in the side until July 1926.

In the last game of that season, he hit 103 against Nottinghamshire, and, in 1927, he reached 1000 runs, but his batting had become totally introspective. Moreover, he bowled less and less.

The 1928 season was a disaster for Essex who won only two matches and finished second from bottom in the Championship. In 32 matches, 39 players were used. Douglas was 46, and that great engine was wearing out. It happens to all, but he found it particularly hard to accept.

He had been a virtual dictator of Essex cricket since the war, but the committee now suggested that he should resign. He refused and fought the committee with the tenacity that he fought all his battles. He had 'done the state some service', and he demanded a respect that was not forthcoming. There were faults on both sides, but he never played for Essex again. Nothing in his life so grieved him as his parting with his beloved county.

In the winter of 1930, he and his father went to Finland to order the timber that would be delivered the following summer. On the return journey, their ship, *Oberon*, collided with its sister ship off the coast of Denmark and sank in four minutes. Douglas and his father were two of the 42 people who were drowned.

The flags at Leyton were lowered to half-mast. The gladiator with his thick black hair, plastered down and parted in the middle would be seen no more. Some doubted that he was a great captain; few doubted that he was a great man.

M	Inns	NOs	Runs	HS	Avge	100s	Ct
459	746	108	17915	210*	28.07	18	265

Overs	Mds	Runs	Wkts	Avge	Best	10/m	5/inn
10552.5	1800	33653	1443	23.32	9/47	21	93

William David Fraser DOW

Born: Langside, Glasgow, Scotland, 27 November 1933.
One of the most noted of Scottish cricketers, Dow was a fast medium pace bowler who was educated at St Aloysius Academy and had played 11 times for his national side with considerable success before appearing for Essex.

Playing as a professional, he appeared for the county against Cambridge University at Brentwood in 1958 and took 4 for 51, bowling Ted Dexter. The following year, he played against Kent at Westcliff but met with no success.

Dow also assisted Cumberland and played rugby for West of Scotland.

M	Inns	NOs	Runs	HS	Avge
2	3	2	9	9*	9.00

Overs	Mds	Runs	Wkts	Avge	Best
55.2	10	171	4	42.75	4/51

Anthony William DURLEY

Born: Ilford, 30 September 1933.
Died: Bedfordshire, 1 January 1993.
Tony Durley joined the staff in 1956 and made his five appearances for the county the following season. He was unable to play in 1958 because of a cartilage operation and left the staff after that. With Buckhurst Hill he was a wicket-keeper batsman, but he did not keep in county matches. He played soccer for Leyton Orient, though not in the first team, and for Ilford, and he represented Essex at table tennis. He moved to Bedfordshire and played for the Luton Town club as well as representing Bedfordshire in the Minor Counties Championship. At the time of his death he was chairman of Bedfordshire CCC.

M	Inns	NOs	Runs	HS	Avge	Ct
5	8	-	38	16	4.75	3

David Edward EAST

Born: Clapton, London, 27 July 1959.
David East replaced Neil Smith as Essex's wicket-keeper in 1981 and held the position in ebullient fashion until a serious finger injury virtually ended his first-class career in 1989, Garnham had arrived on the staff, and East was unable to force his way back into the side after a year's absence. He retired at the end of the 1991 season.

David East was not a stylish wicket-keeper, nor a batsman in the classical mould, but he was a good, exciting keeper and a savage hitter of pace bowling, with an emphasis on the leg side.

Like many others, he was a product of the Ilford Cricket School, Ilford CC and London Schools. He played for Essex 2nd XI, read Biology at the University of East Anglia and played for Northamptonshire 2nd XI in 1979. He returned to Essex in 1980 and made his first-class debut at Edgbaston the following season. Three weeks later, in his second NatWest Trophy match, he held four catches as Essex beat Gloucestershire, and two of them, to account for Zaheer and Hignell, were breathtaking. He took the individual award. He came close to taking his second award in the quarter-final at

Hove when he shared a vital last wicket stand with John Lever, who had coached him at Ilford, and held three catches.

Capped in 1982, he was the winner of the wicket-keeper of the season award in 1983 which was the season in which he caught nine Sussex batsmen in the match at Hove. Four times he had eight victims in a match, and his eight against Kent at Folkestone in 1986 included five stumpings. His outstanding achievement, however, came at Taunton in 1985 when he caught the first eight Somerset batsman to equal Wally Grout's world record.

He could, and did, produce some violent batting. His 134 against Gloucestershire at Ilford in 1988 saved Essex from an innings defeat. He hit five sixes and 19 fours, and his runs came off 113 balls. There was always a sense of bouncy fun in his cricket. He was an ample cricketer who never hid the fact that he was enjoying what he did.

East played hockey for Woodford Wells where he had his wedding reception, and, in the winters, he worked in banking and for the Essex Cricketers' Benefit Association. On his retirement, he took up a position with the wine merchants Lay and Wheeler, played club cricket for Colchester and East Essex and coached the French national cricket team.

M	Inns	NOs	Runs	HS	Avge	100s	Ct	/st
190	254	32	4553	134	20./51	4	480	/53

Overs	Mds	Runs	Wkts	Avge
4.2	-	17	-	-

Sunday League

M	Inns	NOs	Runs	HS	Avge	Ct	/st
110	59	19	510	43	13.03	88	/15

Benson and Hedges Cup

M	Inns	NOs	Runs	HS	Avge	Ct	/st
38	22	5	235	33	13.82	54	/ 1

NatWest Trophy

M	Inns	NOs	Runs	HS	Avge	Ct	/st
21	16	5	142	28	12.91	29	/3

Raymond Eric EAST

Born: Manningtree, 20 June 1947.
To Ray East, cricket was always a game to be enjoyed, and the crowd knew it and warmed to it. Whether he was bowling his slow left-arm with that most beautiful of loops and deceptive spin, batting with determination

and the eagerness to score runs or fielding with dynamic enthusiasm in any position, Ray East had a talent to amuse. His clowning, as he confessed, was his way of coping with his nerves.

Born in Essex, he was brought up in East Bergholt, began work as an apprentice electrician, played village cricket, was spotted

by Peter Smith and asked to go for a trial with Essex. He had played for Suffolk Schools, and in three 2nd XI games for Essex he took 30 wickets at low cost. On the strength of those performances, he was picked to play for the county against Oxford University at Romford, June 1965. He took 3 for 28 and 1 for 17, and the following season he appeared in 13 Championship matches. By the time that Brian Taylor took over as captain and the playing staff was reduced to a minimum, 1967, he was a regular member of the side and captured 61 Championship wickets.

Under Taylor, he matured and prospered, and he became one of the core of players who were to take Essex to the glories of the late 70s and early 80s. He took 92 wickets in 1978, played in two Test trials and did the 'hat-trick' in one of them, but he never played for England. He went with D.H.Robins' side to South Africa, 1973-74, and with the Overseas XI to India 1980-81, and Test cricket is the poorer for not having had the benefit of his infectious humour.

East's quality as a right-handed batsman in the lower order was an immense asset to the county, and his one century came against Hampshire at Chelmsford in 1976. The following year, he returned his best bowling figures, 8 for 30 against Nottinghamshire at Ilford. He also took some outstanding catches in close to the wicket positions. Perhaps his only weakness was one of temperament, that nervousness which he attempted to conceal with his humorous antics.

His last full season was 1983, although he played a few games the following year. He coached at the cricket school and was appointed captain of the 2nd XI. He did an outstanding job in both capacities and as manager of the younger sides. In 1989, he took up an appointment at Ipswich School.

Ray East has played for Suffolk since 1991 and captains the side. His autobiography, published 1983, is called, appropriately enough, *A Funny Turn*.

M	Inns	NOs	Runs	HS	Avge	100s	Ct
405	513	111	7103	113	17.66	1	251

Overs	Mds	Runs	Wkts	Avge	Best	10/m	5/inn
10836.1	3179	25804	1010	25.52	8/30	10	49

Sunday League

M	Inns	NOs	Runs	HS	Avge	Ct
1107.5	105	38	654	25*	9.76	85

Overs	Mds	Runs	Wkts	Avge	Best	5/inn
187.5	104	4504	187	24.08	6/18	4

Benson and Hedges Cup

M	Inns	NOs	Runs	HS	Avge	Ct
55	32	15	259	54	15.23	16

Overs	Mds	Runs	Wkts	Avge	Best	5/inn
418	64	1262	49	25.75	5/33	1

Gillette Cup/NatWest Trophy

M	Inns	NOs	Runs	HS	Avge	Ct
32	23	5	199	38*	11.05	13

Overs	Mds	Runs	Wkts	Avge	Best
257.3	50	657	26	25.26	4/28

George Frederick EASTMAN

Born: Leyton, 7 April 1903.
Died: Eastbourne, Sussex, 15 March 1991.

The younger brother of Laurie Eastman, George Eastman filled the gap for Essex caused by the retirement of Jack Freeman when he stepped in as wicket-keeper in 1926. The post posed problems for the county, for many talented amateurs, like Gilligan and Nicholas, were available only spasmodically. Eastman performed most capably behind the stumps, but his weakness as a batsman meant that he was certain to be replaced as soon as a wicket-keeper of talent who could also bat arrived.

George Eastman appeared regularly in 1927, but he had fewer opportunities in the next two seasons, and the coming of Roy Sheffield brought his end.

He was a professional footballer, a half back with Clapton Orient.

M	Inns	NOs	Runs	HS	Avge	Ct	/st
48	66	28	265	34*	6.97	29	/21

Lawrence Charles EASTMAN

Born: Enfield Wash, Middlesex, 3 June 1897.
Died: Harefield, Middlesex, 17 April 1941.
Laurie Eastman intended to take up medicine as a profession, but World War One ended that ambition. He served on the Western Front and won both the Distinguished Conduct Medal and the Military Medal, and, after the war, turned his attention to cricket.

He played for Essex as an amateur, making his debut against Gloucestershire at Bristol in July 1920, as a medium-pace bowler and taking three wickets in four balls. His third match was against Middlesex at Lord's, and Essex, facing a total of 446, were 184 for 8 when he joined Russell. The pair added 175 by the end of the day, and Eastman made 91.

Two years later, Laurie Eastman became assistant secretary of Essex and began to appear regularly in the county side. He held this position until the end of the 1926 season after which he played as a professional. He was, in the words of J.E.Clay, 'one of those most valued possessions of any county cricket club, a man who year in and year out rendered consistently good service with bat and ball and was, moreover, that fine type of sportsman who was ever ready to sacrifice his own success in the interests of the side.'

He hit his highest score, 161 against Derbyshire at Derby, in 1929, the first season in which he reached 1000 runs. He opened the innings on very many occasions, but he always observed with humour that he batted every position in the order except number 11.

Curiously, in his Benefit Match against Middlesex, at Southend, in 1939, he had an injured knee and was forced to go in last.

He never enjoyed the best of health, and injury kept him out of cricket for much of the 1930 season, but his happy disposition always made him popular with colleagues and crowd.

Standing over six feet in height, he was a natural hitter of the ball, hitting straight and clean. He abandoned his medium-pace for spin and had the ability to turn the ball both ways although it was as a leg-spinner that he was most deadly. It was typical of his intelligence and love of the game that he remarked that he gained most pleasure from slow bowling as he delighted in pitting his brains against the batsman and defeating him with flight and spin.

He was an admirable coach and visited New Zealand three times in that capacity. He also coached in South Africa and toured South America with Brinckman's side in 1937-38. He played for Otago for two seasons 1927-28 and 1928-29, and scored consistently.

In England, all his cricket was played for Essex, for he gained no recognition in representative matches of any kind. Perhaps he was too eager to hit the ball. Going in first in the last three seasons before the outbreak of World War Two, he hit a 1000 runs each year, but he did not score a century. He could take an attack apart from the start – 90 out of 127 in 90 minutes v Kent, 1937; 71 out of 85 in 55 minutes v Hampshire, 1939 – these were typical delights for the spectator, but they were unlikely to encourage selectors.

As World War One had ended his medical career, so World War Two ended his career in first-class cricket. He joined the Civil Defence and played for London Counties in their charity matches around the country. He had the honour of captaining the side when they first appeared at Lord's in July 1940. The match was against British Empire XI, and Eastman's side, which included Jack O'Connor, won by 104 runs. Within 12 months, Eastman was dead. He was on duty as an ARP warden when a bomb exploded close to him. Suffering from severe shock, he was operated on at Harefield Hospital, but he died following the operation.

His brother George Eastman, a wicket-keeper, also played for Essex.

M	Inns	NOs	Runs	HS	Avge	100s	Ct
442	679	49	12965	161	20.57	7	254

Overs	Mds	Runs	Wkts	Avge	Best	10/m	5/inn
9995	2493	26102	975	26.77	7/28	3	29

131.7(eight ball)

Brian Ernest Arthur EDMEADES

Born: Matlock, Derbyshire, 17 September 1941.

Although born in Derbyshire, Brian Edmeades was a graduate of Essex cricket. He moved from Essex Schools to club cricket with West Essex before joining the county staff, and his accent was never anything other than East London. Indeed, his pronunciation of the French title of a popular song gave birth to his nickname *Chanson* or, more familiarly, *Chantz.*

He had a thorough schooling in the 2nd XI under Arnold Quick after joining the staff in 1958, and he was originally seen as a bowler who could bat a bit. A 'precocious straw-haired youth', as Doug Insole affectionately dubbed him, Edmeades bowled medium pace off a comparatively short, hustling run. He came quite quickly off the pitch and was naggingly accurate.

His first-class debut came in 1961 when he played against the South African Fezela

M	Inns	NOs	Runs	HS	Avge	100s	Ct
335	555	69	12593	163	25.91	14	105

Overs	Mds	Runs	Wkts	Avge	Best	10/m	5/inn
3793.1	830	9688	374	25.90	7/37	1	10

Sunday League

M	Inns	NOs	Runs	HS	Avge	Ct
112	99	20	1612	86	20.40	16

Overs	Mds	Runs	Wkts	Avge	Best
677.1	53	2703	115	23.50	4/17

Benson and Hedges Cup

M	Inns	NOs	Runs	HS	Avge	100s	Ct
24	23	3	708	125*	35.40	1	4

Overs	Mds	Runs	Wkts	Avge	Best	5/inn
166.4	30	561	26	21.57	5/22	1

Gillette Cup

M	Inns	NOs	Runs	H.S	Avge	Ct
19	18	2	408	93	25.50	2

Overs	Mds	Runs	Wkts	Avge	Best
189	26	554	26	21.30	4/71

touring side on the Hoffman Ground at Chelmsford. He also played in the Championship matches against Surrey and Sussex that season. At Hove, he took four wickets, including those of Jim Parks and Alan Oakman.

A regular place in the side in 1962 saw him begin to climb up the order, and, in 1964, he hit a maiden first-class century, 135 against Lancashire at Old Trafford, but it was not until 1968 that he began to open the innings.

It was Edmeades' bowling that was still of most value to Essex, and, in 1966, he took 106 wickets at 18.59 runs apiece. This included a haul of 7 for 37 against Glamorgan at Leyton. After that season, his bowling was used less and less, and in his last ten seasons with the county he reached a 1,000 runs five times. In limited-over cricket, he became an invaluable all-rounder.

A good county cricketer and a most loyal and popular club man, Brian Edmeades retired at the end of the 1976 season. He took up a position with Access in Scotland and coached and played, with considerable success, for the Clydesdale club.

His career as a professional cricketer ended in 1981, and he now lives near Nottingham selling sports equipment for Gunn and Moore.

Guy Janison EDWARDS

Born: Kensington, London, 11 May 1881.
Died: Rockcliff House, Upper Slaughter, Gloucestershire, 30 September 1962.
An Old Etonian, Guy Edwards played twice for Essex in 1907. A right-handed batsman, he was the uncle of Alastair McCorquodale, the 100 metres silver medalist at the 1948 Olympics and Middlesex fast bowler.

M	Inns	NOs	Runs	HS.	Avge	Ct
2	3	-	45	21	15.00	2

Herbert Denis Edleston ELLIOTT

Born: Newport, Shropshire, 30 March 1887.
Died: Bognor Regis, Sussex, 26 April 1973.
Educated at Newport Grammar School, Shropshire, Elliott played twice for Essex in 1913 as a bowler. An amateur, he appeared in the home matches against Kent and Northamptonshire in August and had James Seymour of Kent caught by Russell.

M	Inns	NOs	Runs	HS.	Avge	Ct
2	4	-	3	3	0.75	1

Overs	Mds	Runs	Wkts	Avge	Best
23	1	107	1	107.00	1/67

Ronald Ernest EVANS

Born: East Ham, 27 July 1922.
Died: Upminster, 16 June 1993.
Ron Evans first played for Ilford when on leave from the RAF during World War Two. Having served in the Far East, he returned to

the club in 1946 and quickly established himself as a very sound opening batsman. He made the first of his appearances for the Club Cricket Conference in 1947 and was to play for them many times in the next decade. P a r t i c u l a r l y strong on the leg side, he scored 1,000's of runs for Ilford over a period of 20 years and captained the club from 1960 to 1964. He also played for Stoics, Essex Wanderers, The Forty Club and Chinghoppers.

He made a most favourable impression when he first played for Essex in 1950, and he hit 79 in the victory over Kent at Clacton. He appeared in nine matches that season, but thereafter his time for county cricket was very limited, and he last played in 1957.

Ron Evans was a founder director of the Ilford Cricket School in 1957, and he was managing director of J.Evans and Son, funeral directors, the family business he had joined on leaving school, Highfield College, Leigh-on-Sea.

M	Inns	NOs	Runs	HS.	Avge	Ct
17	29	-	482	79	16.62	8

Victor James EVANS

Born: Woodford, 4 March 1912.
Died: Barking, 28 March 1975.
Victor Evans joined the Essex staff in 1929 as a medium pace off-break bowler, but he did not make his first-class debut until 1932. He

was never able to command a regular place in the side, and by far his best season was 1935 when he took 56 first-class wickets. At Southend, he claimed 6 for 47, and 4 for 57 as Gloucestershire were beaten by 63 runs.

He appeared in only ten Championship matches the following season, and in just six in 1937, his last season. In 1938, he became

professional for Golcar in the Huddersfield and District League.

In wartime cricket, he was very successful for London Counties in their charity matches around the country, and even more successful for the Essex County Services side which, with the blessing of the county club, operated in 1944. Evans had some remarkable achievements for this team, and his figures included 9 for 46 against a New Zealand XI at Chelmsford and 6 for 13 against the strong Australian Services XI at High Wycombe. In this match, he took four wickets in four balls.

M	Inns	NOs	Runs	HS.	Avge	Ct
62	96	37	469	23*	7.94	12

Overs	Mds	Runs	Wkts	Avge	Best	10/m	5/inn
1304.4	277	3843	129	29.79	6/47	1	5

Stanley Charles EVE

Born: Stepney, London, 8 December 1925.
Died: Havering, 27 January 1990.
Stan Eve was a right-handed batsman who assisted Essex as an amateur intermittently between 1949 and 1957. He had been noticed in 1943 when, at Lord's, he hit 91 for the Air Training Corps against the Royal Naval College, Dartmouth, and he was a prolific scorer in club cricket with Upminster. He made his debut for Essex against Worcestershire, opening the innings with Dodds, and in his second match, against Warwickshire at Brentwood, he hit 120. He played all the shots in an innings which lasted just over two hours.

He had a neat, enterprising style, ever-ready to attack, and he was a good fielder.

He appeared in 16 matches in 1949, but the next season he was available for only six matches. Between 1952 and 1956, he was unable to play at all because of business commitments. He reappeared against Glamorgan and Gloucestershire at the start of the 1957 season, but thereafter it was business and Upminster.

M	Inns	NOs	Runs	HS.	Avge	100s	Ct
32	51	4	1041	120	22.14	1	17

Frederick Luther FANE

Born: Curragh Camp, County Kildare, Ireland, 27 April 1875.
Died: Kelvedon Hatch, 27 November 1960.

The son of an Army officer who played for Essex in the days before the county was first-class, F.L.Fane was educated at Charterhouse where he was in the XI for three years, heading the batting averages in 1894. Going up to Magdalen College, Oxford, he failed to get his blue as a freshman and did little in his two appearances in the Varsity match, 1897 and 1898. He opened the innings in both years.

He had made his debut for Essex as early as June 1895, when he opened the innings with H.A.Carpenter against Somerset at Leyton and scored 36 and 0. His first century came in 1899 when he made 207 against Leicestershire, so becoming the first Essex player to make a double century as his maiden century. He was a stylish batsman, with a fine off-drive and strong in front of the wicket as befits one who was ever eager to play off the front foot.

A man of means with time to spare, Fane was able to play cricket both winter and summer and toured West Indies in 1901-02, and New Zealand and Australia the following winter. When not touring he was invariably out shooting with his friend Charles Kortright whom he succeeded as captain of Essex in 1904, a position he held until 1906.

F.L.Fane was to become the first Essex cricketer to captain England, but he disliked the job intensely, Sir Home Gordon was to write that only Herbie Taylor, the South African, hated captaining a side more than Fane did. Perhaps Fane's greatest moment as captain was when he led Essex to victory over the Australians by 19 runs in 1905. Wisden recalled -

'Fane finished the match with a remarkable catch, not for any exceptional excellence as a piece of fielding, but from the place where it was made. With a close finish clearly in sight and Buckenham bowling at a great pace, Fane, to save a possible boundary from byes, took up a position practically in line with the wickets and just inside the Pavilion rails – in short, that of very deep long-stop. Frank Laver,

sweeping the ball right round with a curious stiff-armed stroke from the shoulder, lifted it high and straight to where Fane was standing. Though not as a rule the safest of fieldsman, Fane did not fail his side on that occasion.'

His readiness to tour gave him a place on

the MCC side to South Africa, 1905-06, and he hit 143 in the third Test Match in Johannesburg, which he considered the best innings of his career. He went to Australia with A.O.Jones' side in 1907-08 and, when Jones fell ill, Fane led the side in the first three Tests. He had a similar experience in South Africa in 1909-10 when Leveson-Gower stood down from the last two Tests. In short, Fane captained England five times, each time by default.

With men like Fry and Jackson available, Fane was never selected for a Test match in England although he maintained good form and hit a splendid 217 in five hours for Essex against Surrey at The Oval in 1911. Apart from his games for Essex, he played for London County, MCC and the Gentlemen.

At the outbreak of war in 1914, he was commissioned in the Leeds Rifles, a battalion raised by F.S.Jackson, and he served in France. He was awarded the Military Cross 'for conspicuous gallantry and devotion to duty' just prior to the Battle of Bullecourt in 1917.

Fane played only a handful of games for Essex after World War One, the last being in 1922 when he scored 13 against Dublin University at Brentwood. His last first-class match was for Leveson-Gower's XI two years later.

In 1938, at the age of 63, he got married and had two daughters, the younger of whom was born when he was 77. In 1956, he read his own obituary in *Wisden* who had believed that the F.L.Fane who had died was the former Essex captain. In fact, it was his cousin Francis L.Fane. By coincidence, Frederick Fane's father had also read his own obituary.

M	Inns	NOs	Runs	HS.	Avge	100s	Ct
292	512	30	12599	217	26.13	18	141

Overs	Mds	Runs	Wkts	Avge
6.5	-	32	-	-

Harold Alker FARAGHER

Born: Reddish, Lancashire, 20 July 1917.
Harold Faragher appeared for Lancashire 2nd XI in 1935 and showed great promise, but, in the uncertain economic situation of that period, it was decided that he should follow a career in education. He played for Essex in 1949 and 1950 when holidays allowed and hit 71 not out against Middlesex, at Lord's, and 85

not out against Kent, at Maidstone, in his second year when he topped the county averages. He did not play first-class cricket after that season due mainly to the demands of his work. When he retired he was Head of Business Studies at Barking College of Technology.

He played for the Forty Club and, most famously, for Ilford whom he captained for several seasons. His contribution to Essex cricket has been immense, for he was one of the founders of the Ilford Indoor Cricket School where he coached and helped many cricketers of all ages and varying abilities with his good humour, patience, charm and expertise.

Harold Faragher served on the committee of the county club and is the author of small practical handbook, *Let's Play Cricket!*

M	Inns	NOs	Runs	HS.	Avge	Ct
6	9	2	274	85*	39.14	4

Kenneth FARNES

Born: Leytonstone, 8 July 1911.
Died: Chipping Warden, Oxfordshire, 20 October 1941.
The son of a prominent club cricketer, Ken Farnes played from an early age and gained every encouragement from both his father and his Headmaster at the Royal Liberty School, Romford, S.B.Hartley. He joined Gidea Park CC and so impressed Percy Perrin in a match against Essex Club and Ground in 1930 that he was called up to play for the county a few weeks later, against Gloucestershire, at Chelmsford, at the end of June. There was nothing sensational in his debut, but in his second match, at Southend, against Kent, in August, he took 5 for 36 in the first innings and claimed Aidan Crawley as his first first-class wicket. He twice bowled Les Ames in the match, but his performance was over-

considerable height, and it would lift sharply and test the rib cage of any batsman. On a hard, true pitch, he was a difficult adversary; on a pitch giving the bowler any assistance, he was lethal and much feared.

A natural successor to Larwood, he first played for England in the first Test against Australia, at Trent Bridge, in 1934. He took 5 for 102 and 5 for 77, but England lost. It was Farnes who, in this Test, had Chipperfield caught behind for 99 when that batsman was making his Test debut and needed just one for his century at lunch on the second day. Farnes also played at Lord's, but an injured heel hampered him for the rest of the season.

He had a disappointing tour of West Indies although he played in two Tests, but a cartilage injury kept him out of the whole of the 1935 season. He returned fresh and furious in 1936, savaged the Players with a devastating spell of fast bowling at Lord's and was chosen to go with Allen's side to Australia, 1936-37. He appeared in the last two Tests with considerable success, and, in 1938, playing in all four Tests against Australia, he was England's leading wicket-taker in the series. His Test career was to end the following winter with five matches against South Africa.

In 1939, he was unable to play for Essex until August, but in seven matches, he took 33 wickets.

Essex won four and lost one of those games, the other two being ruined by rain. At Clacton, he performed the *hat-trick* against Nottinghamshire, sending back Heane, Hardstaff and Gunn, an impressive trio. In the over before his *hat-trick* , he had had Harris caught behind. He finished with 5 for 30, and Essex won a game in which they had trailed on the first innings.

Clacton, like Southend, was always a happy ground for Ken Farnes. It was there in 1938 that he had match figures of 15 for 113 against Glamorgan, his 8 for 38 in the second innings being the best performance of his great career. A month earlier, he had taken 8 for 43 in the first innings for the Gentlemen as they beat the Players for only the second time since 1914.

Farnes was a most capable close to the wicket fielder, his height enabling him to take catches others could not reach, and although he had no pretensions as a batsman, he did hit 97 not out against Somerset at Taunton in 1936.

shadowed by 'Tich' Freeman who took all ten Essex wickets in the first innings and finished with match figures of 16 for 94.

Ken Farnes had left school and started work in insurance before turning to banking, but, in the autumn of 1930, he went up to Cambridge where he was in the XI for three years, and, by 1933, he was unrivalled as the best amateur fast bowler in the country.

He had accepted a position as a master at Worksop College so that his appearances in county cricket were always limited to later in the season. Tall – he was six feet five inches – handsome and dark, he was a formidable opponent. He brought the ball down from a

A man of charm with great artistic sensitivity, Ken Farnes brought lustre to Essex cricket whenever he was able to play. In his own words, 'I had a passion – or even a mania – for cricket, and first-class cricket was the abstract chief deity . . .I was an unquestioning fanatic.' This enthusiasm shone through all that he did.

At the outbreak of World War Two, Ken Farnes joined the Royal Air Force and trained as a pilot in Canada. Having received his *wings* and with the rank of Pilot Officer, he volunteered for night-flying. He had been back in England only four weeks when the plane which he was piloting on night-flying practice crashed in Oxfordshire, and he was killed. He was 30 years old.

His delightful book, now quite rare, *Tours and Tests,* was published in 1940.

M	Inns	NOs	Runs	HS.	Avge	Ct
79	94	31	590	97*	9.36	42

Overs	Mds	Runs	Wkts	Avge	Best	10/m	5/inn
2265.5	458	7086	367	19.30	8/38	5	28

149 (eight ball)

Geoffrey George FARNFIELD

Born: West Ham, 13 July 1897.
Died: Leamington Spa, Warwickshire, 22 March 1974.
One of 30 amateurs upon whom Essex called in 1921, Farnfield was a right-handed batsman. He opened the innings on one occasion and was one of the more regular faces in the side.

M	Inns	NOs	Runs	HS	Avge	Ct
12	20	1	252	41	13.26	5

Major William Frederick Oliver FAVIELL

Born: Loughton, 5 June 1882.
Died: Nairobi, Kenya, 14 February 1950.
Educated at Forest School, William Faviell was a punishing right-handed batsman and a fast medium pace bowler who was a Regular Army officer. He played for Europeans in India between 1903-04 and 1909-10. In 1905, he headed the batting averages in Ceylon where his regiment was stationed, hitting two centuries against good opposition.

In England, in 1908, he took 7 for 26 and scored 151 for Stoics against St John's School,

Leatherhead, and the same season he played seven matches for Essex.

From 1933 until 1945, he was a major at the Tower of London.

M	Inns	NOs	Runs	HS	Avge	Ct
7	12	4	104	27	13.00	4

Overs	Mds	Runs	Wkts	Avge
5	1	13	-	-

Michael Gwyn FIELD-BUSS

Born: Imtarfa, Malta, 23 September 1964.
Michael Field-Buss played for Essex Schools' sides from the age of ten. He joined the Ilford

club and was taken on the Essex staff as an off-break bowler in 1983. In spite of successes in the 2nd XI with bat and ball, he was restricted to two first team appearances in 1987, and he did not bowl in either match. Released at the end of the 1988 season, he joined Nottinghamshire and has begun to establish himself as a successor to Eddie Hemmings.

M	Inns	NOs	Runs	HS	Avge
2	4	1	56	34*	18.66

Keith William Robert FLETCHER

Born: Worcester, 20 May 1944.
Whatever may happen in the future of Essex cricket, it is certain that the name of Keith Fletcher will never be forgotten. The county club had been in existence for 103 years and had competed in the county Championship for 84 years before, in 1979, it first won a trophy. Then, within the space of six years, under the leadership of Keith Fletcher, Essex won every honour the game has to offer, three Championships, three Sunday League titles and both of the knock-out tournaments. No other captain in the history of the game has led a side to victory in all four competitions.

'The Gnome' succeeded Brian Taylor as captain in 1974 and gave way to Graham Gooch after the 1985 season. He returned to lead the side for another year, 1988, when Gooch felt that he was under too much pressure. If his captaincy of England was to be brief, Fletcher's stewardship of Essex has been exceeded only by J.W.H.T.Douglas.

Fletcher grew and matured with the side he initially led. He was scarred by criticism, hardened by adversity, and he had a deep and lasting understanding of the game founded on a technical and tactical awareness. After Fletcher's retirement in 1988, David Graveney wrote of him in *The Cricketer* -

'Tactically astute, you feel that playing against him any little mistake will be exploited to the full. However, his greatest quality is to maximise every ounce of ability in his team.'

The slightly hunched figure suggested a timidity, a man looking inward, but that image belied the character. Respected and admired, firm in resolution, he had the rare gift of being able to get from cricketers around him a standard of performance that was, in some instances, over and above their innate abilities.

In estimating the man's immense worth as a captain, one is inclined to overlook his greatness as a batsman. At the time of his retirement in 1988, he had scored more runs in a career and more runs for Essex than any other player. He had also held 519 catches, mostly in close to the wicket positions, bowled leg-breaks most effectively on occasion and, in limited-over cricket, scored runs at a brisk rate. As evidence of this, statistics tell us that when Essex won the Sunday League in 1984 Ken McEwan scored his runs at the rate of 76 per 100 balls, Graham Gooch 79 per 100, and Keith Fletcher 112 per 100 balls.

Although born in Worcester, Fletcher is basically a Londoner, for his parents were taking refuge in the Midlands in 1944 after being bombed out of their home in London two years earlier. After the war they settled in Cambridgeshire, and Keith played his first

cricket for the village side of Caldecote. He was 11 years old.

Two years later, he joined Royston and was recommended to Essex. He played for the Young Amateurs and for the Club and Ground, and Trevor Bailey was so impressed by what he saw that Fletcher was offered a contract immediately on leaving school. In July 1962, he made his debut, against Glamorgan at Ebbw Vale. The following season, he was a regular and reached 1000 runs before the end of July. *Wisden* saw him as 'one of the best English batting prospects for a long time . . .he produced an array of well-executed and powerful strokes that delighted spectators'. A fine future was prophesied, and the prophesy was fulfilled.

The first of his 59 Tests came in 1968, against Australia at Headingley. A duck and dropped catches amid a crowd hostile to a southerner preferred to a northern favourite did not prove the best of starts, but by the time he last played for England, as captain in 1982, he had scored 3272 Test runs and hit seven Test centuries.

One of his two double centuries was for England against New Zealand, the other, 228 not out, was for Essex against Sussex at Hastings in 1968. His best bowling performance was to come in the Championship season of 1979 when he took 5 for 41 against Middlesex at Colchester.

In the few minutes when he was not touring with an England party or some other representative side, he would sell and deliver oil to farmers. He is, essentially, a rural person, enjoying rural pleasures. He follows the rural ethic that you only shoot or catch what you are going to eat.

Brought up on uncovered pitches, he was a magnificent player on a damaged wicket and a demolisher of spinners. Outside his 100s and 50s, he played many short knocks which were gems and often match-winners. In the Benson and Hedges Cup Final of 1979, after Gooch and McEwan had savaged the Surrey attack, Fletcher played an innings of 34 which was a glory to watch and which maintained the momentum at a crucial time. Just over a month later, with the Championship won for the first time, he was cheered all the way to the wicket when he went out to bat against Surrey. He was out for four, and he was cheered all the way back to the pavilion.

In August, 1988, he led Essex for the last time in the Championship match at The Oval. The game was ruined by rain, and 'Fletch' was undefeated on nine at the end. He remained with Essex as manager and captain/coach of the 2nd XI, but in 1992, he was appointed England team manager.

Awarded the OBE in 1985, in 27 seasons, he wrote his name indelibly in the annals of Essex cricket.

M	Inns	NOs	Runs	HS	Avge	100s	Ct
574	920	122	29434	228*	36.88	45	519

Overs	Mds	Runs	Wkts	Avge	Best	5/inn
262.5	39	1268	29	43.72	5/41	1

Sunday League

M	Inns	NOs	Runs	HS	Avge	Ct
262	238	39	5726	99*	28.77	87

Overs	Mds	Runs	Wkts	Avge	Best
2.5	-	37	1	37.00	1/4

Benson and Hedges Cup

M	Inns	NOs	Runs	HS	Avge	100s	Ct
83	78	15	2111	101*	33.51	1	21

Overs	Mds	Runs	Wkts	Avge	Best
4.4	-	30	1	30.00	1/25

Gillette Cup/NatWest Trophy

M	Inns	NOs	Runs	HS	Avge	Ct
47	45	4	1036	97	25.27	16

Overs	Mds	Runs	Wkts	Avge	Best
10.3	1	43	2	21.50	1/16

Matthew Kailey FOSH

Born: Epping, 26 September 1957.

A left-handed batsman of great power and ability, Matthew Fosh hit 161 not out for Harrow against Eton at Lord's in 1975 and won his blue at Cambridge in 1977 and 1978. In the first of those years, he won the award as the *Most Promising Young Cricketer of the Year* which is donated by The Cricket Society. He had made his debut for Essex, against Cambridge University, the previous season. He played until 1978 and seemed an outstanding prospect for the future, but he felt that a cricket career was not what he desired and took up an appointment in the city. He was also a rugby blue at Cambridge.

M	Inns	NOs	Runs	HS	Avge	100s	Ct
14	23	-	481	66	20.91		5

Sunday League

M	Inns	NOs	Runs	HS	Avge	Ct
10	9	-	215	45	23.89	1

Gillette Cup

One match, did not bat.

Neil Alan FOSTER

Born: Colchester, 6 May 1962.

That Neil Foster enjoyed the highly successful career at county and international level that he did was a testimony to his character, determination and courage. He was in the sixth form of Philip Morant Comprehensive School when he first played for Essex in 1980,against Somerset, a tall, slim, dark fast bowler with a high, classical action.

In the first match at Ilford Week, May 1980, the Essex side was suddenly struck by a mystery virus. Neither Pont nor Phillip was able to bat, and Gooch was unable to continue his innings through illness. In the next match, depleted through the mystery *plague,* Essex called up Neil Foster to make his first-class debut against Kent, the day after his 18th birthday. He took the wickets of Tavare,

Woolmer and Ealham after his first delivery had gone for four wides, and Essex went on to win by two wickets.

He was not called upon again during the season, and an encouraging one-wicket display against the Sri Lankans constituted Foster's 1981 season. He had come up through Mistley, Wivenhoe and Colchester and East Essex Cricket clubs, had played for Essex Schools and Young England. He forced his way into the Essex side at the beginning of the 1982 season, but, having taken 12 wickets, he suffered a back injury. The injury necessitated an operation, the insertion of a plate into the back, and the complications which followed threatened to end a promising career before it had really started.

With the utmost resolve and determination, Foster fought his way back to fitness. In 1983, he was an integral part of a Championship side, was awarded his county cap and made his Test debut. At his peak, he was England's best strike, bowler as evidenced by his 6 for 104 at Madras in 1985 which set up England's victory over India, and his 8 for 107 against Pakistan at Headingley in 1987 when, in spite of this marvellous effort, England lost by an innings.

In 1986 and 1991, he took 100 wickets in the season, a rare achievement since the contraction of first-class cricket, and on both occasions Essex won the Championship. In the second of those seasons, 1991, he also hit his highest score, 107 not out against Sussex at Horsham, and returned his best bowling figures, 8 for 99 against Lancashire at Old Trafford.

His batting developed from slogging to cultured aggression. He hit cleanly and often, and with his excellent fielding he had every right to be considered an all-rounder. He would add to this by reminding us that he had a trial for Ipswich Town and played for Chelmsford City.

The bowling and the strain took their toll of Foster who found that the virtual disintegration of his knees meant more operations. The seriousness of these injuries was a main factor in prompting him to go to South Africa with Mike Gatting's side, 1989-90, and to suffer the inevitable ban.

Exiled from Test cricket, he showed an unexpected quality as a captain in the absence of Gooch and enjoyed considerable success.

The gentle north Essex burr and the genial smile could never disguise the fact that Foster does not suffer fools gladly, holds firm opinions and speaks his mind. Perhaps, it was part of the aggressive make up of the dedicated fast bowler, but he gave his all to Essex to the very end.

Obviously struggling at the beginning of the 1993 season, he was surprisingly recalled to the England side for the Lord's Test against Australia. A week later, it was announced that he had been forced to retire through injury, the persistent knee problem.

Neil Foster had already taken up a winter post at Holmwood House Preparatory School in Colchester, and he has happily continued full time in the job since his retirement.

M	Inns	NOs	Runs	HS	Avge	100s	Ct
180	200	44	3440	107*	22.05	2	96

Overs	Mds	Runs	Wkts	Avge	Best	10/m	5/inn
5970.3	1333	17626	747	23.59	8/99	7	42

Sunday League

M	Inns	NOs	Runs	HS	Avge	Ct
81	47	16	582	57	18.77	21

Overs	Mds	Runs	Wkts	Avge	Best	5/inn
547.2	32	2394	100	23.94	5/17	1

Benson and Hedges Cup

M	Inns	NOs	Runs	HS	Avge	Ct
49	21	8	278	62	21.38	8

Overs	Mds	Runs	Wkts	Avge	Best	5/inn
483	60	1679	77	21.80	5/32	1

NatWest Trophy

M	Inns	NOs	Runs	HS	Avge	Ct
22	13	2	149	26	13.55	3

Overs	Mds	Runs	Wkts	Avge	Best
244.1	46	751	39	19.25	4/9

Bruce Colin FRANCIS

Born: Sydney, Australia, 18 February 1948.
A stocky and pugnacious right-handed opening batsman who graduated from the Waverley club to the New South Wales Sheffield Shield side, Bruce Francis was registered as Essex's overseas player in 1971 after Lee Irvine had become one of the victims of the Stop the South Africans Tour of 1970 campaign. Francis had excelled with Accrington in the Lancashire League in 1970 when he also appeared in one game for Essex

2nd XI and two games for Northamptonshire 2nd XI.

He hit more than 1500 runs in his first season for Essex, and he scored them quickly, and the following winter he played for Australia against the World XI. He was selected for the tour of England, 1972, which meant that he was lost to Essex, but he was not very successful. He rejoined the county in 1973 and again scored well, but he retired at the end of the season although only 25. He never quite had the stomach for county cricket, and, capable as he was, he never found fielding the favourite part of his game.

He has established himself as an entrepreneur in cricket, playing a part in Packer's World Series Cricket in 1979 and later in 'rebel' tours of South Africa.

M	Inns	NOs	Runs	HS	Avge	100s	Ct
47	84	7	2962	188*	38.46	7	10

Benson and Hedges Cup

M	Inns	NOs	Runs	HS	Avge	Ct
6	6	2	271	76*	67.75	3

Sunday League

M	Inns	NOs	Runs	HS	Avge	100s	Ct
30	29	1	752	107	26.82	2	5

Gillette Cup

M	Inns	NOs	Runs	HS	Avge	Ct
5	5	-	234	87	46.80	3

Henry William Fernehough FRANKLIN

Born: Ford End, 30 June 1901.
Died: Worthing, Sussex, 25 May 1985.
Henry Franklin spent five years in the XI at Christ's Hospital School and won a scholarship to Christ Church, Oxford. He

appeared several times for the university in 1921 and did reasonably well, but he failed to get a blue. He played for Surrey against Oxford University at the end of June, but, within weeks, he was appearing regularly for Essex. He was an aggressive right-handed batsman and a leg-break bowler, but, as *Wisden* later suggested, it must have been 'his beautiful and tireless fielding which kept him his place in a team several of whom were old enough to be his father' rather than a batting average of 6.66 from 17 innings and the wicket of Major Robinson of Gloucestershire at a cost of 221 runs.

It was to be two seasons before the county's faith in him was to be justified. At Leyton, in 1923, he and J.W.H.T.Douglas shared a match-saving ninth wicket stand of 160 in just over two hours against Middlesex. The following year, his last at Oxford, he finally won his blue for cricket and he would have won a blue for hockey but for illness. He did win a blue at rugby and had an outstanding Varsity match. A full back, he was picked for the final England trial, and many believe that he was cruelly unlucky not to win an international cap. He appeared for Old Blues and for Leicester.

On leaving university, he became a master at Radley, and then at Rugby so that he was able to play for Essex only in the school holidays which he did until 1931. In 1940, he became headmaster of Epsom College and remained there until his retirement in 1962.

He captained Essex on occasions in his later years, and his most remarkable innings for the county was a century against Somerset, at Knowle, in 1928, when he hit a six and 17 fours in a vibrant 104.

Franklin was the author of several Latin textbooks, and he chaired a Home Office committee on punishment in prisons. A talented actor and musician, he was a man of wit and humour who was a popular companion.

M	Inns	NOs	Runs	HS	Avge	100s	Ct
73	104	14	1757	106	19.52	2	36

Overs	Mds	Runs	Wkts	Avge	Best
393	45	1596	36	44.33	4/40

Ronald Christian FRANKLIN

Born: Ford End, 9 September 1904.
Died: Prestwood, Buckinghamshire, 28 September 1982.
Educated at Christ's Hospital, Ronald Franklin was the younger brother of Henry Franklin. A right-arm medium pace bowler, he played for Essex in the last match of the 1925 season, against Leicestershire, and bowled George Geary in the second innings.

M	Inns	NOs	Runs	HS	Avge	Ct
1	2	-	1	1	0.50	1

Overs	Mds	Runs	Wkts	Avge	Best
11	1	41	1	41.00	1/20

Alastair Gregory James FRASER

Born: Edgware, Middlesex, 17 October 1967.
The younger brother of the Middlesex and

England bowler Angus, Alastair Fraser was on the Middlesex staff from 1986 to 1989 after which he joined Essex, making his debut in 1991. A fast medium-pace bowler who plays club cricket for Stanmore and who has pioneered playing and coaching in the West Indies during the winter, he was plagued by injury. His bowling rhythm, in particular, was affected, and he was released by Essex at the end of the 1993 season.

M	Inns	NOs	Runs	HS	Avge	Ct
5	5	2	86	52*	28.67	1

Overs	Mds	Runs	Wkts	Avge	Best
39.3	10	139	3	46.33	2/37

Benson and Hedges Cup

M	Inns	NOs	Runs	HS	Avge
1	1	-	6	6	6.00

Overs	Mds	Runs	Wkts	Avge	Best
5.1	-	31	1	31.00	1/31

Sunday League

M	Inns	NOs	Runs	HS	Avge	Ct
8	4	1	25	12	8.33	1

Overs	Mds	Runs	Wkts	Avge	Best
50	-	231	7	33.00	2/39

Alfred James FREEMAN

Born: Edmonton, Middlesex, 2 April 1892.
Died: Chelmsford, 28 April 1972.
One of the famous cricketing family, Alfred was cousin to J.R. and to A.P. 'Tich' Freeman of Kent. A left-arm medium pace bowler, he was employed by Hampstead CC for 47 years, first as bowler and assistant groundsman to his father, and then as groundsman.

He played one match for Essex in 1920, and from 1956 to 1964, he was groundsman for Ilford CC.

M	Inns	NOs	Runs	HS	Avge
1	2	1	1	1	1.00

Overs	Mds	Runs	Wkts	Avge
24	1	95	-	-

Edward Charles FREEMAN

Born: Ladywell, Lewisham, 7 December 1860.
Died: Westbury, Sherborne, Dorset, 16 October 1939.
A member of a famous cricketing family – his son, E.J. played for Essex; his grandson, D.P., for Kent; and, most notably, his nephews, J.R. and A.P. 'Tich' for Essex and Kent respectively – E.C.Freeman was the chief groundsman at Leyton when Essex achieved first-class status. Most of his cricket was played for the county before they became first-class, and his five first-class matches were spread over three seasons, 1894 to 1896.

Having asked the advice of the Surrey groundsman Sam Apted, he learned that he should apply a 'liquid mixture three days before the match' to ensure a good wicket. Unfortunately, he misunderstood the advice and applied the mixture on each of the three days before the match against Surrey with the result that the pitch was treacherous. Thereafter, he was noted for the fine wickets that he produced at Leyton. He later became coach and groundsman at Sherborne School where he was succeeded by his son, E.J.

M	Inns	NOs	Runs	HS	Avge	Ct
5	9	-	95	35	10.55	1

Overs	Mds	Runs	Wkts	Avge
12	3	40	-	-

(five-ball)

Edward John FREEMAN

Born: Ladywell, Lewisham, London, 16 October 1880.
Died: Sherborne, Dorset, 22 February 1964.
Son of the former Leyton groundsman and a  member of a noted cricketing family, E.J.Freeman played for Essex from 1904 until 1912 without ever commanding a regular place in the side. An occasional wicket-keeper and middle-order batsman, he never reached the standard that had been expected of him. His best year was in 1907 when he scored 564 runs, including his highest score, 84 against Nottinghamshire, at Trent Bridge.

He was a fine soccer player who made 27 appearances for Essex and led Leyton Boys in the Corinthian Shield Final against South London in 1896.

He succeeded his father as coach and groundsman at Sherbourne School and represented Dorset.

M	Inns	NOs	Runs	HS	Avge	Ct
55	91	3	1280	84	14.54	14

Overs	Mds	Runs	Wkts	Avge	Best
18	3	50	1	50.00	1/6

John Robert FREEMAN

Born: Ladywell, Lewisham, London, 3 September 1883.

Died: Napsbury, Hertfordshire, 8 August 1958.
Brother of 'Tich' Freeman, the great Kent bowler, and nephew and cousin of the Essex players, E.C. and E.J., John Freeman was one of the Essex stalwarts of the period either side of World War One. A member of one of the great cricketing families, he was a right-handed batsman, a medium pace bowler, and, quite frequently, a competent wicket-keeper.

He was not stylish as a batsman, but he was the true pro-fessional, dedicated, hard-working and very effective.

He first played for Essex in 1905, but it was not until 1909 that he could command anything approaching a reg-ular place. Certainly his best years were after World War One. He reached 1000 runs in a season for the first time in 1919, and although he missed the mark in 1920, he scored 1000 or more in every other season until after his 'official' retirement at the end of 1926.

In 1921, at Northampton, he batted seven hours for his 286 which remains the second highest score for Essex in a county match. Often used as opener, he enjoyed his best season in 1926 when he hit six centuries and scored 1,958 runs. This was his last season on the county staff as he took up a coaching appointment at Merchant Taylor's School. In fact, he assisted Essex once in 1927 and once in 1928 when the county was in need.

M	Inns	NOs	Runs	HS	Avge	100s	Ct/st
336	577	56	14507	286	27.84	26	230/46

Overs	Mds	Runs	Wkts	Avge	Best
96.4	17	365	10	36.50	3/31

Michael Anthony GARNHAM

Born: Johannesburg, South Africa, 20 August 1960.

Mike Garnham was a much travelled wicket-keeper by the time he arrived at Essex in 1989. Born in South Africa of English parents, he found himself moved to Australia at the age of four. He spent time in both Melbourne and Perth before the family moved back to England and settled in Barnstaple.

Educated at North Devon College, he played for Devon while still at school. He went to the University of East Anglia, but left after a year to follow a career as a professional cricketer. He joined Gloucestershire and played three matches for them in 1979. With opportunities limited, he moved to Leicestershire under

special registration, and was their reg-ular wicket-keeper until the end of the 1985 season.

Disillusioned, he retired from first-class cricket and set up his own business manufacturing equipment. He played for Cam-bridgeshire, 1986-88, and made one appearance for Leicestershire in 1988 when that county was hit by injuries.

He played along-side Stuart Turner in the Cambridge-shire side and was persuaded to return to first-class cricket with Essex as a cover for David East. Within weeks of Garnham joining the club, East was injured, and Garnham took over as regular wicket-keeper.

He played for England schools and Young England in the late 1970s and has wintered in Australia. An effective middle-order batsman, he has earned the reputation of scoring runs when they are most needed. He had hit one century, against Oxford University, before joining Essex.

A craftsman who has made furniture which has been sold in two top London stores, Mike Garnham is a man of deep moral and social commitment. In the winter of 1994-95 he plans to drive through the continent of Africa to raise money for Oxfam.

M	Inns	NOs	Runs	HS	Avge	100s	Ct/st
130	176	37	4109	123	29.56	4	266/18

Overs	Mds	Runs	Wkts
4	-	39	-

Sunday League

M	Inns	NOs	Runs	HS	Avge	Ct/st
82	58	14	662	40*	15.04	63/13

Benson and Hedges Cup

M	Inns	NOs	Runs	HS	Avge	Ct/st
25	16	8	161	27*	20.12	27/4

NatWest Trophy

M	Inns	NOs	Runs	HS	Avge	Ct/st
14	10	4	115	53*	19.16	12/5

William Thomas GARRETT

Born: Camberwell, London, 9 January 1876.
Died: Buckhurst Hill, 16 February 1953.
The son of a man who had made money as a grocer before becoming manager of the Elms Farm, Leyton, a sports club with a cluster of cricket pitches, William Garrett appeared as an amateur for Essex between 1900 and 1903. A middle order right-handed batsman, he seemed to reserve his best performances for the matches against Warwickshire. At Leyton, in 1900, Essex followed-on 394 in arrears, but Garrett batted for four hours and remained unbeaten on 64 to save the match.

The following season, at Edgbaston, he hit 92, and when Warwickshire came to Leyton he made 76. He assisted Surrey 2nd XI in 1904 and 1905, and he was the landlord at The King's Head, Loughton, for many years. His father had been licensee at The Red Lion, Billericay, after his days at The Elms Farm.

M	Inns	NOs	Runs	HS	Avge	Ct
15	25	1	516	92	21.50	4

Overs	Mds	Runs	Wkts	Avge	Best
44	8	142	1	142.00	1/72

Jack Sydney Bates GENTRY

Born: Wanstead, 4 October 1899.
Died: Loxwood, Sussex, 16 April 1978.

Jack Gentry had a distinction that was rare for one of his generation in that he played for three counties. Educated at Christ's Hospital, he played most of his cricket for the Battersea club, but he appeared in one match for Hampshire in 1919, made ten appearances for Surrey in 1922-23, and played for Essex against Yorkshire at Leyton in August 1925. The match was ruined by rain.

Gentry was a slow left-arm bowler with a rather peculiar delivery, and although he did not spin the ball greatly, he was very accurate. He could play little first-class cricket due to his work in the Civil Service. He had a distinguished career and was awarded the Companion of the Order of the Indian Empire and the CBE.

M	Inns	NOs	Runs	HS	Avge
1	-	-	-	-	-

Overs	Mds	Runs	Wkts	Avge
8	1	20	-	-

Paul Antony GIBB

Born: Brandsby, Yorkshire, 11 July 1913.
Died: Guildford, Surrey, 7 December 1977.
Paul Gibb is always likely to be remembered as one of cricket's eccentrics, for he was a private man who conformed to no predetermined pattern.

He was educated at St Edward's School, Oxford, where, in a strong XI, his record was good rather than outstanding. On leaving school, he was employed by Sir Julien Cahn, the cricket-loving millionaire, and he went with Cahn's side to Canada, Bermuda and the United States in 1933. In 1934, he made his first-class debut, for Scotland against the Australian touring side, opening the innings with C.S.Dempster, the New Zealand Test player. That autumn, he went up to Emmanuel College, Cambridge, and narrowly got his blue as a freshman, again opening the innings.

A fortnight after the Varsity match, Gibb made his debut for Yorkshire and hit 157 not out in four and a quarter hours against Nottinghamshire. He became only the second player to score a century on the occasion of his debut for Yorkshire. That winter, he captained the Yorkshire side in Jamaica.

In 1936, he took over the wicket-keeping duties at Cambridge when S.C.Griffith was injured. Amid much criticism, Gibb retained

the wicket-keeping spot to the exclusion of Griffith the following season. There was even more controversy in 1938 when Gibb hit a century in his fourth and final Varsity match, made a double century against Free Foresters and was chosen as England's wicket-keeper in the Test match at Old Trafford. Certainly, he was not among the top flight of keepers at the time, and this is what aroused the criticism. In the event, the match was abandoned without a ball being bowled and Gibb was injured and unable to play in the Headingley Test. Wood, the regular Yorkshire 'keeper, played at The Oval.

Gibb went to South Africa, 1938-39, and played in all five Tests as an opening batsman, with Ames, fit again, keeping wicket. Gibb hit 93 and 196 on his Test debut and made 120 in the fifth Test. He played no cricket in 1939, and during World War Two, he flew Sunderlands and Catalinas for Coastal Command.

He returned to Yorkshire in 1946, and, batting at number six, was England's wicket-keeper in the first two Tests against India. He went to Australia that winter as first choice 'keeper, but he was dropped after the first Test, and he became a solitary character. He kept a moving and revealing diary which was published in the early issues of *Wisden Cricket Monthly*, two years after Gibb's death.

Paul Gibb, bespectacled and prematurely bald, a slight figure, now disappeared from cricket, but in 1951 came more controversy and sensation when it was announced that he was to play for Essex as a *professional*. He was the first cricket blue ever to turn professional, and his membership of MCC was placed in abeyance.

It is probably true to say that Gibb kept wicket for Essex better than he had ever done before. Perhaps it was the regular practice that helped him to develop his skills. In 1952, he established what was then a county record with 66 catches and 17 stumpings, and the following year, he had 79 victims.

He became a popular figure at Essex, consuming large quantities of ice-cream which seemed to have no effect on his weight, and he travelled the county circuit in a small van which contained most of his belongings and was invariably his sleeping accommodation.

He hit 1000 runs in each of his first three seasons for Essex, and again in 1955. In 1951, his first season, he hit four centuries, including one against his old county, Yorkshire.

As a batsman, he had inexhaustible patience, relying on his very strong back play and allowing the runs to come. A Test average of 44.69 gives evidence of his ability, but he was not a batsman of flair. As *Wisden* so aptly commented, 'Two Gibbs on a side could have been difficult and three intolerable: one was often invaluable.'

Gibb appeared in the first three matches of the 1956 season, but he injured a thumb against Leicestershire and was forced out of cricket for a month. He reappeared against Lancashire at Old Trafford in June, was out for 0 and did not play again. He retired at the end of the season and was a first-class umpire from 1957 to 1966. He also spent his winters in South Africa and coached at schools. One of his pupils at Hilton College, Durban, was Mike Procter.

He worked in a London store, and he then became a bus driver with the Alder Valley Bus Company, living alone in a caravan at Shamley Green. In the summer before his death, he was persuaded to attend the Centenary Test in Melbourne. It took much persuasion to make him go, and when he arrived he wore contact lenses and a wig so that he went unrecognised for much of the time by his former friends and colleagues. He has a unique place in Essex cricket history.

M	Inns	NOs	Runs	HS	Avge	100s	Ct/st
145	250	12	6328	141	26.58	8	230/46

Overs	Mds	Runs	Wkts	Avge
0.5	-	4	-	-

Archibald Lesley GIBSON

Born: Kingsclere, Hampshire, 4 September 1877.
Died: Nakuru, Kenya, 29 July 1943.
An outstanding cricketer at Winchester where he was in the XI for three seasons and topped the batting tables in the last two with averages over 50, Archie Gibson first played for Essex against Surrey, at Leyton, in 1895, when still at school. On leaving Winchester, he went to Russia where he lived for two years, and he then became a tea planter in Ceylon.

A sound and patient batsman, he hit 218 for Dimbula against Dikoya, at Radella, which, for some time, was the highest score in important cricket on the island. He appeared for Essex when on leave and played in 17 matches in 1910, his last season for the county.

In 1919, he played for Pelham Warner's XI against Oxford University, and that was his last first-class game in England although, at the age of 50, he played first-class cricket in Ceylon for the Up-Country XI.

M	Inns	NOs	Runs	HS	Avge	Ct
23	36	3	492	71	14.90	6

Overs	Mds	Runs	Wkts	Avge
6	-	16	-	-
(five-ball)				

Sir Kenneth Lloyd GIBSON

Born: Kensington, London, 11 May 1888.
Died: Marylebone, London, 14 May 1967.
An outstanding wicket-keeper who was able to give little time to cricket, Kenneth Gibson was from a military family. He was in the Eton XI in 1906 and 1907, toured Egypt with MCC in 1909 and played for Essex, when available, from 1909 to 1912.

A steeple-chase rider and a handicapper, he enjoyed his best season in 1911 when he took seven catches and made two stumpings in the match against Derbyshire at Leyton. This record of nine dismissals remains an Essex record although it was equalled by David East. Six of Gibson's victims came in the first innings.

It was in 1911 that he was chosen for the Gentlemen against the Players at both The Oval and Lord's, and the first of these matches was looked upon as a Test trial. His last first-class appearance was for the Army in 1920.

He fought in both World Wars and was mentioned in dispatches when with the Dragoon Guards in World War One. His father was created First Baron Gibson in 1926, and Kenneth Gibson succeeded to the title.

M	Inns	NOs	Runs	HS	Avge	Ct/st
36	55	6	795	75	16.22	53/9

Overs	Mds	Runs	Wkts	Avge	Best
1.5	-	9	1	9.00	1/9

Frank William GILLIGAN

Born: Denmark Hill, London, 20 September 1893.
Died: Wanganui, Wellington, New Zealand, 4 May 1960.

The eldest of three brothers who played first-class cricket, Frank Gilligan was the only one of the three who did not captain England although he won his blue at Oxford in 1919 and led the side the following season. Educated at Dulwich College, he was an excellent wicket-keeper and a useful batsman although not a stylist. Had he been regularly available, he would have solved the county's wicket-keeper problems in the 1920s, but he was a teacher available only in the summer holidays.

Gilligan assisted Essex from 1919 to 1929, and, in 1928 at Cheltenham, he caught two and stumped four Gloucestershire batsmen when he was leading the Essex side in the absence of Douglas.

He took up a post as headmaster of Wanganui Grammar School in New Zealand, and he held the position for 19 years. In 1955, he was awarded the OBE for his services to education.

M	Inns	NOs	Runs	HS	Avge	Ct/st
79	108	27	1808	78*	22.32	87/33

Overs	Mds	Runs	Wkts	Avge
0.2	-	6	-	-

Rev. Canon Frank Hay GILLINGHAM

Born: Tokyo, Japan, 6 September 1875.
Died: Monaco, 1 April 1953.
Frank Gillingham is the most renowned clergyman ever to play for Essex. He is also the only Essex cricketer to have been featured in *Vanity Fair* where, on 15 August 1906, Spy's cartoon was entitled *Cricketing Christianity*.

Gillingham was brought to England at the age of eight and was educated at Dulwich College. He gained a place in the cricket XI in 1891 and 1892, and, on leaving school, worked for a time in the City. He answered a calling to enter the church and forsook the business world for St John's Hall, Highbury, and Durham University where he thrived as a cricketer and a rugby player.

When he was ordained in 1899 he became curate at Leyton and so qualified for Essex by residence. Leyton was essentially a sporting parish, for Gillingham's predecessor had been captain of the XI at Durham, and his successor was a Cambridge cox. Gillingham himself was immensely popular. He would play cricket in the street with the boys of the parish, and he once dispatched a fire balloon from the pulpit. He played for Essex Club and Ground before making his Championship debut in 1903, and he hit 116 against Leicestershire in the last home game of the season.

The following year, he topped the Essex batting averages and on his first appearance at Lord's, he hit 201 against Middlesex. Tall and strong, at home on any wicket, but a better player of pace than spin, Gillingham was particularly strong in front of the wicket. An admirable fielder who kept wicket on occasions, he was a batsman who believed in hitting the ball hard.

Had he been able to play regularly, Gillingham would have been a prolific runscorer and would most probably have played Test cricket. As it was , he represented the Gentlemen three times against the Players and scored more than 10,000 runs in first-class cricket.

He became Chaplain to the Forces, and, in 1906, was with the South Wales Borderers on Salisbury Plain. He was the most popular of preachers, and, in 1939, was appointed Chaplain to the King. A renowned after-dinner speaker who delivered his witty anecdotes without the vestige of a smile, he was a kind, gentle man who offered understanding without condemnation and who enhanced the lives of all those with whom he came in contact.

In May 1927, Essex beat the New Zealand tourists at Leyton, and the match was memorable in that, as an exploratory venture, commentary on the game was broadcast. The broadcast was of a limited nature, but it marked the birth of cricket coverage on radio. The commentator was Canon Gillingham.

He played for Essex over a period of 25 years, keeping a promise to play in Russell's benefit match against Surrey, at Leyton, in 1928. He had shared seven century partnerships with Russell over the years. Gillingham played no more first-class cricket after 1928.

M	Inns	NOs	Runs	HS	Avge	100s	Ct
187	307	21	9160	201	32.02	19	91

Overs	Mds	Runs	Wkts	Avge
1.2	-	13	-	-

Christopher GLADWIN

Born: East Ham, 10 May 1962.
Chris Gladwin's path to the county side was through Langdon Comprehensive School, Newham, Essex Schools and Wanstead CC. He played for the 2nd XI at the age of 16. He made his first-class debut in 1981, and three years later, he hit 1396 runs. To many he appeared to be a left-handed version of

Graham Gooch with whom he opened the innings. There was talk of his being a prospective England player, but he was troubled by a back injury, and his form fell away.

He played in South Africa, 1986-87, and he began the 1987 season well. His form again lapsed, however, and, as he was carrying a little too much weight, he had become less mobile in the field. He was released at the end of the 1987 season.

A cheerful young man, Chris Gladwin played a few matches for Derbyshire in 1989, and he assisted Suffolk in 1988 and 1990. His club cricket remained in Essex with Old Brentwoods. He is now concerned with the administration of a sports centre.

M	Inns	NOs	Runs	HS	Avge	100s	Ct
67	114	7	2953	162	27.59	1	31

Overs	Mds	Runs	Wkts	Avge
21	1	71	-	-

Sunday League

M	Inns	NOs	Runs	HS	Avge	Ct
30	30	1	580	75	20.00	5

Benson and Hedges Cup

M	Inns	NOs	Runs	HS	Avge	Ct
11	11	-	205	41	18.63	2

NatWest Trophy

M	Inns	NOs	Runs	HS	Avge	Ct
4	4	-	26	15	6.50	1

Andrew Kenneth GOLDING

Born: Colchester, 5 October 1963.

A slow left-arm bowler who went from Colchester Royal Grammar School to St Catherine's College, Cambridge, where he read Geography, Andrew Golding captained the England Schools team to Zimbabwe and played one match for Essex in 1983 against

the New Zealanders. He claimed the wicket of wicket-keeper Ian Smith twice in the match.

The following year, he was up at Cambridge and got his blue in 1986. He was on the Essex staff from 1987 until 1989. A rugby injury disrupted his final 2nd XI season, and he retired at the end of 1989 to take up a post at Ipswich School.

Like many Essex players, he has since played for Suffolk and plays his club cricket for Wivenhoe.

M	Inns	NOs	Runs	HS	Avge
1	2	2	8	6*	-

Overs	Mds	Runs	Wkts	Avge	Best
28	3	97	2	48.50	1/44

Graham Alan GOOCH

Born: Whipps Cross, Leytonstone, 23 July 1953.

At the end of the 1993 season, Graham Gooch stood surveying the cricket world, an Alexander with no more worlds to conquer. He had played in more than 100 Tests, had captained England in victory and defeat, had scored more runs in Test cricket than any other English batsman and had scored more than 100 hundreds in first-class cricket. He had scored more centuries for Essex than any other cricketer, and he had captained the county since 1989, having been captain in 1986 and 1987. He had scored more runs in the Sunday League, in the Benson and Hedges Cup and in the 60-over knock-out competition than any other batsman, and he had scored a triple century for England. In 1991, he had been awarded the OBE for services to cricket.

His career had not been without its upsets. His Test career had begun in 1975 with a 'pair' against Australia, and he would have played more Test matches had he not gone to South Africa as captain of a 'rebel' tour and suffered

a ban. He played two seasons for Western Province in the Currie Cup.

Gooch had not been an outstanding player with Essex Schools, but Bill Morris at the Ilford Cricket School and the Ilford CC rated him very highly. He toured with the England Youth side, and he could bat, bowl and keep wicket.

In 1973, Brian Taylor called upon him to play in some Sunday League games. He batted low in the order and bowled little. In the Championship match against Northamptonshire at Westcliff, he batted at number five, scored 18 and did not bowl. The following season, in 15 matches, he scored 637 runs, including his maiden first-class century. This 114 not out against Leicestershire at Chelmsford showed the shape of things to come. Essex, needing 242 to win, were 154 at the fall of the sixth wicket and seemed doomed to defeat. In under two hours, Gooch hit three sixes and eight fours, took charge of the innings, and Essex won by two wickets with an over to spare. The apprentice precision tool-maker now turned his attention to professional cricket.

The following season he reached 1000 runs for the first time and was chosen, perhaps prematurely, for England. One of the great careers of modern times had been launched, and Gooch began to grow with the first great Essex side around him.

The significant turning point in his career was when he began to open the innings in 1978. He regained his place in the England side and toured Australia that winter.

England calls in Tests and the World Cup restricted him to ten Championship matches for Essex in 1979, but he had begun to gain the reputation of being able to destroy any attack in the country. His contribution to the county's first triumph, the winning of the Benson and Hedges Cup in 1979, was enormous.

At Northampton, he hit 83 as Essex won by three runs. At Chelmsford, on 19 May, he and Lilley hit 223 in 36 overs for the first wicket against Oxford and Cambridge. Gooch hit 19 fours and two sixes in his 133. Four days later, he made 66 as Sussex were beaten with ease. His one failure came at The Oval where Surrey were narrow victors, but by then Essex had already qualified for the knock-out stages of the competition.

In the quarter-final, against Warwickshire at Chelmsford, he lost Lilley with just two runs scored, and it was eight overs before Gooch himself opened his account. By the time he was leg before to Willis in the 55th and final over of the innings, he had hit a six and 19 fours and made 138. These were the days before fielding restrictions, and Warwickshire had men circling the boundary in the closing overs, and still Gooch pierced the cordon and sent the ball crashing to the fence.

He was top-scorer, 49, in the close semi-final victory over Yorkshire, and then came that glorious day at Lord's in July when he and McEwan batted as men do in dreams. Gooch's 120 was the first century ever made in a Benson and Hedges Final, an innings of the highest quality, with three sixes and 11 fours. It brought him the Gold Award, and Essex their first trophy.

This was simply the start of years of plenty as Gooch played a major part in every success. In 1984, he established an Essex record with 2539 runs in the season as the county won the Championship. The following season, he and Brian Hardie began the NatWest Final with a stand of 202, a record for the competition; and the following day, they went up to Trent Bridge and hit 239, a Sunday League record. Gooch had already claimed the record for the highest individual score, 176 against Glamorgan at Southend in 1983.

In 1990, he and Paul Prichard shared a second wicket partnership of 403 against Leicestershire at Chelmsford, the highest partnership for any Essex wicket.

Even in one of the least successful of Essex seasons, he hit a century in each innings in the last match of the season just a few weeks after giving up the England captaincy.

Amid this abundance of runs and records, Gooch had also found time to take well over 200 first-class wickets and to make nearly 500 catches, many of them brilliant efforts at slip where he excelled in his early days.

The style has changed over the years. The drooping moustache, 'Zap', still suggests a mournful expression and none of the power has been lost. He still ambles in to bowl and produces deliveries sharper and nastier than expected from slow medium. But there has been a change. His batting is more circumspect than it was in 1979. Responsibility and age have seen to that. Like any great artist, he has moved from the unbridled flamboyance of youth to the golden wisdom of age and experience.

M	Inns	NOs	Runs	HS	Avge	100s	Ct
346	569	54	26719	275	51.88	79	344

Overs	Mds	Runs	Wkts	Avge	Best	5/inn
2309.1	581	6368	192	33.16	7/14	3

Sunday League

M	Inns	NOs	Runs	HS	Avge	100s	Ct
249	244	21	7906	176	35.45	12	91

Overs	Mds	Runs	Wkts	Avge	Best
912.2	44	4143	139	29.81	4/33

Benson and Hedges Cup

M	Inns	NOs	Runs	HS	Avge	100s	Ct
101	100	11	4607	198*	51.76	12	62

Overs	Mds	Runs	Wkts	Avge	Best
606.5	62	2118	69	30.69	3/24

Gillette Cup/NatWest Trophy

M	Inns	NOs	Runs	HS	Avge	100s	Ct
50	49	4	2383	144	52.95	6	23

Overs	Mds	Runs	Wkts	Avge	Best
273.1	37	847	28	30.25	3/31

Cecil Henry GOSLING

Born: Barrington, Hall, Hatfield Broad Oak, 22 February 1910.
Died: Barrington Hall, Hatfield Broad Oak, 19 May 1974.

Although he was in the side at Eton, C.H.Gosling, a nephew of R.C.Gosling who played for Essex in the late 19th century, did not get his blue at Oxford where, in 1929, he played in the match against Middlesex, took a catch and was unable to bat in either innings through injury. He was not selected again.

He won a blue for fives, and he appeared for Essex against Hampshire and Gloucestershire at the end of June 1930. Thereafter his time was spent in business. He was Deputy Lieutenant for Essex in 1949.

M	Inns	NOs	Runs	HS	Avge	Ct
2	4	-	61	33	15.25	2

Robert Cunliffe GOSLING

Born: Hassobury, Farnham, Essex, 15 June 1868.
Died: Hassobury, Farnham, Essex, 8 April 1922.

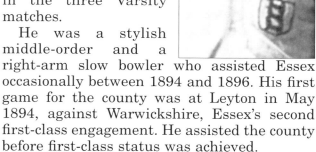

One of four brothers who played for Eton where he was in the XI for three years, Robert Gosling gained his blue in each of his three years at Cambridge. He was dismissed only once in the three Varsity matches.

He was a stylish middle-order and a right-arm slow bowler who assisted Essex occasionally between 1894 and 1896. His first game for the county was at Leyton in May 1894, against Warwickshire, Essex's second first-class engagement. He assisted the county before first-class status was achieved.

An outstanding inside-forward in soccer, Gosling played for Old Etonians and won five caps for England between 1892 and 1895. He scored twice in his five matches.

His nephew, Cecil, played for Essex in 1930.

M	Inns	NOs	Runs	HS	Avge	Ct
4	8	1	55	21*	7.85	

Leonard GRAHAM

Born: Leyton, 20 August 1901.
Died: Kensington, London, 21 December 1962.

Leonard Graham played two games for Essex in 1926 as a middle-order right-handed batsman. He was better known as the Millwall half-back who played for England against Scotland and Wales in 1925.

M	Inns	NOs	Runs	HS	Avge	Ct
2	3	1	14	12	7.00	2

David Anthony Athelston GRAY

Born: Kensington, London, 19 June 1922.

A slow left-arm bowler who captained Winchester in 1941 and who was leading wicket-taker for the college in that season and in the previous season, David Gray joined the RAF on leaving school. Commissioned, he was a flight-lieutenant when, in 1944, he was awarded the DFC.

He went up to Caius College, Cambridge, after the war and played for the university, 1947, in the first two matches of their programme, against Sussex and against the South Africans. The third match was with Essex, and he appeared for the county against his university.

M	Inns	NOs	Runs	HS	Avge
1	1	-	6	6	6.00

Overs	Mds	Runs	Wkts	Avge	Best
29	5	63	1	63.00	1/34

William Johns GRAY

Born: Chelmsford, 26 November 1864.
Died: Chelmsford, 18 December 1898.

William Gray opened the Essex innings in the match against Yorkshire at Halifax in July 1894. It was a game in which Essex fielded two or three new faces. Gray was the brother of the actor, Alfred Gray.

M	Inns	NOs	Runs	HS	Avge
1	2	-	4	2	2.00

Brigadier Michael Arthur GREEN

Born: Clifton, Gloucestershire, 3 October 1891.
Died: Kensington, London, 28 December 1971.

A regular army officer, a right-handed batsman, an all-round sportsman and a much-travelled man, M.A.Green played club cricket for Wimbledon and made his debut for Gloucestershire in 1912. A member of the Army Reserve, he was called up in 1914. In World War One, he served three years in France, spent some time on a staff course in Cambridge and was posted as Brigade Major of a Division in Egypt shortly before the Armistice.

He also served in India where he played first-class cricket for the Europeans, and, when in E n g l a n d, appeared for Gloucestershire until 1928. He played racquets, squash, rugby and soccer for the Army, and he also played soccer for Casuals and Surrey, and rugby for Harlequins and Surrey.

Green had intended to give up first-class cricket, but, stationed in Colchester, he appeared for Essex during Colchester week in 1930 at the invitation of Brian Castor who thought that his presence in the Essex side might draw the garrison crowd. Although Green contributed little, Essex beat both Somerset and Glamorgan during the week. Those were his last games in first-class cricket for a county.

He spent much of the 1930s in the Gold Coast and Sierra Leone and fought in World War Two. He was secretary of Worcestershire, 1945 to 1951, and was manager of the MCC side to South Africa, 1948-49, and joint-manager of the side to Australia and New Zealand, 1950-51.

His autobiography, *Sporting Campaigner*, was published in 1956.

M	Inns	NOs	Runs	HS	Avge	Ct
2	4	-	27	13	6.75	1

William Thomas GREENSMITH

Born: Middlesbrough, Yorkshire, 16 August 1930.

Bill Greensmith was one of the great servants of Essex cricket. A successful club cricketer with Buckhurst Hill for whom his brother also played as a left-handed batsman, Bill Greensmith arrived at Essex in 1947 highly recommended by Andy Sandham, the Surrey coach.

He made his debut in 1947, but as a young leg-break and googly bowler, he took some time to establish himself because of the demands of national service and the continuing good form of Peter Smith. Greensmith played for the Combined Services between 1949 and 1951, and it was in this last

season that, available again for Essex on a regular basis, he took 53 wickets in all matches.

His development as a cricketer was impressive, and he was capped in 1952 when his batting advanced. Like all young leg-spinners, he did not have a consistent control of length, but he could turn the ball sharply and was very effective on his day. In 1953, hitting mainly on the leg side, he made 138 not out in four hours ten minutes against Kent at Blackheath, but it was not until 1955 that his full potential as an all-rounder was seen. He took 84 wickets and scored 698 runs, and he maintained this form the following season when he took 8 for 59 against Gloucestershire at Bristol.

Troubled by injury in 1957, he lost form the following year, but he re-established himself in 1961 and enjoyed two good seasons. Granted a benefit in 1963, he was unwell for a period, and it seemed that his bowling art had totally deserted him. He finished the year with only one Championship wicket, that of Grieves, the Lancashire captain, and he retired at the end of the season.

M	Inns	NOs	Runs	HS	Avge	100s	Ct
371	550	149	8042	138*	20.05	1	147

Overs	Mds	Runs	Wkts	Avge	Best	10/m	5/inn
7322.1	1747	20711	720	28.76	8/59	2	21

Colin GRIFFITHS

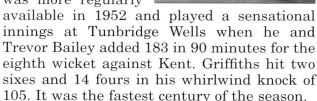

Born: Upminster, 9 December 1930.
A right-handed batsman from Brentwood School, Colin Griffiths played in three matches in 1951, the first of them against the South African tourists, and gave indication of considerable potential. He was also particularly impressive with his fielding.

A member of the Westcliff club, he was more regularly available in 1952 and played a sensational innings at Tunbridge Wells when he and Trevor Bailey added 183 in 90 minutes for the eighth wicket against Kent. Griffiths hit two sixes and 14 fours in his whirlwind knock of 105. It was the fastest century of the season.

That proved to be the high point of his brief career. In eight matches the following season, his highest score was 17, and he was not seen again.

He worked in the city and later played for Wimbledon.

M	Inns	NOs	Runs	HS	Avge	100s	Ct
27	41	3	615	105	16.18	1	4

Overs	Mds	Runs	Wkts	Avge
3	-	22	-	-

Arthur Stanley GRIMWOOD

Born: Walthamstow, 8 September 1905.
Died: Chingford, 2 July 1986.
A left-handed batsman who was on the staff at Leyton in the mid-1920s and played in four matches in 1925, Arthur Grimwood was also a slow left-arm bowler.

M	Inns	NOs	Runs	HS	Avge
4	6	-	26	15	4.33

Overs	Mds	Runs	Wkts	Avge
1	-	5	-	-

Trayton Golding GRINTER

Born: Leytonstone, 12 December 1885.
Died: Frinton, 21 April 1946.
Tray Grinter joined the wine merchants Cockburn and Company (Leith) Ltd on Mafeking Day, 1900, and 33 years later, he was chairman of the company. In the years before World War One, he was recognised as one of the finest batsmen in club cricket in the country. For South Woodford, between 1909 and 1914, he hit 45 centuries, including six in succession in the first of those seasons. It was in that year that he was first asked to appear as an amateur for Essex. He played in three matches, hitting 49 not out against Lancashire at Leyton, and finishing third in the batting averages.

Serving with the Artists' Rifles in World War One, he was severely wounded in the left arm, and it was feared that he would never play again. J.H.Douglas, father of the Essex captain, persuaded him to play for Wanstead, and he captained the club from 1921 until 1925. In spite of his great handicap, which meant that he virtually batted one-handed and used a specially made light bat, narrow at the top so that he could grip it with his damaged left hand, he continued to score heavily and reached 100 centuries in club cricket by 1924. He also appeared for Essex in 1921, making 15 and 5 against Kent.

Having moved to Walton-on-Naze, he decided the journey to Wanstead was now too much for him, and from 1927 onwards he played for Frinton CC which he transformed from a village side to a power in Essex cricket. In 1942, at the age of 57, he completed 200 centuries in club cricket.

He later turned his attention to golf with great success. For a man who had been shot to pieces in World War One and who had undergone two serious operations later in life, his achievements were phenomenal.

Many cricketers in Essex owed him much, not least of them was Tom Pearce whom he employed and to whom he gave the time to assist Essex as much as he did. The county cricket club will be ever grateful to him.

M	Inns	NOs	Runs	HS	Avge	Ct
8	13	1	201	49*	16.75	2

William Charles GUNARY

Born: Dagenham, 5 August 1895.

Died: Upminster, 26 January 1969.
A market gardener by profession, Bill Gunary was a fast left-arm bowler who took a host of wickets for Ilford CC. In 1929, he was invited to play for Essex against Leicestershire at Leicester at the end of August. Rain affected the match, and Gunary failed to take a wicket. He said afterwards, however, that he learned much from the professionals about how to play cards.

His son played for Essex 2nd XI in the 1950s.

M	Inns	NOs	Runs	HS	Avge	Ct
1	1	-	0	0	0.00	1

Overs	Mds	Runs	Wkts	Avge
19	6	58	-	-

Sidney HADDEN

Born: Hastings, Sussex, 26 August 1877.
Died: Whipps Cross, Leytonstone, 2 November 1934.
One of several wicket-keepers used by the county in the years immediately after World War One, Sid Hadden first appeared at the end of the 1912 season. He was by then already 35 years old so that he was very much at the veteran stage when Essex called upon him in 1920.

M	Inns	NOs	Runs	HS	Avge	Ct/st
6	5	2	29	17*	9.66	5/1

Henry HAILEY

Born: Limehouse, London, 7 April 1851.
Died: Southend-on-Sea, 24 September 1932.
Henry Hailey was a right-handed batsman of considerable ability who was 40 years old when he first played for the county in 1891. He was in the Essex side that played in the inaugural first-class match against Leicestershire in 1894, and he hit 50 in the return match with the same county at Leicester in August.

The following season, he hit 66 not out against MCC at Lord's, but he was not seen again after 1895.

M	Inns	NOs	Runs	HS	Avge	Ct
13	22	5	301	66*	17.70	5

Brian Ross HARDIE

Born: Stenhousemuir, Scotland, 14 January 1950.
'If I knew that I had to go into battle and that I was going to get killed,' said Ian Greig, the Surrey captain, 'the man I'd want alongside me would be Brian Hardie because I would know then that I would die laughing.'

Another county captain, Chris Cowdrey, hearing that Gooch and Hardie had shared a big opening partnership in a Sunday League match, commented, "Hardie. He's the one! You think you're going to get him out every ball, but you never do."

Brian Hardie, 'Lager', was one of the most respected batsmen on the county circuit, and, as a short-leg, he had no superior anywhere in the country. He had played for Scotland in first-class matches for three seasons before coming south to join Essex in 1973. He frequently opened the innings, but he also batted at number five, concreting a position which had been an Essex weakness.

An innings of four runs in 142 minutes against Hampshire in his second season gave Hardie the reputation of being a stonewaller, a very slow scorer, but this was to prove a false assumption. Ever looking to play forward, he came to clump the ball with the full face of the bat, and he put many an attack to the broadsword.

He made his highest score, 162, against Warwickshire, in 1975, and he equalled it against Somerset at Southend ten years later. He shared in all the Essex triumphs up to his retirement at the end of the 1990 season, and he hit 103 not out in four hours against Northamptonshire, at Northampton, in 1979, to steer the county to their first title.

When Essex won the NatWest Trophy in 1985 he hit 110 off 149 balls as he and Gooch put on 202 for the first wicket. The following day, against the same opponents, Nottinghamshire, at Trent Bridge, Hardie and Gooch began the match with a partnership of 239, which remains a first wicket record for the Sunday League.

Hardie had a style of his own. He pushed forward with the utmost determination, and if he was not pleasing in the aesthetic sense, he breathed character and resolve which were highly entertaining. There was always the right blend of courage and joy in his cricket. He was infectious. You were happy when you watched him.

With several young players pressing for first team places, 'Lager' played only 11 Championship matches in his last season. He usually deputised for Gooch when the skipper was on Test duty, and he captained the side on occasions. In his 11 matches, he hit 650 runs, with two centuries, and averaged 65.00. He was at the top until the end.

He spent some winters coaching in New Zealand. His elder brother Keith, who played ten times for Scotland as a most capable all-rounder, emigrated there.

In the autumn of 1990, Brian Hardie took up the post of sports master at Brentwood School and quickly made an impression with his personality, dedication and expertise.

M	Inns	NOs	Runs	HS	Avge	100s	Ct
374	601	78	17945	162	34.31	27	346

Overs	Mds	Runs	Wkts	Avge	Best
47	3	254	3	84.67	2/39

Sunday League

M	Inns	NOs	Runs	HS	Avge	100s	Ct
236	219	21	5621	109	28.39	3	66

Overs	Mds	Runs	Wkts	Avge	Best
4.5	-	24	1	24.00	1/4

Benson and Hedges Cup

M	Inns	NOs	Runs	HS	Avge	100s	Ct
85	80	16	1943	119*	30.36	2	27

Gillette Cup/NatWest Trophy

M	Inns	NOs	Runs	HS	Avge	100s	Ct
34	34	1	1143	110	34.64	1	13

Overs	Mds	Runs	Wkts	Avge	Best
8	1	16	1	16.00	1/16

Steriker Norman HARE

Born: Tottenham, Middlesex, 31 March 1900. Died: Meadle, Buckinghamshire, 30 September 1977.

A club cricketer with Ilford, S.N.Hare had one

of the shortest and most remarkable careers in first-class cricket. He had been educated at Chigwell School, and he made his debut for Essex against Derbyshire at Leyton, May, 1921. He was put at number ten in the order, and when he joined Douglas, the captain, the score was 145 for 8. The pair added 251, and the stand was broken when Hare was caught at mid-off for 98. He drove and cut strongly and hit ten fours, but he was described as being a little weak on the leg side.

Hare travelled west with the county for the next two matches. He scored 15 and 4 against Gloucestershire and bagged a 'pair' against Somerset at Bath. That was the end of his first-class career which spanned ten days.

He worked for the Anglo-Persian Oil Company and would never have been regularly available. He was awarded the CBE for his business acumen and diplomacy.

M	Inns	NOs	Runs	HS	Avge	Ct
3	5	-	117	98	23.40	1

J. HARRIS

One of the enigmas of Essex county cricket, Harris – we cannot even be sure of the initial 'J' – was a wicket-keeper with the Beckton club. A professional, he played for the county in two matches in 1905.

M	Inns	NOs	Runs	HS	Avge	Ct
2	3	1	0	0*	0.00	4

James George William HARROLD

Born: 26 March 1892.
Died: Epsom, Surrey, 7 October 1950.
A soccer player with Leicester City and Millwall, James Harrold won an amateur international cap for England. He appeared intermittently as an off-break bowler for Essex between 1923 and 1928.

M	Inns	NOs	Runs	HS	Avge	Ct
11	19	3	88	17	5.50	13

Overs	Mds	Runs	Wkts	Avge	Best
30	1	123	3	41.00	1/15

Ronald Charles HARVEY

Born: Ingatestone, 7 May 1934.
Educated at Rainford Secondary School, Chelmsford, Ronald Harvey was a professional with Essex in 1952. He was on National Service in 1953 and 1954, and he was he not seen again after his one match which was for the county against Tom Pearce's XI in May 1952. He was a right-arm medium pace bowler and left-handed batsman, and he played for Chelmsford.

M	Inns	NOs	Runs	HS	Avge
1	2	2	12	12*	-

Overs	Mds	Runs	Wkts	Avge	Best
16	1	88	3	29.33	3/88

Sir Frank Cyril HAWKER

Born: Epping, 21 July 1900.
Died: Hastings, Sussex, 22 February 1991.
The grandson of John Bastow, an Essex player of the days before the county was first-class, and the brother-in-law of Tom Pearce, Cyril Hawker was in the City of London School XI from 1917 to 1919, but his business career was to prevent him from playing first-class cricket.

He was an executive director of the Bank of England, and later chairman of the Chartered Bank, and of the Standard and Chartered Bank. He held many other business posts.

He was president of MCC, 1970-71, and played once for Essex, against Lancashire, at Old Trafford, 1937, batting at number eight. He was a prolific scorer in club cricket, particularly for Old Citizens, and for Southgate whom he captained for many years. He occasionally assisted the British Empire XI in their charity matches during World War Two.

M	Inns	NOs	Runs	HS	Avge
1	2	-	26	16	13.00

Allan Frederick George HAYZELDEN

Born: Leytonstone, 10 January 1904.
Died: Harefield , Middlesex, 10 April 1955.
A talented amateur right-arm fast bowler who was educated at Merchant Taylors School, Hayzelden played for Essex against Worcestershire at Leyton in May 1929, and took the wicket of B.W.Quaife. In July two years later, he appeared against Kent at Colchester and helped Nichols to bring about a ten-wicket victory. Among his victims on that occasion were Hardinge and Frank Woolley.

M	Inns	NOs	Runs	HS	Avge	Ct
2	3	1	5	4*	2.50	3

Overs	Mds	Runs	Wkts	Avge	Best
37.5	6	110	6	18.33	3/30

Edward Wyndham HAZELTON

Born: Buckingham, 8 May 1894.
Died: Great Dunmow, 13 March 1958.
An Army officer, Hazelton played for Essex against the Australian Imperial Forces at Leyton in 1919. His first-class career extended longer than that, however, for he appeared for MCC in 1930. Educated at Wellingborough School, he played for Buckinghamshire from 1912 until 1931.

Hazelton bowled right-arm medium pace or leg-breaks, and although he had no success in his one game for Essex, he captured 23 wickets for 544 runs in his seven other first-class matches.

M	Inns	NOs	Runs	HS	Avge
1	2	-	8	8	4.00

Overs	Mds	Runs	Wkts	Avge
18	1	77	-	-

Arthur Edward HEATLEY

Born: Kemp Town, Brighton, Sussex, 25 October 1865.
Died: Ingrave, 1 July 1941.
An amateur, Arthur Heatley played against Yorkshire in the match at Halifax in 1894. He and Walter Mead added 43 for the ninth wicket in Essex's second innings. He took three catches in the first innings and one in the second, but he did not appear again.

M	Inns	NOs	Runs	HS	Avge	Ct
1	2	1	20	13*	20.00	4

Overs	Mds	Runs	Wkts	Avge
1	-	10	-	-

(five-ball)

Raymond Maurice HEAVEN

Born: Shoreham-by-Sea, Sussex, 8 October 1918.
Studying as an accountant in the late 1930s, Ray Heaven was granted a special arrangement which enabled him to continue his studies and play cricket in the summer months.

An all-round sportsman, he won the Essex Junior Lawn Tennis Championship in 1936 and played soccer in the Olympian League. Having watched him in the nets, Essex engaged him as a leg-break bowler and right-handed batsman for the 1939 season.

Described as a leg-break bowler from Westcliff, in fact he did not bowl in the one first-class match in which he appeared, against Yorkshire at Sheffield when Essex won by an innings, a fortnight before the outbreak of World War Two. He joined the Royal Navy but was invalided out in 1941. He played for the London Counties, the British Empire XI and Essex County Services in wartime cricket. He retired from first-class cricket after the war in order to follow his career in accountancy.

Ray Heaven has retired to the Peak District and contributed a charming article to the *Essex CCC Yearbook, 1993.*

M	Inns	NOs	Runs	HS	Avge	Ct
1	1	1	5	5*	-	4

Patrick Anthony HECTOR

Born: Islington, London, 29 July 1958.
Pat Hector came onto the Essex staff after his success with the Essex Schools' sides. He was educated at Warren Comprehensive School, Chadwell Heath, and played for the Romford and Gidea Park club. A fast medium-pace right-arm bowler and hard-hitting batsman, he played three matches in June 1977, against Cambridge University, Hampshire and Leicestershire. He hit 40 and took 3 for 61 in the first, and had three good Leicestershire wickets for 56 in his final game, but he was not retained on the staff.

M	Inns	NOs	Runs	HS	Avge
3	5	1	75	40	18.75

Overs	Mds	Runs	Wkts	Avge	Best
56	7	190	7	27.14	3/56

Reuben HERBERT

Born: Lansdown, Cape Town, South Africa, 1 December 1957.

Coached by his father, a master at Barstable School, Basildon, Reuben Herbert was a product of Essex Schools Cricket. He was a heavy scorer in junior cricket and for Orsett and Thurrock in the Essex League, but Essex valued him mostly as an off-break bowler. He first played for the county in 1976, but his appearances were limited, and he left the county after the 1980 season.

He coached in Holland, captained Westcliff and sold sports goods. He played for Suffolk, 1984 to 1986, and for Hertfordshire in 1987. He also played representative cricket for the Minor Counties and led the Essex C.A. side.

M	Inns	NOs	Runs	HS	Avge	Ct
6	9	1	62	14*	7.75	5

Overs	Mds	Runs	Wkts	Avge	Best
36.4	3	148	3	49.33	3/64

Sunday League

M	Inns	NOs	Runs	HS	Avge	Ct
3	2	1	9	8	9.00	1

Overs	Mds	Runs	Wkts	Avge	Best
19	-	119	2	59.50	1/24

John Percy HERRINGSHAW

Born: Derby, 22 May 1892.
Died: Yapton, Sussex, 13 November 1974.

A slow left-arm bowler who appeared for Essex as a professional in 1921 and 1922 with limited success.

M	Inns	NOs	Runs	HS	Avge	Ct
9	14	5	94	18	10.44	7

Overs	Mds	Runs	Wkts	Avge	Best
150.2	28	498	9	55.33	2/48

George Frederick HIGGINS

Born: Mile End, London, 25 December 1868.
Died: Woodford Green, 19 August 1951.

George Higgins assisted Essex as an amateur during their first two years as a first-class county. He made his debut in the rather strange game against Yorkshire at Halifax in July 1894, when Essex fielded several players who had not been seen before. A right-handed batsman, Higgins appeared in Essex's first Championship match, against Warwickshire at Edgbaston, May 1895. He batted at number four and hit 118 and shared a fourth wicket stand of 205 with Burns. So Higgins was the first Essex centurion in first-class cricket.

He did not appear after 1895.

M	Inns	NOs	Runs	HS	Avge	100s	Ct
9	17	-	306	118	18.00	1	2

Harry Mountford HILLS

Born: Mayland, 28 September 1886.

A leg-break bowler and right-handed batsman, Harry Hills had his career interrupted by World War One. He was first seen against Kent at Gravesend and against Lancashire at Leyton, in 1912. He appeared in 11 other matches before the war, and he was in the side for the opening match of the 1919 season, against the Australian Imperial Forces at Leyton, but after that he was seen no more.

M	Inns	NOs	Runs	HS	Avge	Ct
14	21	4	139	26	8.17	7

Overs	Mds	Runs	Wkts	Avge	Best	5/inn
191.1	9	738	15	49.20	5/63	1

Colin HILTON

Born: Atherton, Lancashire, 26 September 1937.

Colin Hilton's stay with Essex was very brief.

He played for Lancashire from 1957 to 1963 and, initially, he had had much success. He took 92 wickets in 1962 when he was capped. He left Lancashire after one more season, however, and joined Essex on special registration. A right-arm fast bowler, he 'proved rather more a liability than an asset and he resigned at the end of the season. Unable to master the front-foot law, Hilton was no-balled no fewer than 230 times during the summer.'

M	Inns	NOs	Runs	HS	Avge	Ct
24	23	9	128	29*	9.14	12

Overs	Mds	Runs	Wkts	Avge	Best	5/inn
630.3	96	1999	58	34.46	6/86	1

Gillette Cup

M	Inns	NOs	Runs	HS	Avge
2	1	1	2	2*	-

Overs	Mds	Runs	Wkts	Avge	Best
26	6	73	5	14.60	4/47

Augustus Bernard HIPKIN

Born: Brancaster, Norfolk, 8 August 1900.
Died: Carluke, Lanarkshire, 11 February 1957.
Known as *Joe* Hipkin to the Leyton crowd because of his similarity in appearance to Joe Beckett the boxer, Bernard Hipkin was a burly

cricketer, a slow left-arm bowler and a hard-hitting left-handed batsman. In the early 1920s, Essex were desperately short of bowling, and Johnny Douglas discovered Hipkin and engaged him for the 1923 season. The Essex skipper must have wondered about

his decision when he was caught by Hipkin who was fielding substitute for Middlesex. The catch ended a ninth wicket partnership of 160 between Douglas and Franklin.

Hipkin had made his debut against Sussex at Leyton in the opening match of that 1923 season, claiming A.E.R.Gilligan as his first wicket. He took 43 wickets that year, and the following season he took 116 wickets in all matches. This, it seemed, was the bowler for whom Essex had been looking, but, to the despair of Douglas, Hipkin had flattered to deceive. He became more intent upon hitting the ball hard and appeared to lose interest in his bowling. His number of runs increased as his number of wickets declined. In 1927, he hit 946 runs, with centuries against Glamorgan and Oxford University, but his total of wickets dropped to 34. Douglas worked him hard and disciplined him strongly, but the decline continued, and by 1931, his last season with Essex, he had virtually ceased to bowl, and he was a shadow of the man who had performed the hat-trick against Lancashire in 1924.

Hipkin was a soccer player, keeping goal for Leyton, Charlton Athletic and Chatham, and this, no doubt, played a part in his ability as a good fielder and catcher.

On being released by Essex, he secured a post as player-coach with Uddingstone CC in Glasgow, and he was later with the West of Scotland club, enjoying marked success at both clubs.

M	Inns	NOs	Runs	HS	Avge	100s	Ct
232	326	55	4239	108	15.64	2	209

Overs	Mds	Runs	Wkts	Avge	Best	10/m	5/inn
5432	1267	13377	518	25.82	8/71	3	18

Robin Nicholas Stuart HOBBS

Born: Chippenham, Wiltshire, 8 May 1942.
When he left Essex in 1975, Robin Hobbs was the only genuine leg-break bowler in county cricket. Many believed that, in a game of changing attitudes and changing structure, he would be the last leg-break bowler to play for England. Happily, the quality leg-spinners from Pakistan and India and the deeds of Shane Warne, coupled with the advent of Ian Salisbury, have brought leg-break bowling back into fashion as a match-winning force.

The son of a Chingford cricketer who was serving in the RAF at Chippenham, Robin Hobbs was soon moved from his birthplace to

Scotland and eventually to Essex. Educated at Raines Foundation School, Stepney, he bowled quickish leg-breaks and was in the Chadwell Heath side by the age of 15.

Leaving school, he went into insurance, and a century for the Employers Liability Insurance Company won him a Jack Hobbs bat under the scheme then operated by the old London evening paper, *The Star.*

He came under the eye of Kent and was given a trial at Canterbury and received winter coaching at Eltham. He was now playing for Chingford, however, and his talent was recognised by Trevor Bailey and Doug

Insole who signed him for Essex. Making his debut for the 2nd XI in May 1960, Hobbs took 6 for 39 in his second match, against Kent. The following season he played in 12 first team matches and took 23 wickets.

With Bill Greensmith the first choice leg-spinner, Phelan having completed his National Service, and Jim Laker having been recruited, Hobbs could find no place in the Essex side in 1962, but he took 55 wickets for the 2nd XI.

In 1963, Robin Hobbs established himself in the Essex Championship team and began to attract the attention of the national selectors. He played for MCC against Surrey, appeared in the Scarborough Festival and toured East Africa with an MCC side under M.J.K.Smith. He took 81 wickets in 1964, and, in 1967, when he captured 101, he played in all three Tests against India and one against Pakistan. The following winter he toured West Indies and played in the first Test.

An exciting fielder, Hobbs was no mean batsman, capable of stubborn defence or violent hitting as the occasion demanded. In 1968, at Ilford, he and Stuart Turner added 192 for the eighth wicket against Glamorgan in two hours. Both batsmen reached maiden first-class centuries. In his last season with Essex, 1975, Hobbs hit 100 in 44 minutes against the Australians as Chelmsford.

Hobbs' best bowling performance was against Glamorgan at Swansea in July 1966, when he took 8 for 63 in the first innings and had match figures of 13 for 164.

In 1972, he took 102 wickets at 21.40 runs each, but already increasing emphasis on one-day cricket was beginning to have its effect on leg-spinners. In spite of some excellent bowling performances in limited-over cricket, Robin Hobbs appeared in all 16 Sunday League matches in the 1971 season without bowling a ball. It was in this season that he played the last of his seven Test matches.

Somewhat frustrated, one feels, by the attitudes that were prevalent towards spinners, and leg-spinners in particular, in the early 70s, Robin Hobbs retired from Essex cricket in 1975 and played for Suffolk for three seasons. It came as a great surprise when he returned to first-class cricket in 1979 as captain of Glamorgan. He gave up the captaincy, but played three seasons for the Welsh county, finally retiring in 1981. His last match was *against* Essex, at Colchester, and he took 5 for 85 in the second innings. He played one more season for Suffolk, but thereafter restricted himself to games for Copford and for Jim Parks' *Whitbread Wanderers Eleven.*

Since leaving Essex he has been employed as an area representative for Barclaycard.

M	Inns	NOs	Runs	HS	Avge	100s	Ct
325	429	102	4069	100	12.44	2	222

Overs	Mds	Runs	Wkts	Avge	Best	10/m	5/inn
7322.3	1897	19844	763	26.00	8/63	5	32

Sunday League

M	Inn	NOs	Runs	HS	Avge	Ct
93	64	21	591	54*	13.74	31

Overs	Mds	Runs	Wkts	Avge	Best	5/inn
84.4	4	470	22	21.36	6/22	1

Benson and Hedges Cup

M	Inns	NOs	Runs	HS	Avge	Ct
14	10	2	81	40	10.12	3

Overs	Mds	Runs	Wkts	Avge	Best
44	5	133	3	44.33	2/21

Gillette Cup

M	Inns	NOs	Runs	HS	Avge	Ct
19	15	2	155	34	11.92	4

Overs	Mds	Runs	Wkts	Avge	Best
90.1	19	304	18	16.88	4/55

George William HOCKEY

Born: Ipswich, Suffolk, 1 January 1905.
Educated at Ipswich School, George Hockey played for Essex as an amateur between 1928 and 1931. A right-handed batsman, he occasionally assisted Suffolk between 1935 and 1948.

M	Inns	NOs	Runs	HS	Avge	Ct
19	33	5	305	23	10.89	4

Overs	Mds	Runs	Wkts	Avge
5	2	20	-	-

Graham Wade HORREX

Born: Goodmayes, 27 December 1932.
A right-handed opening batsman, Graham Horrex was educated at Brentwood School and played for the Brentwood club. He was a noted squash player who represented Essex at that sport. He played cricket for the county in 1956 and 1957 as an amateur, but he had little success.

M	Inns	NOs	Runs	HS	Avge
7	13	-	141	41	10.84

Richard HORSFALL

Born: Todmorden, Yorkshire, 26 June 1920.
Died: Halifax, Yorkshire, 25 August 1981.
Dick Horsfall played in the Lancashire League at the age of 16, and he first came to the notice of Essex with his achievements in services cricket towards the end of World War Two. He was qualified to play for the county in 1947 and hit 170 against Hampshire at Bournemouth in his first season. Very much a hard-wicket batsman who liked to hit the ball hard in front of the wicket, he had undergone a serious back operation before he began his county career, and, in spite of his joyful approach to the game, he was never fully fit and often in pain.

Tall, fair and slim, Horsfall was a chain-smoker and, for all his good humour, a cricketer with a very nervous disposition. He was always at his best when runs were needed quickly and when he could play his natural game without reproach. His one double century was made against Kent at Blackheath in four and a half hours in 1951. He and Paul Gibb added 343 for the third wicket, which stood as an Essex record for over 30 years.

Good in the outfield, he was never happy close to the wicket, but as a batsman, he was always an entertainer. He enjoyed a fine season in 1953, hitting 1731 runs, but this was followed by two poor seasons, and Essex released him at the end of the 1955 season.

He joined Glamorgan, but he played only five matches for them, and it was apparent that a career which had promised so much had never quite been fulfilled. A very popular man, he returned to Todmorden where he kept a public house.

M	Inns	NOs	Runs	HS	Avge	100s	Ct
207	349	25	9583	206	29.59	17	85

Overs	Mds	Runs	Wkts	Avge	Best
12	2	41	1	41.00	1/4

William George HUBBLE

Born: Leyton, 20 June 1898.
Died: Bishops Waltham, Hampshire, 14 December 1978.
A left-handed amateur batsman, Hubble

opened the Essex first innings against Cambridge University at Colchester in June 1923. A slow left-arm bowler, he took two wickets for three runs in 28 balls in Cambridge's second innings, claiming Wright and Leonard Crawley as his victims.

M	Inns	NOs	Runs	HS	Avge
1	1	-	0	0	0.00

Overs	Mds	Runs	Wkts	Avge	Best
17.4	3	60	2	30.00	2/3

Mervyn Gregory HUGHES

Born: Eurora, Victoria, Australia, 23 November 1961.

It may surprise many to know that Merv Hughes, Australia's demon bowler with the threatening moustaches, played one game for Essex. He had made his debut for Victoria in the 1981-82 season, and, in 1983, he came to England on an Australian Esso Scholarship. He took 60 wickets for Essex 2nd XI in Championship matches alone, a phenomenal performance, and he played in the 1st XI match against the New Zealand tourists with considerable success. Later, of course, he became a force in Test cricket.

Cricket has been his life, and he has pursued no other career. When the play, *An Evening with Gary Lineker,* opened in Australia its name was changed to *An Evening with Merv Hughes,* but Merv says it has nothing to do with sport.

M	Inns	NOs	Runs	HS	Avge
1	2	-	10	10	5.00

Overs	Mds	Runs	Wkts	Avge	Best
31.2	2	162	6	27.00	4/71

Lieutnant Colonel Francis Edgar HUGONIN

Born: London, 16 August 1897.

Died: Stainton-in-Cleveland, North Yorkshire, 5 March 1967.

Educated at Eastbourne College, Hugonin went straight from school into the Army at the outbreak of World War One. A Regular Army officer in the Royal Artillery, he was a most capable wicket-keeper and player for Essex when stationed at Colchester in 1927 and 1928. He played also for Berkshire and often for Free Foresters, and between 1930 and 1937, he was the Army's regular wicket-keeper. Indeed, his last first-class appearance was for the Army against Cambridge University at the end of May 1937. His final victim was Paul Gibb, later to be an Essex wicket-keeper also, whom he stumped.

In World War Two, he was taken prisoner by the Japanese when Singapore fell, and E.W.Swanton was to write of him poignantly after his death:

'Far-East prisoners of war will recall the value of his leadership in circumstances of the utmost difficulty at Saigon, and he will have a special place in the affections of all the fellow-cricketers with whom he shared the rigours of captivity on or around the Burma-Siam railway.'

M	Inns	NOs	Runs	HS	Avge	Ct/st
6	8	3	42	17	8.40	8/1

Alan HURD

Born: Ilford, 7 September 1937.

Educated at Chigwell School, Alan Hurd was a fine off-break bowler whose appearances for Essex were restricted to his three summer vacations while up at Clare College, Cambridge, where he won his blue in all three years, 1958-60.

Following a successful season with Cambridge in 1958, he made a sensational debut for Essex. In the match against Kent at Clacton, he had Wilson caught off the first ball he bowled for the county, and he finished with figures of 6 for 15. In the second innings, he took 4 for 62.

He played for the Gentlemen against the Players at Lord's, but he was never quite as successful for Essex in his last two seasons as he had been in his first.

A left-handed batsman, he was a renowned rabbit, at one time entering the record books with his string of noughts.

He left first-class cricket to take up a teaching post at Sevenoaks School, and he played club cricket for Sevenoaks Vine.

M	Inns	NOs	Runs	HS	Avge	Ct
35	34	14	115	20*	5.75	5

Overs	Mds	Runs	Wkts	Avge	Best	10/m	5/inn
818.4	225	2221	84	26.44	6/15	1	5

Geoffrey Charles HURST

Born: Ashton-under-Lyne, Lancashire, 8 December 1941.

A naturally gifted athlete, Geoff Hurst was on the Essex staff in the early 1960s, but his only first-class appearance was against his native county, Lancashire, at Liverpool at the end of June 1962. Unbeaten in his first innings, he was bowled for 0 in his second so that he did not score a run in his single appearance.

A brilliant fielder and an occasional wicket-keeper, he was, of course, lost to cricket because of his outstanding soccer career with West Bromwich Albion, West Ham United and Stoke City. One of the famous West Ham trio in England's World Cup winning side, Hurst scored a hat-trick in the famous victory over West Germany at Wembley to become the only man ever to have hit three goals in a World Cup Final.

M	Inns	NOs	Runs	HS	Avge	Ct
1	2	1	0	0*	0.00	1

Nasser HUSSAIN

Born: Madras, India, 28 March 1968.

Nasser Hussain first played for Essex Schools at the age of eight. Recommended as a leg-break bowler by Bill Morris of Ilford Cricket School, he appeared against Sussex Schools at Eastbourne and was in a winning side.

Coached at the Ilford School, at the County School at Chelmsford, and at Forest School, he

was soon recognised as a batsman of outstanding ability. He thrived at Durham University, and he was in the Combined Universities' side that reached the quarter-finals of the Benson and Hedges Cup in 1989. At Taunton, the Universities lost by three runs to Somerset in spite of an innings of 118 from Hussain who won the Gold Award.

He first played for Essex in 1987 and has already shared in the three record partnerships for the county; an unbroken 347 with Mark Waugh for the third wicket v Lancashire; 314 with Salim Malik v Surrey for the fourth wicket; and 316 v Leicestershire with Mike Garnham for the fifth wicket.

Chosen for England's tour of West Indies, 1989-90, he played in three Tests, but then suffered a broken arm while playing tennis. The injury halted his international career, but he regained his Test place in the Ashes series of 1993 and was chosen for the tour of West Indies the following winter.

He has also toured with England 'A' parties and played grade cricket in Australia. As an additional asset to his forceful and confident right-handed batting, Hussain has proved himself to be an outstanding fielder in close to the wicket positions.

One of his brothers, Mehriyar or 'Mel', was on the staffs of both Worcestershire and Hampshire while another brother, Abbas, played for the U.A.U. Nasser's father 'Joe' captained Ilford for a time and has a business interest in the Ilford Indoor Cricket School.

M	Inns	NOs	Runs	HS	Avge	100s	Ct
120	178	23	6738	197	43.47	18	153

Overs	Mds	Runs	Wkts	Avge	Best
46	2	307	2	153.50	1/38

Sunday League

M	Inns	NOs	Runs	HS	Avge	Ct
83	73	14	1608	76	27.25	35

Benson and Hedges Cup

M	Inns	NOs	Runs	HS	Avge	Ct
14	12	2	237	59	23.70	6

NatWest Trophy

M	Inns	NOs	Runs	HS	Avge	100s	Ct
12	11	1	458	108	45.80	1	9

Barry James HYAM

Born: Romford, 9 September, 1975.
A student at Havering Sixth Form College who played his early cricket for Romford and Gidea Park Colts, Barry Hyam was called into the Essex side for the penultimate game of the 1993 season when neither Garnham nor Rollins was available to keep wicket. The match was against Glamorgan at Cardiff, and he performed admirably. He is with the Orsett and Thurrock club.

M	Inns	NOs	Runs	HS	Avge	Ct
1	2	-	1	1	0.50	2

Robert Wilberforce James Gerard HYNDSON

Born: Cape Town, South Africa, 1894.
Died: Bradford, Yorkshire, 27 September, 1943.
A middle-order batsman and change bowler, Hyndson played for Essex against the Australian Imperial Forces at Southend in 1919. His brother played for Surrey in 1927 and in several Army matches.

M	Inns	NOs	Runs	HS	Avge
1	2	-	7	6	3.50

Overs	Mds	Runs	Wkts	Avge
14	1	71	-	-

Mark Christopher ILOTT

Born: Watford, Hertfordshire, 27 August 1970.
Son of the president of Watford Town CC, Mark Ilott learned his cricket at the club and with Hertfordshire Colts. A left-arm fast medium pace bowler, he appeared for Hertfordshire at all levels, appearing in the Minor Counties' side in 1987 and 1988 when he joined Essex and played against Cambridge University and Northamptonshire.

Injury hampered his early development, but by 1990, he was establishing himself as the natural successor to John Lever. He went with England 'A' to Pakistan, 1990-91, but, after playing in the match against Cambridge University at the beginning of the 1991 season, he was out for the rest of the summer with a back injury.

Ilott demonstrated his complete recovery with 64 wickets in 1992. He won a place in the England 'A' side to Australia, and, in 1993, he appeared in three Tests in the Ashes series and returned career best bowling figures in the match against Surrey at The Oval. He toured South Africa with England 'A' in 1993-94.

M	Inns	NOs	Runs	HS	Avge	Ct
68	72	18	716	51	13.25	18

Overs	Mds	Runs	Wkts	Avge	Best	10/m	5/inn
2136.3	453	6668	215	31.01	7/85	1	10

Sunday League

M	Inns	NOs	Runs	HS	Avge	Ct
46	23	6	139	24	8.17	5

Overs	Mds	Runs	Wkts	Avge	Best
340	26	1481	58	25.53	4/15

Benson and Hedges Cup

M	Inns	NOs	Runs	HS	Avge
12	3	1	19	14	9.50

Overs	Mds	Runs	Wkts	Avge	Best	5/inn
105.5	16	320	20	16.00	5/21	1

NatWest Trophy

M	Inns	NOs	Runs	HS	Avge	Ct
8	4	2	50	26	25.00	2

Overs	Mds	Runs	Wkts	Avge	Best
84.1	9	324	10	32.40	2/23

John Herbert INNS

Born: Writtle, 30 March 1876.
Died: Writtle, 14 June 1905.
Described as a good wicket-keeper and one of the finest fielders in England, John Inns played as a professional for Essex between 1898 and 1904. His opportunities for keeping wicket were limited by the consistency of Tom Russell. He died at the age of 29.

M	Inns	NOs	Runs	HS	Avge	Ct
10	14	3	73	28	6.63	8

Overs	Mds	Runs	Wkts	Avge
5	1	15	-	-

Douglas John INSOLE

Born: Clapton, London, 18 April 1926.
Doug Insole's record as a player puts him among the very greatest of Essex cricketers. When one adds his contribution as captain and chairman of the county club he becomes a giant among men.

Born across the border in Middlesex, he moved to Highams Park at the age of four. He learned his early cricket from his father, a great enthusiast, and his skill was nurtured both at elementary school and at Sir George Monoux Grammar School, Walthamstow. His progress was interrupted when he was evacuated to Herefordshire during the war, but by then he had represented Essex and London Schools.

In many ways he was a self-taught batsman. He was never to be a great stylist, very much an on-side batsman, but he was a very effective player. When his school returned to London he first began to appear for Chingford in 1943 and 1944 and met with considerable success.

After two years in the Army he went up to St Catharine's College, Cambridge, and made his first-class debut for the university against Yorkshire in May. The purists had dismissed his chances of playing in the side, but he scored heavily in the trials, and hit 44, 49 and 58 in his first three first-class innings.

He made 161 not out against Hampshire at Portsmouth, averaged over 42 and rarely failed. At the end of the season, he found his form with Essex, hit 109 not out against Lancashire at Clacton and reached 1000 runs in all matches, a feat he was to accomplish 12 times more before his retirement at the end of the 1963 season.

In his second season, 1948, he again prospered at Cambridge, but played only a handful of matches for Essex. Captain of Cambridge in 1949, he led the light blues to a brilliant and unexpected victory over Oxford. His own batting throughout the season was consistently good and his fielding was outstanding. He had, at various times at Cambridge, kept wicket with distinction. His captaincy was inspiring, ever looking to win, never lacking enthusiasm.

He topped the Essex batting averages by a vast margin, hitting 850 runs average 65.38.

Against Yorkshire at Colchester in July he hit 219 and was awarded his county cap.

In 1950, Insole initially shared the captaincy of Essex with Tom Pearce, but he took over from Pearce in June and remained in charge of the county until the end of the 1960 season. At Cambridge, he had first formed his friendship with Trevor Bailey, and these two were to form the backbone of Essex cricket for a decade.

Insole was an inspiring captain. He set a wonderful example in the field and raised Essex standards in this department. He bowled useful medium pace if required, and he was a capable wicket-keeper. He was to score centuries against the other 16 first-class

counties and to play nine times for England in a period when the country was rich with batsmen. He was vice-captain to Peter May on the tour of South Africa, 1956-57, hit a century in the third Test and finished top of the Test match averages in batting and second to May for the whole tour.

Three times he reached 2000 runs in a season, and, in 1955, he scored more runs than any other batsman in the country, 2427. He played for the Gentlemen against the Players on 18 occasions and captained the amateurs. He was an England selector for nine years, chairman of the TCCB for three, and an MCC committee member from 1956 to 1980. He also managed two England sides to Australia, and he has remained a powerful voice in English cricket. He was, rightly, appointed CBE for services to the game.

For two years before going to Cambridge he had played inside-right for Walthamstow Avenue, and it was in this position that he played for the university for three seasons, captaining the side in 1948 when he came close to winning an amateur international cap for England. He was a founder member of the famous Pegasus side, and the first man to captain the club. He appeared for Corinthian Casuals in the FA Amateur Cup Final of 1955-56. In so many ways, his life ran parallel to that of his friend, Trevor Bailey.

It was to Bailey that Insole handed over the captaincy of Essex in 1961 although he was to make occasional appearances until the end of the 1963 season. His work for Essex cricket did not end there. He was chairman of the county from 1976 to 1978 and again from 1984 until 1993, and he has been a driving force in the success of the club, demanding standards, encouraging the development of players and urging positive cricket, that quest for victory that does not fear defeat. What Essex County Cricket Club has achieved since 1979 owes a tremendous amount to Doug Insole.

In a life marked by personal tragedies, he has never failed to give his all to the club and to the game as a whole. His commitment to his business has been equally unrelenting. He has enjoyed a highly successful career as marketing director of Trollope and Colls Holdings Ltd, a position to which he was first appointed in 1975.

He has a penchant for jazz, has been a JP for Chingford, a member of the Football Association Council and of the Sports Council, and he has written an interesting early autobiography, *Cricket From the Middle*. A man with a zest for life and an appetite for work, he will always remain a giant among the cricketers of Essex.

Doug Insole has one dubious distinction, however. He is the only Essex bowler ever to have been no-balled for 'throwing'. The match was that against Northamptonshire at Northampton in 1952.

M	Inns	NOs	Runs	HS	Avge	100s	Ct/st
345	574	54	20113	219*	38.67	48	279/1

Overs	Mds	Runs	Wkts	Avge	Best	5/inn
1284.1	259	4061	119	34.12	5/22	1

Ronald Charles IRANI

Born: Leigh, Lancashire, 26 October 1971.
A tall right-arm medium pace bowler and right-handed batsman, Ronnie Irani played for Young England sides with considerable success as an all-rounder, but he appeared in only nine first-class matches for Lancashire between 1990 and 1993. Rejecting the offer of a new contract for the 1994 season, he joined Essex. An injury to John Stephenson and the retirement of Derek Pringle gave him an immediate place in the side,  and he responded with some outstanding performances. He had career best performances with both bat and ball, and, at Worcester, in June, he hit 119 and shared a fourth-wicket partnership of 245 with Graham Gooch. His century and this stand enabled Essex to move to a thrilling and totally unexpected victory. In his first NatWest game, against Sussex, he took the individual award. On the evidence of his form in his first season with Essex, Irani is destined for the highest honours.

M	Inns	NOs	Runs	HS	Avge	100s	Ct
18	29	6	965	119	41.95	2	6

Overs	Mds	Runs	Wkts	Avge	Best
249.4	42	834	28	29.78	4/27

Sunday League

M	Inns	NOs	Runs	HS	Avge	Ct
16	16	-	185	35	11.56	2

Overs	Mds	Runs	Wkts	Avge	Best
58.2	6	248	11	22.54	3/22

Benson and Hedges Cup

M	Inns	NOs	Runs	HS	Avge
2	-	-	-	-	-

Overs	Mds	Runs	Wkts	Avge	Best
14	1	89	1	89.00	1/61

NatWest Trophy

M	Inns	NOs	Runs	HS	Avge
2	2	-	41	30	20.50

Overs	Mds	Runs	Wkts	Avge	Best
24	2	125	4	31.25	4/59

Brian Lee IRVINE

Born: Durban, South Africa, 9 March 1944.
When the ruling was introduced in 1968 that counties were to be allowed immediate registration for an overseas player Essex signed Lee Irvine. Little was known of him, and he was certainly not in the same salaried  class as Nottinghamshire's Gary Sobers, but for two years he was to delight Essex supporters. He was a free-scoring, left-handed middle-order batsman, a brilliant fielder and a very useful wicket-keeper. He reached 1000 runs in both of his seasons with the county, and in the first, 1968, he hit more sixes than any other batsman in the county.

He had made his first-class debut for a Western Province Invitation XI in 1962-63, and had then assisted Natal until the end of his time with Essex when he was to return home and join Transvaal. Surprisingly, perhaps, he hit only one century for Essex, and that was at Swansea in his second season.

Lee Irvine returned to South Africa and took up a marketing position with a building society which brought about his move to Transvaal. His two seasons with Essex had helped him to mature as a batsman, and the county can claim, with justification, that they turned him into a Test cricketer. He played in the four Test-series against Australia, 1969-70, South Africa's last before their excommunication, and hit 353 runs, average 50.42 including the last century before the exile. He was chosen for tours of England and Australia, both of which were cancelled.

He is in the trade finance industry and runs his own company. He was also the organiser of the Datsun Double Wicket event, which brought together cricketers of all creeds and colour, and a South African Test selector.

Interestingly, it was Lee Irvine who, in an after-dinner speech, gave the first hints of the cricket revolution which was to result in Kerry Packer's World Series.

M	Inns	NOs	Runs	HS	Avge	100s	Ct
54	89	12	2674	109	34.72	1	40

Overs	Mds	Runs	Wkts	Avge	Best
18	-	70	1	70.00	1/39

Sunday League

M	Inns	NOs	Runs	HS	Avge	Ct
16	15	1	311	63	22.21	8

Overs	Mds	Runs	Wkts	Avge
0.4	-	6	-	-

Gillette Cup

M	Inns	NOs	Runs	HS	Avge	Ct
4	4	1	84	36*	28.00	2

Victor Edmund JARVIS

Born: Hampstead, London, 30 September 1898.
Died: Stokenchurch, Buckinghamshire, 30 April 1975.

Victor Jarvis played two matches for Essex as an amateur in 1925. He was a slow left-arm bowler from Leigh-on-Sea who bowled round the wicket. He batted right-handed.

M	Inns	NOs	Runs	HS	Avge
2	4	-	44	37	11.00

Overs	Mds	Runs	Wkts	Avge
6	-	23	-	-

Cecil Victor JENKINSON

Born: Ilford, 15 May 1891.
Died: Pembury, Kent, 6 November 1980.

One of several wicket-keepers upon whom Essex called in the early 1920s in an attempt to solve a problem position, Jenkinson was an amateur who appeared against Hampshire, Sussex and Lancashire in 1922, all away matches, and against Middlesex at Lord's and Worcestershire at Leyton the following year. He became the county scorer for several years in the 1950s and 1960s.

M	Inns	NOs	Runs	HS	Avge	Ct/st
5	6	2	9	8	2.25	4/4

Lindsey Crawford Stapleton JERMAN

Born: Old Fletton, Huntingdonshire, 23 April 1915.

'Jerry' Jerman was educated at Rhyl Grammar School and worked in Essex as area

sales manager for Dunlop tyres. He played for Chelmsford from 1947 to 1951, and then for Romford for many years after that. He captained both clubs as he did the Club Cricket Conference. A fast medium pace bowler, he had considerable success for

Essex 2nd XI in the Minor Counties Championship, and, in 1950, he made his first-class debut against Combined Services at Chelmsford. He did not take a wicket and fell victim to Brian Close.

The following season he entered cricket folklore. Playing against Surrey at Southchurch Park at Southend, he joined Trevor Bailey with the score at 314 for 9, and Bailey more than 20 runs short of a century. Bailey 'farmed' the bowling carefully, but eventually Jerman had to face his first ball in the County Championship, and the bowler was Jim Laker. 'Jerry' promptly hit that first ball into the lake for six. The last wicket realised 42, and Bailey finished on 104 not out. It was in that match that Jerman got his one first-class wicket, bowling the Surrey captain M. R.Barton.

He served on the Committee for many years and has been a passionate worker for the Supporters' Association which has raised vast sums of money for the club. His commitment to the county has been total.

M	Inns	NOs	Runs	HS	Avge	Ct
3	2	-	8	8	4.00	2

Overs	Mds	Runs	Wkts	Avge	Best
82	20	222	1	222.00	1/39

Arthur Sannox JOHNSTON

Born: Hornsey, Middlesex, 16 March 1863.
Died: Well Hall, Eltham, London, 8 August 1929.
Arthur Johnston was educated at Mill Hill School and made three appearances for Middlesex before first playing for Essex in their pre-first-class days in 1889. His first first-class match for Essex was against Yorkshire at Leyton in 1894, and he made infrequent appearances over the next two seasons.

He was a capable right-handed batsman and a good fielder. He was an even better golfer and was the amateur champion in 1895.

M	Inns	NOs	Runs	HS	Avge	Ct
7	12	1	235	63	21.36	3

Anthony Mervyn JORDEN

Born: Radlett, Hertfordshire, 28 January 1947.
Tony Jorden went from Monmouth School to Fitzwilliam College, Cambridge in October

1967, but he had made his debut for Essex at Leicester in 1966. A fast medium pace bowler, he won his blue in all three years at Cambridge and captained the side in 1969 and 1970, an unusual honour.

He played for Essex at the end of the summer term at Cambridge, and his best season for the county was 1968 when he hit 59 not out against Somerset at Chelmsford and took 4 for 29 at Northampton.

Jorden left first-class cricket after 1970 and, a chartered surveyor, he is a director of Leighton Goldhill Ltd. He played club cricket for Blackheath and for Luton when he also assisted Bedfordshire, 1975-77.

Good a cricketer as he was, Tony Jorden is far better known as a rugby player. He got his blue at Cambridge, played for Blackheath, Bedford, Eastern Counties, London and Barbarians, and was England's full-back in seven internationals. He was later a coach to Wasps and to the London Division.

M	Inns	NOs	Runs	HS	Avge	Ct
60	85	20	704	59*	10.83	36

Overs	Mds	Runs	Wkts	Avge	Best
1140.4	170	3501	117	29.92	4/29

Gillette Cup

M	Inns	NOs	Runs	HS	Avge	Ct
4	4	2	29	21	14.50	1

Overs	Mds	Runs	Wkts	Avge	Best
48	4	156	10	15.60	3/41

Colonel Ronald Cecil Graham JOY

Born: Colchester, 30 July 1898.
Died: Holly Hill House, Ditchingham, Norfolk, 12 December 1974.

One of the many Regular Army officers who assisted Essex in the 1920s, Ronald Joy married a daughter of Frank Penn, the Kent cricketer who played for England against Australia in 1880. A right-arm fast medium pace bowler with a high action, Joy was in the Winchester XI in 1916 and first played for Essex in 1922.

He was a successful club cricketer and frequently assisted the Army. He also played first-class cricket for the Europeans and Hyderabad between 1929 and 1932. His last game for Essex was in 1928. Joy was awarded the DSO in 1942.

M	Inns	NOs	Runs	HS	Avge	Ct
13	16	2	142	35	10.14	10

Overs	Mds	Runs	Wkts	Avge	Best
131.4	23	398	12	33.16	3/41

Michael Scott KASPROWICZ

Born: South Brisbane, Queensland, Australia, 10 February 1972.

A right-arm fast bowler who made his first-class debut in 1989 at the age of 17, Michael Kasprowicz was signed as the Essex overseas player in 1994. In some ways, this was a break with tradition, but the loss of both Foster and Pringle had weakened the county attack, and Kasprowicz was seen as the ideal replacement. In 1992-93, he had taken 51 wickets in the Australian season and was desperately unlucky not to have been chosen for the tour of England in 1993. He quickly settled at Essex and played a major part in the county winning their first three Championship matches in 1994. His big hitting provided an unexpected bonus.

M	Inns	NOs	Runs	HS	Avge	Ct
17	24	4	326	44	16.30	9

Overs	Mds	Runs	Wkts	Avge	Best	5/inn
527.3	92	1869	60	31.15	6/71	2

Sunday League

M	Inns	NOs	Runs	HS	Avge	Ct
15	12	-	61	17	5.08	2

Overs	Mds	Runs	Wkts	Avge	Best
94.4	6	458	11	41.63	2/38

Benson and Hedges Cup

M	Inns	NOs	Runs	HS	Avge	Ct
2	-	-	-	-	-	1

Overs	Mds	Runs	Wkts	Avge	Best
15	0	72	2	36.00	2/52

NatWest Trophy

M	Inns	NOs	Runs	HS	Avge
1	1	-	13	13	13.00

Overs	Mds	Runs	Wkts	Avge	Best	5/inn
12	2	60	5	12.00	5/60	1

Henry David KEIGWIN

Born: Lexden, Colchester, 14 May 1881.
Died: Nr Thiepval, France, 20 September 1916.
The elder brother of Richard Keigwin, H.D. enjoyed much success in the St Paul's XI, but failed to get a blue at Cambridge. He scored heavily for Peterhouse, twice reaching 1000 runs before the end of May and, in 1904, sharing stands of 318 and 244 with his brother. He appeared for Essex in 1906 and 1907 when he became director of music at Glenalmond in Scotland. He appeared in representative matches for Scotland.

He served in the Lancashire Fusiliers in World War One and while fighting in France as a second lieutenant, he was killed in action.

A third Keigwin brother, Herbert Stanley, played first-class cricket for Cambridge and London County before emigrating to Bulawayo, Rhodesia.

M	Inns	NOs	Runs	HS	Avge	Ct
4	6	-	69	20	11.50	1

Overs	Mds	Runs	Wkts	Avge	Best
56	14	179	4	44.75	1/23

Richard Prescott KEIGWIN

Born: Lexden, Colchester, 8 April 1883.
Died: Polstead, Suffolk, 26 November 1972.
The younger of two brothers who played for Essex, Richard Keigwin was a sportsman of outstanding ability. Educated at Clifton College,he won his blue in each of his four years at Cambridge, 1903-1906, and it was during his first year at Cambridge that he made his debut for Essex. He was a sound right-handed middle-order batsman, who opened on occasions, and a very useful off-spinner. He obtained his blue for soccer, hockey and racquets as well as cricket, and he played for Essex and England at hockey. He was also a county player at soccer.

He was a most successful coach at the Royal Naval College, Osborne, and his appearances for Essex were limited to 20 in 16 years. He played his last game for Essex in 1919, and two years later, having become a master at Clifton College, he played the first of his nine games for Gloucestershire. He also represented Gloucestershire at soccer and lawn tennis, and, after spending some time in France, he became an expert in pelota. After spending 16 years at Clifton, he became warden of Wills Hall, Bristol.

An exceptional Danish scholar, he was the foremost translator of Danish literature into English and the leading authority on the works of Hans Christian Andersen. For his services to Danish literature, the Danish government made him a knight of the Order of Danneborg. He served Danish cricket as well as he did Danish literature.

He instigated an MCC tour of Denmark in 1922 and led the party himself, and he took another MCC party three years later.

M	Inns	NOs	Runs	HS	Avge	Ct
20	32	3	455	75	15.68	3

Overs	Mds	Runs	Wkts	Avge	Best
164.2	24	639	14	45.64	4/49

Charles John Michael KENNY

Born: Wallington, Surrey, 19 May 1929.
Captain of Ampleforth College in 1947, Charles Kenny was considered to be a right-

arm fast medium pace bowler of well above average ability. He first played for Essex against Gloucestershire at Colchester in 1950 and claimed the England batsman George Emmett as his debut victim.

Kenny won his blue at Cambridge in 1952, and, following the university season, he appeared in 14 Championship matches for Essex and took 32 wickets, proving to be a most valuable addition to the attack. Unfortunately, little was seen of him in 1953, and he dropped out of county cricket after that season.

He played club cricket for Hampstead and made the last of his three appearances for Ireland in 1955. He played for Free Foresters with considerable success until 1962.

M	Inns	NOs	Runs	HS	Avge	Ct
18	14	6	26	16	3.25	4

Overs	Mds	Runs	Wkts	Avge	Best	5/inn
415.3	84	1212	39	31.07	5/80	1

Terence KENT

Born: Battersea, London, 21 October 1939.
A slow left-arm bowler and right-handed batsman, Terry Kent made his debut for Essex against Cambridge University in May 1960. The following season, he took 4 for 54 against Northamptonshire at Wellingborough, but he could never command a regular place in the side and left the staff after the 1962 season.

He played club cricket for Walthamstow and Addiscombe.

A professional footballer, Kent played one match for Southend United as a half-back in 1958 before being transferred to Millwall where he played reserve team soccer.

M	Inns	NOs	Runs	HS	Avge	Ct
10	10	4	74	23*	12.33	5

Overs	Mds	Runs	Wkts	Avge	Best
211	64	561	15	37.40	4/54

Ian Metcalfe KING

Born: Leeds, Yorkshire, 10 November 1931.

A slow left-arm bowler and left-handed batsman, Ian King joined the Warwickshire staff in 1949 and made 53 appearances for that county between 1952 and 1955. He had been educated in Worcester and had played for Kidderminster before playing for Warwickshire, and in 1956, he went into the Birmingham League with Aston Unity.

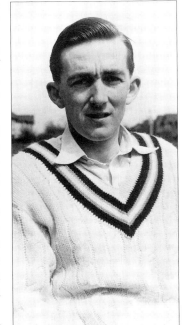

King joined Essex on special registration in 1957. He proved to be economic and fielded admirably, but his bowling lacked penetration, and he decided to take over his family business in Birmingham, and returned to league cricket.

M	Inns	NOs	Runs	HS	Avge	Ct
28	36	21	131	33	8.73	29

Overs	Mds	Runs	Wkts	Avge	Best
525.5	197	1146	34	33.70	4/25

Robert Jasper Stuart KING

Born: Leigh-on-Sea, 10 May 1909.
Died: Westcliff-on-Sea, 11 May 1992.
A leg-break bowler and right-handed batsman from Felsted School, Stuart-King, as he was also known, played for Essex against Nottinghamshire at Trent Bridge in 1928, a few weeks after leaving school.

He had captained Felsted and had enjoyed a highly successful season, topping both the batting and the bowling averages.

M	Inns	NOs	Runs	HS	Avge	Ct
1	1	-	3	3	3.00	-

Overs	Mds	Runs	Wkts	Avge
7	-	20	-	-

Barry Rolfe KNIGHT

Born: Chesterfield, Derbyshire, 18 February 1938.
Barry Knight was one of Essex's great all-round cricketers. He reached the 'double' in four consecutive seasons, 1962-65, and in the second and the last of those seasons, he accomplished the feat in Essex matches alone. Educated at East Ham Grammar School, he made his debut for Essex against Worcestershire in May 1955. He batted number nine, scored 22 and did not bowl.

A bowler of above medium pace and a hard-hitting batsman, he could not play a full season until 1959 when his national service was completed. He took 100 wickets for Essex, topped the bowling averages and was only five runs short of the 'double' in all matches. He made his maiden century against Worcestershire at Leyton.

The following season he appeared for the Players against the Gentlemen, and it was no surprise when he was selected for the tour of Pakistan and India, 1961-62. His Test debut came against India in December 1961, and in the next eight years, he was to play another 28 Tests for England, established as the country's leading all-rounder. In February 1963, he and Peter Parfitt added 240 for England's sixth wicket against New Zealand, and this remains

a record for England's sixth wicket against any country.

Barry Knight had enjoyed his best season in English cricket in the summer immediately before that tour. Against Middlesex at Brentwood, he hit the highest score of his career, 165, and he and Roger Luckin added 206 for the sixth wicket which equalled the county record and has not been bettered since. Late that summer, he played an astonishing innings of 88 against Warwickshire at Edgbaston. His innings included 21 fours.

In 1963, he took 8 for 69 against Nottinghamshire at Trent Bridge, his best bowling performance, but three years later, he left the county. There was dissension as to who should succeed Trevor Bailey as captain, and Knight, one of the contenders, resigned and later joined Leicestershire although Essex opposed the move. He had first played for Wanstead 1st XI at the age of 16, and it was hard to see him as anything but an Essex man. He was only 28 when he left the county. Arguably, he was never quite the same player after his

move to Leicestershire for whom he played until 1969.

In September 1969, he joined Adidas as their promotions manager in Australia, and in 1971, he opened a coaching centre in Sydney. He is now the owner of three indoor cricket schools, and he is permanently resident in Australia.

M	Inns	NOs	Runs	HS	Avge	100s	Ct
239	399	42	8798	165	24.64	8	171

Overs	Mds	Runs	Wkts	Avge	Best	10/m	5/inn
6287.5	1213	17162	761	22.55	8/69	8	39

Gillette Cup

M	Inns	NOs	Runs	HS	Avge	Ct
6	6	-	129	52	21.50	2

Overs	Mds	Runs	Wkts	Avge	Best	5/inn
76.3	13	206	15	13.73	5/41	1

Nicholas Verity KNIGHT

Born: Watford, Hertfordshire, 28 November 1969.

Nick Night is one of the long line of distinguished Felsted cricketers to have played for Essex. A left-handed batsman and excellent fielder, he

went to Loughborough University and played for the Combined Universities in the Benson and Hedges Cup in 1990 and 1991, captaining the side in his last year. It was in this season that he first played for the county, scoring 388 runs in eight completed innings and hitting a match-winning 101 not out against Lancashire at Old Trafford.

Tall and elegant, he gave early indication of a sound temperament. An all-round sportsman, he has played for Essex and Young England at hockey.

M	Inns	NOs	Runs	HS	Avge	100s	Ct
46	74	8	2454	157	37.18	7	59

Overs	Mds	Runs	Wkts	Avge	Best
16.4	0	93	1	93.00	1/61

Sunday League

M	Inns	NOs	Runs	HS	Avge	Ct
45	39	7	746	61*	23.31	19

Overs	Mds	Runs	Wkts	Avge	Best
14	-	85	2	42.50	1/14

Benson and Hedges Cup

M	Inns	NOs	Runs	HS	Avge	Ct
6	5	2	56	26*	18.66	2

NatWest Trophy

M	Inns	NOs	Runs	HS	Avge
4	4	1	113	81*	37.66

Charles Jesse KORTRIGHT

Born: Furze Hall, Fryerning, Ingatestone, 9 January , 1871.
Died: Brookstreet, South Weald, 12 December 1952.

Regarded as the fastest bowler of his day and by many as the fastest bowler of all time, Charles Kortright was a six-footer of splendid physique and abundant stamina. He scorned the idea of swing and spin and insisted that a fast bowler should concentrate on length, direction and speed, and that he should make good use of the yorker. Concerning his pace, he would relate a tale that, in a club match at Wallingford, he bowled a ball which rose almost vertically and went out of the ground without a second bounce, so that he was the first man to bowl *six* byes.

Born into a wealthy family, Kortright was to boast later that he did not have to earn a living, for he and his sisters were well provided for. He was educated at Brentwood School and had one year in the XI, when he was 13, before moving to the larger Tonbridge School where the standard was far higher and where he had to wait another three years before winning a place in the school side.

On leaving Tonbridge, Kortright joined Brentwood CC and came to the notice of Essex for whom he first played in 1889. Although the county had not attained first-class status at that time, Kortright's performances attracted attention of good judges, and, in June 1893, he was asked to play for MCC against the Australian touring side. He was most impressive. He took 3 for 57 in the first innings, and then he 'hit so freely that MCC were in the end able to head their opponents by five runs'. Batting again, the Australians reached 104 for three. At this point, Kortright was put on to bowl and 'worked a wonderful change'. According to *Cricket: A Weekly Record of the Game,* 'No one, indeed, but Mr Bruce, who carried out his bat for 46 could do anything with him. He finished up the innings, as he had the first, by bowling Messrs Trumble and Jarvis with consecutive balls. He

took 5 wickets for 72 runs, and considering that it was his first trial in a big match, it was a fine performance.'

In spite of this glowing start and the fact that he was chosen for the Gentlemen against the Players at Lord's a month later and took 7 for 73 and 2 for 67, Kortright was never to play for England nor, it seems, was he asked to tour although he was not constrained by thoughts of work.

When Essex entered first-class cricket the following season he was in the side for the opening match against Leicestershire and became the first bowler to take a first-class wicket for the county when he bowled Holland – Warren had been run out earlier. In Essex's debut in the County Championship in 1895, he took 8 for 94 in the first match, against Warwickshire, at Edgbaston. He maintained excellent form for the next three seasons, and 70 per cent of wickets he obtained for Essex were captured without the help of any other member of the side.

A back injury kept Kortright out of the side for the whole of the 1899 season. He had been at his very best the previous year, and it is likely that he would have won selection for England in 1899 as Richardson was past his best, and Lockwood injured. In 1898, Kortright had also scored the first of his two centuries.

It was apparent when he returned to cricket in 1900 that he was not the force he had been, and by the time of his retirement at the end of the 1907 season, he had almost ceased to bowl. In 1900, at Leyton, he hit 131 in under two hours against Middlesex, and he captained Essex in 1903. His last match for the county was at Leyton, in June 1907, against Middlesex, when he scored 4 and, bowling two overs in the second innings, took the wicket of 'Plum' Warner.

In retirement, he dabbled on the stock exchange, but mostly enjoyed his hobbies of bird-watching and golf. He was a passionate golfer and played first at Chelmsford and Romford before beginning his long association with his beloved Thorndon Park club. He was essentially a country gentlemen with all the sporting pursuits that description suggests.

He has been the subject of two interesting books, *Korty* by Charles Sale, and *The Demon and The Lobster* by Anthony Meredith.

M	Inns	NOs	Runs	HS	Avge	100s	Ct
160	255	18	4182	131	17.64	2	167

Overs	Mds	Runs	Wkts	Avge	Best	10/m	5/inn
886	625	9036	440	20.53	8/57	8	35

2145.3 (five-ball)

James Charles LAKER

Born: Frizinghall, Bradford, Yorkshire, 9 February 1922.
Died: Putney, London, 23 April 1986.

Jim Laker was, in the opinion of many, the greatest off-break bowler to have represented England. His match figures of 19 for 90 and 46 wickets in the series against Australia in 1956 give ample support for this view.

He played for Surrey from 1946 to 1959, and he parted with some ill-feeling after the publication of his book *Over To Me*. Happily, his rift with the county with which he is most closely associated was later healed.

Laker played league cricket and had business interests, but Trevor Bailey persuaded him to play for Essex as an amateur in 1962. He assisted the county for three seasons although he was not able to play regularly. He gave a much needed boost to the spin department and was the perfect model for some aspiring young bowlers.

He became a well-known commentator and was also a journalist. He was the author of *Cricket Contrasts* and the subject of a biography by Don Mosey.

M	Inns	NOs	Runs	HS	Avge	Ct
30	29	8	248	28	11.80	11

Overs	Mds	Runs	Wkts	Avge	Best	10/m	5/inn
979.5	279	2367	111	21.32	7/73	2	7

Arthur William Edwards LAPHAM

Born: 1879.
Died: Portsmouth, Hampshire, 9 February 1964.
A useful all-round cricketer, Arthur Lapham played for Wiltshire from 1906 until 1913. In 1921, he appeared in three Championship matches for Essex and finished second in the bowling averages.

M	Inns	NOs	Runs	HS	Avge
3	5	-	31	16	6.20

Overs	Mds	Runs	Wkts	Avge	Best
29.2	-	90	5	18.00	2/25

Albert Edward LASHBROOKE

Born: West Ham, 30 November 1883.
Died: West Hulme, Oldham, Lancashire, 2 October 1963.
A professional opening bowler, Lashbrooke played against Lancashire at Old Trafford in 1908. He scored 0 and 9, and he took the wicket of Whitehead in the second innings. He did not appear in first-class cricket again.

M	Inns	NOs	Runs	HS	Avge
1	2	-	9	9	4.50

Overs	Mds	Runs	Wkts	Avge	Best
17	-	61	1	61.00	1/26

Alan Braden LAVERS

Born: Melbourne, Victoria, Australia, 6 September 1912.
A very useful all-round cricketer who captained Buckhurst Hill for many years, Alan Lavers' career with Essex stretched from  1937 to 1953 although he was never able to play regularly. He was one of several fine club cricketers who played for Essex in the years either side of World War Two who had learned their cricket at Chigwell School. Making his debut against Kent at Gravesend in 1937, Lavers was used initially as a batsman, and in the five matches he played that season he bowled only four overs. The following season, at Sheffield, he claimed Hutton, Smailes and Wood as his first victims in first-class cricket, and one feels that, had he been able to play more, he would have posed problems for the best batsmen with his off-breaks which were generally bowled round the wicket at a pace quicker than was usual.

He was commissioned in the Army during World War Two, and he ran a family business which was concerned with the making of brushes. His last match for Essex was against Leicestershire at Colchester in July 1953, when he scored 40 and 42 not out.

M	Inns	NOs	Runs	HS	Avge	Ct
25	44	2	695	42*	16.54	6

Overs	Mds	Runs	Wkts	Avge	Best
156	29	483	13	37.15	4/68

3 (eight-ball)

Terence Patrick LAWRENCE

Born: Waltham Abbey, 26 April 1910.
Educated at Uppingham, Lawrence went up to Cambridge and appeared in the Freshman's

Match in 1930, and in the Senior's Match the following season, but he played no first-class cricket while at university.

He assisted Hertfordshire between 1929 and 1931, and, as a right-handed middle-order batsman, he played a few games for Essex between 1933 and 1935. He reappeared in major cricket when he played for Berkshire in 1947.

His father was Sir Walter Lawrence who had his own cricket ground at Hyde Hall, Sawbridgeworth, and who donated the Lawrence Trophy for the fastest century of the season.

M	Inns	NOs	Runs	HS	Avge	Ct
7	14	-	133	39	9.50	3

John Morton LEIPER

Born: Woodford Green, 17 February 1921.

In 1937 and 1938, Jack Leiper dominated cricket at Chigwell School. In 1938, when he was captain, he hit 911 runs and took 77 wickets in school matches alone, and he also assisted Woodford Wells and Sir Julien Cahn's XI. Here was an outstanding schoolboy cricketer with a glittering future in the game, but then came World War Two.

He was in every sense of the word, an all-round cricketer, an attacking left-handed batsman, a right-arm fast medium pace bowler, and a wicket-keeper who kept for Essex 2nd XI on several occasions. War service allowed him only occasional matches for the British Empire XI, and his first-class career was to be restricted to two matches for Essex in 1950 in which he took the wicket of Martin Young of Gloucestershire and hit 44 against Somerset, sharing a ninth wicket stand of 79 with Trevor Bailey.

His son Robert also played for Essex. Jack Leiper ran his own credit trade business.

M	Inns	NOs	Runs	HS	Avge	Ct
2	4	-	50	44	25.00	1

Overs	Mds	Runs	Wkts	Avge	Best
32	5	79	1	79.00	1/38

Robert James LEIPER

Born: Woodford Green, 30 August 1961.

Son of Jack Leiper, Robert Leiper is a left-

handed batsman who was educated at Chigwell School and enjoyed considerable success for Essex Schools and for England Young Cricketers. Like his father, he assisted Woodford Wells and since leaving Essex has flourished in club cricket and for the Essex League side.

He joined the county staff in 1980, but he was given few opportunities although he played until 1984. In 1981, he hit 49 against the Australians and won the individual award for the match, but, although he prospered in the 2nd XI, he appeared in only one Championship match the following season.

Bob Leiper is now running his own company which is active in the computer industry.

M	Inns	NOs	Runs	H.S	Avge	Ct
2	4	-	53	49	13.25	2

Benson and Hedges Cup

M	Inns	NOs	Runs	HS	Avge
1	1	-	7	7	7.00

John Kenneth LEVER

Born: Stepney, East London, 24 February 1949.

It was hard to accept at the end of the 1989 season that J.K. would never again slide in from one end to open the Essex bowling. He had been with the county for 22 years and during that time he had taken more first-class wickets for the county than any bowler save Morris Nichols, Peter Smith and Trevor Bailey. At the end of his career, too, he stood supreme as the leading wicket-keeper in both the Sunday League and the Benson and Hedges Cup.

In first-class cricket, he took 100 wickets in a season four times, which, since the shortened programme after 1969, has been bettered only by Derek Underwood. He had also become a useful batsman, and he would move easily across the outfield, pick up and throw in one movement. He had one of the smoothest run-ups to the wicket that the game has known, and there was a beauty in his left-arm fast medium-pace delivery. He batted right-handed, and perhaps the greatest glory of his game was that he did not seem to be trying. It was all so effortless. He moved as if silk.

From the start, he placed great emphasis on physical fitness, and he had a commitment to the game, an attitude, that was an example to all. He was yet another product of Essex Schools' cricket and of the Ilford Indoor School where he was nurtured by Bill Morris. Morris always believed that if J.K. had applied himself more to his batting when he was younger, he could have become an all-rounder in the Bailey mould.

Lever played 2nd XI cricket at the age of 16, and he was only 18 when, on the occasion of his first-class debut, he bowled Roger Knight, now secretary of MCC. In his first County Championship match, on his own club ground at Valentine's Park a month later, he captured the wickets of Ron Headley (twice), Ormrod, Kenyon and Graveney as Essex drew with Worcestershire. One of the great careers of modern times had begun.

Within a year, Essex had entered their austerity period, operating with a limited staff under the captaincy of Brian Taylor. They were brave, fit and determined young men who worked very hard, and towards the end of his career, Lever maintained that he owed much to those years. He learned to bowl because he had to bowl. There was no one else.

He suffered the trials and disappointments of the early 1970s, but gradually the nucleus of one of the greatest of Essex sides developed, and in 1976, 'Jake' won the first of his 21 Test caps. He was bowling at a time when there were several good new-ball bowlers in England, and he always had to struggle for his Test place. Fifteen years later and the selectors only problem would have been who to choose to share the new ball with J.K.

In his first Test, he scored 53 and took ten wickets to bowl England to an innings victory over India, and he enjoyed a splendid series. Two years later, wrongfully omitted from England's World Cup squad, he was the spearhead of an Essex attack that won the Benson and Hedges Cup and the County Championship. After the disappointments, he was to play a major part in all the triumphs.

It was in 1984, another Championship year, that he took 116 wickets in the season and returned his best figures, 8 for 37 in a massive victory over Gloucestershire at Bristol. He was relentlessly accurate, varied his pace and moved the ball late as only the very best can do.

His best batting performance had come 14 years earlier at Cardiff when, going in as night-watchman, he had hit 91 in five hours 35 minutes. His later batting became quicker than that.

Although he played less in his last year, 1989, he remained in peak condition to the end, and, in his last match, he took seven Surrey wickets for 48 runs at Chelmsford.

J.K.'s greatest asset and that which he conveyed to others was that he loved what he was doing. He worked hard, helped others, put everything into every game and enjoyed every minute of it. He was a model of all that can be good in a professional cricketer.

On his retirement, he took up a post at Bancroft's School. He was awarded the MBE .

M	Inns	NOs	Runs	HS	Avge	Ct
443	446	168	2830	91	10.18	160

Overs	Mds	Runs	Wkts	Avge	Best	10/m	5/inn
12531.4	2786	34699	1473	23.54	8/37	11	77

Sunday League

M	Inns	NOs	Runs	HS	Avge	Ct
291	116	70	409	23	8.89	72

Overs	Mds	Runs	Wkts	Avge	Best	5/inn
2044.1	232	7619	386	19.74	5/13	4

Benson and Hedges Cup

M	Inns	NOs	Runs	HS	Avge	Ct
90	26	18	104	13	13.00	21

Overs	Mds	Runs	Wkts	Avge	Best	5/inn
904.1	175	2789	149	18.72	5/13	2

Gillette Cup/NatWest Trophy

M	Inns	NOs	Runs	HS	Avge	Ct
44	27	19	97	15*	12.13	3

Overs	Mds	Runs	Wkts	Avge	Best	5/inn
450	105	1219	70	17.41	5/8	1

Derek Cyril LEVICK

Born: Ealing, Middlesex, 27 May 1929.
A right-handed batsman who was educated at Acton County High School, Levick showed promise in the Essex 2nd XI and played against Leicestershire at Westcliff in 1950. An amateur, he appeared in two more Championship games the following season without making his mark. He had the reputation for being an aggressive batsman and a good fielder.

M	Inns	NOs	Runs	HS	Avge	Ct
3	6	-	14	6	2.33	1

Jonathan James Benjamin LEWIS

Born: Isleworth, Middlesex, 21 May 1970.
Although born in Middlesex, Jonathan Lewis, was moved to Chelmsford at the age of three and was educated at King Edward VI Grammar School. He took a degree in Sports Studies at

Roehampton Institute of Higher Education. A man with an interest in several sports, he excelled at cricket, played for the Chelmsford club and joined the Essex staff in 1990, having already played for the 2nd XI.

With Gooch, Waugh and Pringle unavailable, Lewis was given his first-class debut against Surrey at The Oval in September 1990. He hit 166 not out off 200 balls with 15 fours and so became the first Essex batsman to score a century in his first first-class innings.

He played in only two matches the following season, but, in 1992, he appeared in 13 matches and hit a vital 133 against Sussex at Hove. Correct in method, sound in temperament, Jon Lewis would seem to have a most important part to play in the future of Essex cricket.

Lewis has played club cricket in Zimbabwe during the winter months.

M	Inns	NOs	Runs	HS	Avge	100s	Ct
45	76	12	2422	136*	37.84	4	29

Overs	Mds	Runs	Wkts
8	1	32	-

Sunday League

M	Inns	NOs	Runs	HS	Avge	Ct
19	14	3	149	23	13.54	5

NatWest Trophy

M	Inns	NOs	Runs	HS	Avge	Ct
2	2	1	25	24*	25.00	1

Alan William LILLEY

Born: Ilford, 8 May 1959.

A product of Essex Schools' cricket and the Lord's groundstaff, Alan Lilley had a wonderful entry to first-class cricket. Chosen for the last game of the 1978 season, against Nottinghamshire at Trent Bridge, he scored 22 and 100 not out. Essex were set to score 222 in two and a half hours, and Lilley and Gooch began with a partnership of 159, and Alan Lilley then scored 43 of the last 63 runs wanted as Essex won with 5.1 overs to spare. He hit four sixes and nine fours.

It was planned that he would open in all the one-day matches in 1979, but he was caught nibbling outside the off stump for 0 in both the quarter and semi-final of the Benson and Hedges Cup, and Mike Denness played in the final. This was unlucky for Lilley who, in the first match of the campaign, had shared a sensational record opening stand with Gooch of 223 in 36 overs against the Combined Universities of Oxford and Cambridge.

A strong, powerful man who could bowl medium pace and keep wicket if required, Alan Lilley was a magnificent fielder. His catching of Mike Gatting in the semi-final of the Benson and Hedges Cup at Chelmsford in 1985 will never be forgotten by those who saw it. Gatting aimed a vicious square cut at Turner only to be brilliantly picked up low at cover by Lilley. Essex were beaten in the final that year as they were in 1989 when Alan Lilley scored 95 not out against Nottinghamshire.

Not capped until 1986, Lilley never commanded a regular place in the Championship side, but he was always an invaluable member of the squad with a great sense of fun which included carrying his skipper across the dressing-room. He played grade cricket in Australia, coached for many years at the Ilford Cricket School and at Chelmsford, and was offered a post at Chigwell School. He chose instead to remain with Essex as Youth Development Officer and has enjoyed great success in the position.

Alan Lilley played his club cricket for Ilford and Wanstead.

M	Inns	NOs	Runs	HS	Avge	100s	Ct
120	190	15	4495	113*	25.69	3	67

Overs	Mds	Runs	Wkts	Avge	Best
86.3	4	565	8	70.62	3/116

Sunday League

M	Inns	NOs	Runs	HS	Avge	Ct
134	115	11	1657	60	15.93	20

Overs	Mds	Runs	Wkts	Avge	Best
4.3	-	23	3	7.67	2/0

Benson and Hedges Cup

M	Inns	NOs	Runs	HS	Avge	100s	Ct
45	37	4	741	119	22.45	1	11

Overs	Mds	Runs	Wkts	Avge	Best
3	-	11	1	11.00	1/4

NatWest Trophy

M	Inns	NOs	Runs	HS	Avge	100s	Ct
17	15	2	352	113	27.08	1	1

Overs	Mds	Runs	Wkts	Avge	Best
8	3	33	2	16.50	2/19

Peter John LINDSEY

Born: Matlock, Derbyshire, 29 May 1944.
An off-spin bowler who played club cricket for both Buckhurst Hill and Wanstead, Peter Lindsey was a man of great charm who was on the Essex staff in the mid-60s. He appeared in only one first-class match, against Oxford University at Oxford in May 1964.

M	Inns	NOs	Runs	HS	Avge
1	1	1	7	7*	-

Overs	Mds	Runs	Wkts	Avge	Best
18	6	50	1	50.00	1/8

Reverend Charles Gough LITTLEHALES

Born: Bulphan, 20 May 1871.
Died: Wickham Bishops, 28 August 1945.
A very good wicket-keeper at Forest School, Littlehales played no first-class cricket while at Oxford. His first appearance for Essex was against Leicestershire at Leyton in 1896. He did not keep wicket but opened in the second innings when Essex needed 82 to win. He made 21.

His duties as a clergyman restricted his playing opportunities, and he last appeared in 1904.

M	Inns	NOs	Runs	HS	Avge	Ct/st
6	10	1	109	23	12.11	4/1

Jesse LITTLEWOOD

Born: Holmfirth, Huddersfield, Yorkshire, 8 April 1878.
Died: Kidderminster, Worcestershire, 27 October 1942.
Son of a Lancashire professional, Jesse Littlewood was on the Essex staff as a bowler and played in one match in 1905. His brother also played for Lancashire during the same period.

M	Inns	NOs	Runs	HS	Avge	Ct
1	1	1	5	5*	-	1

Overs	Mds	Runs	Wkts	Avge
11	1	36	-	-

George Melbourne LOCKS

Born: Leytonstone, 24 May 1889.
Died: Redbridge, 17 September 1965.
One of the long list of amateurs who played for Essex in 1928. George Locks appeared against Lancashire and Yorkshire in the away fixtures. As these counties finished first and fourth in the Championship, Locks faced a stiff entry into first-class cricket. A fast medium pace bowler, he took the wickets of McDonald at Liverpool, and of Arthur Mitchell and Bedford at Sheffield, but he did not play again.

M	Inns	NOs	Runs	HS	Avge
2	4	2	5	3*	2.50

Overs	Mds	Runs	Wkts	Avge	Best
73	11	227	3	75.66	2/86

George Marshall LOUDEN

Born: Forest Gate, 6 September 1885.
Died: Amersham, Buckinghamshire, 28 December 1972.
George Louden was a stockbroker in the City, and, as such, his appearances in county cricket were very limited although he first played for the county in 1912 and last appeared in 1927. He came to Essex and made his rare appearances as an amateur after considerable success with the Ilford club, and it is a measure of his ability that he played eight times for the Gentlemen against the Players between 1919 and 1925, and that at Lord's in 1923, he took the wickets of Hobbs, Hearne, Hendren, H.Smith and Tate at a personal cost of 49 runs. In the opinion of Pelham Warner, the

selectors made a mistake in not picking him to play against the Australians in 1921.

A kind and gentle man, Louden was a tall, slim handsome fast-medium pace bowler with a beautiful high action. He did not have the strongest of physiques, but the economy of his style enabled him to bowl for long spells although Johnny Douglas was criticised for over-bowling him. He was able to move the ball both ways, but it was surprising pace off the wicket that was his greatest asset.

He performed the hat-trick against Somerset at Southend in 1921 and was always a force to be reckoned with when he was available for Essex. Even in his last match, against Sussex in 1927, the final game of the season at Hove, he took 4 for 32 and, with Nichols, bowled Essex to a ten-wicket victory.

M	Inns	NOs	Runs	HS	Avge	Ct
82	125	33	844	74	9.17	54

Overs	Mds	Runs	Wkts	Avge	Best	10/m	5/inn
3040.1	552	9066	415	21.84	8/36	5	33

Frank Alfred LOVEDAY

Born: Hackney, London, 14 September 1892.
Died: Bluebell Common, North Walsham, Norfolk, 18 October 1954.
'Of those new to first-class cricket, F.Loveday, of the Beckton club, showed good promise as a batsman, scoring 253 runs in eight innings. He specially distinguished himself in the Lancashire match at Leyton by twice helping Russell to score over 100 runs for the first wicket. Possessing great patience he should, with increased experience, become something more than a defensive player.' So said *Wisden* of Frank Loveday after his first season with Essex, 1921. Apart from his innings of 53 and 44 against Lancashire, the left-handed opener had scored 81 in three and a half hours against Somerset a month earlier, and there did seem reason for optimism.

Loveday had played for Cambridgeshire in 1914 and had learned his cricket at City of London School. Fourth in the Essex batting averages in 1921, he appeared in only one match in the following season, making 'a pair' against Lancashire. Four innings in 1923 failed to rekindle the form of his first season, and he was not re-engaged.

M	Inns	NOs	Runs	HS	Avge	Ct
7	14	-	321	81	22.29	2

William Guy LOVELL

Born: Whitehaven, Cumberland, 16 February 1969.
Guy Lovell's career began late, for he played little or no cricket until he joined Millom CC when he was in his teens. He was with Leicestershire for two years before joining the Lord's groundstaff. In June 1990, he joined Essex.

A slow left-arm bowler, he found his opportunities very limited, and he retired from the game in 1992, having played in one Sunday League match in 1991.

Sunday League

M	Inns	NOs	Runs	HS	Avge
1	-	-	-	-	-

Overs	Mds	Runs	Wkts	Avge
6	-	34	-	-

Alfred Perry LUCAS

Born: Westminster, London, 20 February 1857.
Died: Great Waltham, 12 October 1923.
When Essex became a first-class county in 1894 the captain of the side was A.P.Lucas. He was already 37 years old, and he had played for two other counties.

'Bunny' Lucas first played for Surrey in 1874, shortly after leaving Uppingham. He had been coached at school by H.H. Stephenson, the captain of the first England side to tour Australia, and he was recognised as a young batsman of exceptional talent. He was still 17 when he played for the Gentlemen of the South against the Players of the North, and he performed admirably against the finest bowling of the day.

He went up to Clare College, Cambridge, won his blue as a freshman and was in the XI for four years, 1875 to 1878. A few months after leaving university he was in Lord Harris' side for the tour of Australia and played in the Test match. He also played in four Tests in England, often opening the innings, and last appeared in 1884. By that time, he had joined Middlesex and he appeared for them irregularly until 1888.

Lucas was a great friend of Charles Green, and it was at the request of Green, the great benefactor of Essex cricket and the driving force behind the county attaining first-class status, that Lucas joined Essex in 1889. He was appointed captain in 1892.

He led the side in the inaugural first-class

match, against Leicestershire, but as the season progressed he dropped lower in the order and was absent on occasions. Owen deputised for him, and, at the end of the season, business pressures forced Lucas to

stand down, and Owen became captain for 1895. Lucas did lead the side on several occasions in 1901, and he played for the county until 1907 when he was 50. By the end of his life, he had lost his hearing.

Relieved of the cares of captaincy, Lucas showed glimpses of his best form with Essex in 1895. In July of that year, at Taunton, Essex scored 692, which was to remain a record for 65 years, and 'Bunny' Lucas hit an immaculate 135 at number seven. In 1902, at Leyton, he made 103 against Derbyshire, and he was then 45 years old and appearing only irregularly. He was, as *Wisden* wrote, 'one of the finest of batsmen – almost unique in his combination of perfect style and impregnable defence. It may fairly be said of him that no defensive batsman of any generation was more worth looking at. He played the ball so hard and his style was so irreproachable that one could watch him for hours without a moment of weariness.'

Lucas was also a right-hand slow round-arm bowler good enough to claim 155 wickets in his career, but by the time he joined Essex, he bowled little.

M	Inns	NOs	Runs	HS	Avge	100s	Ct
98	153	21	3554	135	26.92	2	50

Overs	Mds	Runs	Wkts	Avge	Best
15	1	90	1	90.00	1/17

5 (five-ball)

Roger Alfred Geoffrey LUCKIN

Born: High Easter, Pleshley, 25 November 1939.

Roger Luckin played for Essex in just two seasons, but he made his mark in that time. Son of a great servant of Essex, Sam Luckin, whose efforts on behalf of the club as supporter and committee member are commemorated by a plaque in the Chelmsford pavilion, Roger was educated at Felsted and coached by Ray Smith. A left-handed batsman, he played club cricket for both Brentwood and Chelmsford where he appeared alongside Geoff Hurst whose fielding he still remembers as being breath-taking.

Luckin's debut came in the opening match of the 1962 season, against Somerset at Taunton. This was the game in which Peter Spicer also made his debut, and if Luckin's innings was less spectacular than Spicer's, he still scored a creditable 30. Although batting low in the order, at number eight, he displayed great consistency in his first few matches and hit 53 against Middlesex at Lord's in his fifth game.

When Middlesex came to Brentwood a month later Luckin hit 14 fours in an innings of 82, and he and Barry Knight shared a sixth wicket stand of 206 which equalled the county record and which has yet to be bettered.

In all, Luckin played in 26 matches in 1962 and scored 651 runs, but the following season he could play in only three games and he retired from first-class cricket at the end of the year. Like many other amateurs, he had to put the needs of business first.

An accountant with Moores and Rowland in Suffolk, he restricted his cricket to the Gentlemen of Essex, the Gentlemen of Suffolk and to the Felsted Robins of which he is president. He has also appeared for MCC in many 'out' matches, and is one of the old club's most reliable match-managers.

In 1969, he agreed to play for Cambridgeshire and played for them with considerable success until 1972. He lives near Bury St Edmunds and retains his passion for the game and for the county for which he played for all too brief a time.

M	Inns	NOs	Runs	HS	Avge	Ct
29	46	3	735	82	17.09	8

Ronald Victor LYNCH

Born: Stratford, 22 May 1923.
Ron Lynch's contribution to Essex cricket, and to the game in general, cannot be measured by his three appearances for the county as an amateur in 1954.

At the end of World War Two, he joined an American firm, International Harvesters, who imported a variety of hardware components. He played his club cricket for Ilford before later moving to Chingford. A slow left-arm bowler and a useful batsman, he was highly successful in club cricket and was invited to play in three matches for the county in June 1954.

His first game was against Nottinghamshire at Brentwood, and it was ruined by rain. The second was at Rushden, against Northamptonshire, where he captured the wickets of Livingston, Barrick, Jakeman and Starkie in a 29-over spell, but again the match was ruined by rain. The same fate awaited him at Liverpool where Trevor Bailey and Doug Insole approached him and said that they felt that he had had a poor deal and that they would like him to play in the remaining eight games of the season.

Delighted, Lynch asked his employers for unpaid leave, but they told him that his services were too valuable and he could not be spared.

He recalls with amused regret that a fortnight later he played truant to appear for Essex 2nd XI, and nobody seemed to notice that he was absent. He later moved to work at a staff bureau in Chadwell Heath, and he finished his working days with Associated Newspapers concerned with computer projects.

His involvement with cricket has never slackened. He was the founder chairman of the Essex League, and he has twice been chairman of the Club Cricket Conference. Few men have done so much for the game in Essex and elsewhere.

M	Inns	NOs	Runs	HS	Avge	Ct
3	3	2	7	6*	7.00	2

Overs	Mds	Runs	Wkts	Avge	Best
43	15	107	4	26.75	4/64

Lewis William LYWOOD

Born: Walthamstow, 23 December 1906.
Died: Caterham, Surrey, 31 October 1971.
Resident and working in Surrey, Lewis Lywood played for that county as a fast bowler in 1927 and 1928, but he was so severely savaged by Hammond and B.H.Lyon of Gloucestershire in his second match that he was not engaged. Born in Essex, he was able to assist his native county in 1930. He played against Worcestershire and Northamptonshire, capturing the wickets of Cox and Jupp in his second match, but he was not retained on the staff.

He returned to work in the Croydon Town Hall and was a much feared fast bowler with outstanding performances for Croydon

Municipal Officers in South London club cricket.

M	Inns	NOs	Runs	HS	Avge
2	3	-	12	7	4.00

Overs	Mds	Runs	Wkts	Avge	Best
26	3	83	2	41.50	1/7

Michael Stephen Anthony McEVOY

Born: Jorhat, Assam, India, 25 January 1956.
Educated at Colchester Royal Grammar School, Michael McEvoy trained as a teacher at Borough Road College. He played for British Colleges and for England Young Cricketers and scored consistently for the Colchester and East Essex club. A fine all-round sportsman, he assisted Colchester RFC and joined the Essex staff in 1976.

As an opening right-handed batsman and medium pace bowler, he had several opportunities in the county side when Gooch was on international duty. In 1980, he appeared in 16 Championship matches and scored 600 runs. He played in ten the following season and took three wickets against Middlesex at Lord's, but that was his last season for Essex. He played for Cambridgeshire in 1982 and toured East Africa with the Minor Counties the following winter.

He joined Worcestershire in 1983 and played for them for two seasons, hitting a century against Warwickshire at Edgbaston in his first year. Since 1985 he has played for Suffolk and has appeared for the Minor Counties. He is with the Sudbury club.

M	Inns	NOs	Runs	HS	Avge	Ct
43	74	1	1371	67*	18.78	42

Overs	Mds	Runs	Wkts	Avge	Best
30	8	103	3	34.33	3/20

Sunday League

M	Inns	NOs	Runs	HS	Avge	Ct
12	8	2	64	15	10.66	4

Benson and Hedges Cup

M	Inns	NOs	Runs	HS	Avge
1	1	-	13	13	13.00

Kenneth Scott McEWAN

Born: Bedford, Cape Province, South Africa, 16 July 1952.
Once, while making a century against Kent at Tunbridge Wells, Ken McEwan straight drove, square cut and pulled Derek Underwood to the boundary in the space of one over. Each shot was executed with regal charm, and never a hint of arrogance. He batted, as did the ancients, upright, correct and magisterial. He was incapable of profaning the art of batting, incapable of an ineloquent gesture.

Ken McEwan's ancestors were inn-keepers in Scotland in the 19th century, and they were later to become connected to the great breweries of Edinburgh. McEwan's great-great grandfather died and left a widow and seven children. The widow surveyed the economic situation in Scotland and decided to emigrate to Australia in 1846. An outbreak of disease on the boat meant that the passengers were set ashore at what is now Port Elizabeth in Eastern Province. The McEwans moved inland and, eventually, Ken's branch of the family became farmers at Glen Lex. His mother, Molly Scott from whom he takes his middle name, was also of Scottish descent.

Brought up in a sporting atmosphere, Ken McEwan was educated at Queen's College, Queenstown, which was run on a rigid English Public School system and which employed cricket coaches from England, usually Sussex county cricketers. The school's most famous sportsman was Tony Greig, one of Ken McEwan's early heroes and influences, and the standards were high. McEwan excelled as a tennis player, surprisingly left-handed, as a rugby player and as a cricketer who captained the school and won his cap for the South African Schools' side. Ian Greig had become his 'fag' at school.

Ken McEwan did his National Service in the Navy and, at the instigation of Tony Greig, came to England to play 2nd XI cricket for

Sussex. He made his first-class debut for Eastern Province, played for Northamptonshire 2nd XI and had another season with Sussex. That the southern county did not engage McEwan will remain one of the mysteries of cricket forever, but they chose instead to sign the Indian spinner Joshi, and with the West Indian Geoffrey Greenidge on the staff, they could find no room for another overseas player.

To his surprise, McEwan was invited to play

for Essex in a friendly match in Scotland. Some weeks later, he was signed as the replacement for Bruce Francis, and he played his first first-class match in England, for T.N.Pearce's XI against the West Indies in the Scarborough Festival, September 1973.

The following season, 1974, he scored 1056 runs, and this was to prove to be his lowest aggregate in an English season. He scored more than 1000 runs in each of his 12 seasons

with Essex and passed 2000 in 1983.

Nervous, unassuming, even shy, ever laughing at the antics and jokes of his colleagues for whom he was a wonderful audience, Ken McEwan scored his first century for Essex in his sixth match, against Middlesex at Ilford. There were to be 51 more in the next 11 seasons. He was still short of his 22nd birthday when he first played for Essex, and as he matured and gained more experience of English wickets over the next few years the runs began to flow. He hit six centuries in 1976 and eight in 1978. He was a jewel in county cricket.

He made his highest score, 218, against Sussex at Chelmsford in 1977, and in 1979, he hit 208 not out against Warwickshire at Edgbaston. This innings was played in early season when, with 836 in 13 innings, McEwan helped to send Essex soaring to the top of the County Championship, a position they were never to relinquish. Invariably batting at number three, he was also a hero in the Benson and Hedges Cup, and his innings of 72 and his 124-run, 95-minute partnership with Gooch in the final will live long in the memory.

McEwan was part of Essex's success in all four competitions, and he ended on the highest of notes. He scored 46 not out as Essex won the NatWest Trophy, and, eight days later, he hit 62 against Yorkshire as Essex clinched the Sunday League title. He was named Man of the Match. It was 15 September 1985, and it was his last match for Essex.

McEwan also played in Sheffield Shield winning sides with Western Australia and Currie Cup winning sides with Western Province whom he assisted on his return to South Africa. He came out of retirement to play for Border when they were promoted to the Currie Cup, 1991-92.

He left county cricket to return to farm in South Africa. Why did he leave when there were so many runs still left him and Jack O'Connor's record number of centuries was in touching distance? The answer is that he was of that generation of South African cricketers who had been deprived of international cricket through politics. In his own words, 'I am tired of travelling up and down the motorways of England with no prospect of Test cricket at the end of it.' In fact, he did play in unofficial 'Tests' against the West Indians, but de Klerk and Mandella were too late for Ken McEwan.

One will remain ever grateful to Essex for making it possible for Ken McEwan to be seen in action for 12 English summers. His presence graced and illuminated the game. Ken McEwan was one of the great glories of cricket and we shall cherish what he gave us.

M	Inns	NOs	Runs	HS	Avge	100s	Ct
282	458	41	18088	218	43.37	52	197

Overs	Mds	Runs	Wkts	Avge	Best
46.1	3	301	4	75.25	1/0

Sunday League

M	Inns	NOs	Runs	HS	Avge	100s	Ct
180	178	19	5531	162*	34.78	9	52

Overs	Mds	Runs	Wkts	Avge
2	-	7	-	-

Benson and Hedges Cup

M	Inns	NOs	Runs	HS	Avge	100s	Ct
63	60	6	1925	133	35.64	3	21

Gillette Cup / NatWest Trophy

M	Inns	NOs	Runs	HS	Avge	100s	Ct
27	27	3	842	119	35.08	1	11

Overs	Mds	Runs	Wkts	Avge
1	-	5	-	-

Charles Percy McGAHEY

Born: Hackney, London, 12 February 1871.
Died: Whipps Cross, Leytonstone, 10 January 1935.
In a county that has been rich in characters for over a century, there has never been a more loved nor more fascinating character than Charles McGahey. He and Perrin played together for more than 20 years, and, in the minds of the public, they were inseparable, 'The Essex Twins'.

It is easy to see why they were so linked. They played many big stands together. They were both very big men. They were both magnificent players of fast bowling. They were

both amateurs, and, in their years with the county, they were practically inseparable, yet they were very different men.

Perrin was the more stylish, the better batsman; McGahey was a fine batsman, a very useful leg-break bowler, and a far better fielder than Perrin. Perrin was thoughtful, somewhat dour, a wealthy man who came to have a strong influence in cricket's corridors of power in his later years. McGahey died in poverty, earning a modest wage as the Essex scorer. He was, wrote Charles Bray, 'Gay and witty, constantly getting into scrapes in his younger days and having little appreciation of the value of money. A happy-go-lucky character, an optimist who always believed that something would turn up to enable him to earn enough money to live on.'

For Charlie McGahey, the patron saint was Mr Micawber.

The son of a railway clerk, a member of a rising middle-class, McGahey was an all-round sportsman. He was a capable cyclist and a soccer full-back of considerable ability. He could well have played as a professional, but that was not the way of his world, and he graduated from Forest Gate Alliance and Ilford Park to Ilford and Clapton. In 1892, he played for Millwall in the London Charity Cup Final. Later he was to play for City Ramblers, London and Middlesex. He also assisted Clapton Orient and crossed the great divide between Tottenham Hotspur and Arsenal.

He was really a self-taught cricketer, playing initially on Wanstead Flats, and then moving to Romford and on to Leyton. In 1893, at a time when Essex was still a second-class county, he was invited to play against Derbyshire at Leyton. He scored 37, but against Yorkshire and Leicestershire he failed to make an impact.

McGahey was a natural hitter, and it was necessary for him to find discretion and to establish a sound defence if he were to succeed at county level. It took him time, but he achieved it. He was, by nature, a driver, and he defended by 'playing forward half-cock', according to C.B.Fry.

He was in the Essex side for the inaugural first-class match, against Leicestershire in 1894, and the following season, when the county entered the Championship for the first time, he hit 147 against Somerset at Taunton when Essex reached 692.

From this point on, McGahey began to prosper, but his health was suspect. He ended the season exhausted, and it was feared in 1897 that he was suffering from a lung complaint. That winter, he went to Australia at the expense of C.E.Green, and his health improved dramatically. A second trip in 1901-02 with MacLaren's side gave him greater strength, and it also provided him with his two opportunities of playing Test cricket.

The McGahey/Perrin partnership began to take shape towards the end of the 19th century, and the legends grew quickly. None of their stands remain in the record book, but Perrin's 343 not out against Derbyshire in 1904 remains the highest score made for the county, and McGahey's 277 against the same opposition, at Leyton, a year later, has since been bettered only by J.R.Freeman.

The feat by the 'Twins' which really captured the public imagination was their

part in the victory over Lancashire at Old Trafford in 1898. Essex needed 336 in the fourth innings to win a match in which the previous highest total had been 254 in Lancashire's first innings. Essex were 34 for 0 at the end of the second day, but Owen and Carpenter were both out next morning with the score on 88. Perrin and McGahey then added 191. Perrin and Turner were out at the same total, but McGahey hit 145 and took Essex to an historic victory.

Fry considered that McGahey's 145 'would have been a splendid achievement under the most favourable circumstances; against the bowling of Briggs, Mold and Cuttell, in the fourth innings of a match, it must be considered one of the great performances of cricket.'

McGahey reached 1000 runs in a season on ten occasions, and in 1901, he made 1838 runs in all matches. He hit two other double centuries as well as the 277 against Derbyshire. He was a very fine batsman, and, in 1898, he and Perrin became the first Essex batsmen to score 1000 runs in county matches alone.

McGahey succeeded Fane as captain in 1907 and held the position until the end of the 1910 season. His form was never affected, but the job was never really one for Charlie.

For several years, he was assistant secretary at Essex, and he last played for the county in 1921 when he was 50. The one match he appeared in was at Colchester, against Hampshire, and he made 6 and 0.

He was a wonderful character, an integral part of cricket folk-lore. It was he who gave Robertson-Glasgow the nickname of 'Crusoe'. Falling to the Somerset bowler one day, he was asked by a colleague what had happened. 'Bowled by a bugger I thought died 300 years ago,' he said, 'Robinson Crusoe.'

Perrin told how once when on 99, McGahey shouted 'Come One'! but missed the ball and was bowled. As he passed the bowler he said, 'Lucky for you I wanted a drink.' Cricket was a game to be enjoyed for Charlie McGahey.

And he liked his drink. He lived for many years at The Three Blackbirds, a public house in Leyton owned by Bill Golding, chairman of Leyton FC and an Essex committee member, and he ever had a reputation for generosity and good humour.

He was a fool only unto himself. 'He knew what it was to be poor in the autumn of his life,' wrote Charles Bray. 'It may have been his own fault but never did I know him to be bitter or complaining. He was a most lovable person.'

In that autumn of his life, he became the Essex scorer, from 1930, and in the winter he was on the turnstiles at Leyton FC. Tom Pearce recalled the perpetual cry, 'Could I have a sub from next week's wages, skipper, I'm hearts of oak.'

He loved his pint of Bass, and Home Gordon told how he once took over the scoring at Horsham while Charlie went for a drink, only to find that he was on the book for an hour. There is also the suspicion that the famous 'missing run' in the Holmes/Sutcliffe 555 stand against Essex came about because Charlie was either downing a pint or getting rid of one.

To the end he was the friend to and philosopher of the Essex team. No man went to him for counsel or encouragement without coming away a better and happier man.

On Christmas Day, 1934, he slipped on a greasy pavement and damaged a finger. Septic poisoning set in, and he died in Whipps Cross Hospital a fortnight later. He was, indeed, a most lovable man and a very fine cricketer.

M	Inns	NOs	Runs	HS	Avge	100s	Ct
400	685	61	19079	277	30.57	29	140

Overs	Mds	Runs	Wkts	Avge	Best	10/m	5/inn
2855.1	547	9481	306	30.98	7/27	3	12
148 (five-ball)							

Colin Donald McIVER

Born: Hong Kong, 23 January 1881.
Died: Worcester College, Oxford, 13 May 1954.
Colin McIver was a most capable batsman/wicket-keeper who played for Essex from 1902 until 1922, but business limited his appearances. As a schoolboy at Forest School, he was outstanding, being in the XI for five seasons and captain in his last, 1901. It was in that season that he drew particular attention, scoring 1003 runs in ten completed innings.

He made his first appearance for Essex in 1902 when a freshman at Oxford, and he won his blue in the two following years. He also won his blue for soccer, playing centre-forward in the Oxford side in 1904. Two years later, when he was with Old Foresters, he played wing-half for England in the amateur international in Paris when France were beaten 15-0.

It was not until 1913 and 1914 that McIver was able to play with any regularity for Essex. In 1913, he hit 110 against Lancashire at Leyton and followed this at the end of July with innings of 134 and 44 against Hampshire, and 80 and 53 against Kent on the same ground. He formed a fine opening partnership with Russell and kept wicket admirably.

The partnership with Russell blossomed in 1914, and against Leicestershire at Leyton, in July, they established an Essex first wicket

record with a stand of 212. In two hours before lunch on the first day, they scored 186. McIver, who made 90 on this occasion, was particularly noted for his cover-driving and for his cutting. He hit two more centuries at Leyton that season and passed 1000 runs in all matches. Then came World War One.

He played little in 1919, appeared quite regularly in 1920, and then faded from the side, playing just once in 1922. As *The Daily News* observed, Essex were looking to him to keep wicket in that post-war period, but he was now beyond 40.

McIver continued his involvement with cricket all his life. He helped H.D.G.Levenson-Gower to organise the Eastbourne Festival, and he was deeply concerned for his local cricket team, Ashtead in Surrey, where he lived for so long. Each year, his friend Levenson-Gower would take a side to Ashtead.

McIver's last first-class match was for MCC in 1934 when he was 53, and he continued to play for MCC and for Grasshoppers until he was past 60. He died suddenly on a visit to Worcester College, Oxford.

M	Inns	NOs	Runs	HS	Avge	100s	Ct/st
59	101	6	2544	134	26.77	4	47/13

Overs	Mds	Runs	Wkts	Avge	Best
10.2	3	25	1	25.00	1/4

Malcolm MACKINNON

Born: Toward Point, Argyle, Scotland, 11 May 1891.
Died: Sunningdale, Berkshire, 13 February 1975.
A right-handed batsman and off-break bowler, Mackinnon played no first-class cricket while at Oxford, and his working life was spent in

India where he played for the Stragglers of Asia and for the Europeans between 1927 and 1935.

He played three matches for Essex in the summer of 1927.

M	Inns	NOs	Runs	HS	Avge
3	4	-	55	31	13.75

Steven John MALONE

Born: Chelmsford, 19 October 1953.

A right-arm bowler who was genuinely quick but erratic, Steve Malone played his first cricket in mid-Essex before moving to Hadleigh and Thundersley. On the Essex staff from 1975 until 1978, he appeared in only two first-class matches, one in his first year and one in his last, both were against Cambridge University. He later played for Hampshire and for Glamorgan, and more recently for Wiltshire where he now lives.

Overs	Mds	Runs	Wkts	Avge	Best	10/m	5/inn
41	7	101	2	50	.50	1/28	

John William MARSTON

Born: Rosario, Argentina, 25 October 1893.
Died: Lambeth, London, 9 July 1938.

A leg-break and googly bowler educated at Haileybury, John Marston played for Essex against the West Indian tourists at Ilford in 1923, and against Somerset on the same ground the following year. In the second innings against Somerset, he captured the wickets of MacBryan and Considine.

M	Inns	NOs	Runs	HS	Avge	Ct
2	4	1	12	6	4.00	1

Overs	Mds	Runs	Wkts	Avge	Best
28	1	112	2	56.00	2/47

Arthur Dalby MARTIN

Born: Hackney, London, 9 November 1888.
Died: Northwood, Middlesex, 12 July 1958.

An amateur bowler who played one match in 1920 and appeared against Northamptonshire and Middlesex in 1921, Martin was particularly successful in the match at Northampton. He captured the wickets of W.W.Timms, stumped, Tomkins and Beers in an 11-over spell.

M	Inns	NOs	Runs	HS	Avge	Ct
3	3	-	0	0	0.00	1

Overs	Mds	Runs	Wkts	Avge	Best
51	1	210	5	42.00	3/43

Eric Gordon MARTIN

Born: Rock Ferry, Cheshire, 4 February 1907.
Died: Chelsea, London, 27 January 1928.

A medium pace bowler, Eric Martin appeared for Essex in two matches as an amateur in 1928. He was also a useful middle-order batsman.

M	Inns	NOs	Runs	HS	Avge	Ct
2	4	-	25	13	6.25	1

Overs	Mds	Runs	Wkts	Avge	Best
44	4	140	2	70.00	1/63

Oswald MARTYN

Born: Clapham, London, 10 January 1887.
Died: Patcham, Sussex, 14 September 1959.

Oswald Martyn, an amateur, appeared for Essex against Northamptonshire, at Southend in July 1922. Essex won by ten wickets after rain had delayed the start. Martyn batted at number four.

M	Inns	NOs	Runs	HS	Avge	Ct
1	1	-	0	0	0.00	1

William Henry James MAYES

Born: Marylebone, London, 17 July 1885.
Died: Esher, Surrey, 5 February 1946.

A right-arm fast bowler, Mayes played for Essex against Middlesex as an amateur at Leyton in May 1914. This was the occasion on which Middlesex scored 464 for one declared, with Tarrant making 205 not out, J.W.Hearne 106 not out, and Anson 90. Mayes suffered no worse than anyone else in the Essex attack.

M	Inns	NOs	Runs	HS	Avge
1	2	-	2	2	1.00

Overs	Mds	Runs	Wkts	Avge
14	-	69	-	-

Harold MEAD

Born: Walthamstow, 13 June 1895.
Died: Epping, April 1921.
A son of the great Walter Mead, Harold Mead, a slow left-arm bowler and a lower order right-handed batsman, played alongside his father in the opening match of the 1913 season, against Derbyshire at Leyton. He also appeared against Middlesex, at Lord's, and he played in two more matches the following season.

He joined the Essex Regiment on the outbreak of war, and he was severely wounded in 1915. In truth, he never really recovered from his wounds, and he died before his 26th birthday.

M	Inns	NOs	Runs	HS	Avge	Ct
4	8	2	19	8*	3.16	3

Overs	Mds	Runs	Wkts	Avge	Best
55.4	5	194	3	64.66	2/84

Walter MEAD

Born: Clapton, London, 1 April 1868.
Died: Shelley, Ongar, 18 March 1954.
Walter Mead was known as 'The Essex Treasure', and no man more deserved such a title. He was small in stature, sported a little black moustache and bowled medium-pace off-breaks, and the occasional lethal leg-break, with an easy action. It seemed that he could, and on occasions did, bowl for ever without losing length or direction. He served Essex for the best part of 20 years, and his commitment never wavered, save for two years when there was a disagreement.

He played for Middlesex Colts when he was 16, and he was engaged by the Clapton club. He then became professional to Broxbourne CC and established a residential qualification for Essex.

Mead's debut for Essex came at the beginning of the 1890 season. Against Surrey at The Oval, he took 5 for 101 in the second innings, and his debut was greeted with the comment, 'He bowls with judgment, and fielded well, too, in addition.' He was engaged as a bowler at Lord's, and he made his first-class debut for MCC at Cambridge in May 1892, claiming the wicket of Gerry Weigall. It was the first of 1916 wickets in the first-class game.

Even on a good wicket, he could turn the ball sharply at medium pace, and he hurried batsmen into their shots. Above all, he varied his bowling most intelligently.

In 1893, Essex were suddenly given a fixture against the Australians when the tourists' original opponents, Cambridge Past and Present, found that they were unable to raise a side. There was some scepticism that Essex were fit to meet with the mighty visitors, but the county achieved a worthy draw, and Mead took 9 for 136 an 8 for 69 to become a national hero. Sadly, first-class status for Essex was still a year away, and, in the record books, 'Tich' Freeman remains the only man to have taken 17 wickets in a match on two occasions.

Mead was, of course, in the Essex side for the inaugural first-class match, against

Leicestershire at Leyton in May, 1894. He took 6 for 49 in the first innings, and a great county career was launched. He took 94 wickets in all matches that season. The following season, he captured 179 at 14.55 runs each.

It was in this season, 1895, that he established an Essex record when he too 8 for 67 and 9 for 52 against Hampshire at Southampton at the end of July. Ten of his victims were clean bowled. Mead finished fifth in the first-class bowling averages, and his reputation as one of the finest bowlers in the country was assured, nor did that reputation lessen in the years that followed.

The outstanding bowling performances tumbled over each other. In 1896, he took 9 for 75 against Leicestershire at Leyton; and there were 9 for 40 against Hampshire at Southampton in 1900. In 1899, he appeared against Australia at Lord's. Hill and Trumper hit centuries, Australia won by ten wickets, and Mead claimed only the wicket of the Australian wicket-keeper Kelly. Incredibly, Walter Mead never played for England again although many far lesser bowlers have won a host of Test caps. It was small consolation that he was chosen nine times for the Players.

It is interesting to note that C.B.Fry, who thought Mead 'the hardest trier imaginable', wrote, in 1899, when analysing the Essex man's bowling, 'One of his best balls is a plain straight one off which you may easily be caught at the wicket. You must also look out for another upon which he puts vigorous leg-break, but which on the contrary turns slightly from the off.' So was it Bosanquet who invented the googly?

Mead was a sound fielder at cover point, and although he made no claims to being a great batsman, he hit 119 against Leicestershire at Leyton in 1902 and could make runs when they were needed.

But it was bowling that was his life, and when he bowled a particularly good ball to a batsman which he did frequently, he would cock his head on one side and wink.

His relations with the county were always good until, at the end of the 1903 season, he asked for an increase in his winter's pay. Essex, as ever at that time, were in a difficult financial position, and his demand was refused. In 1904 and 1905, he did not appear for Essex, playing for MCC and London County, but the rift was healed, and Mead returned to county cricket in 1906 and captured his usual 100 wickets.

By 1913, it was apparent that his days as a great bowler were nearing their end. He played in 12 Championship matches, twice alongside his son Harold, and took 29 wickets at 26.20 runs each, which still placed him third in the county averages, but he was 45 and a spark had gone. In his last match for Essex, he sent down only one over, and his final wicket had come at Hove at the end of July when he had Chaplin of Sussex caught.

He remained on the Lord's groundstaff until 1918, and he coached and was umpiring Essex minor matches with his zest for the game until the end.

M	Inns	NOs	Runs	HS	Avge	100s	Ct
332	469	125	3843	119	11.17	1	151

Overs	Mds	Runs	Wkts	Avge	Best	10/m	5/inn
8147.2	4037	28423	1472	19.30	9/40	30	117
4529 (five-ball)							

Gordon Christopher MELLUISH

Born: Marylebone, London, 25 August 1906.
Died: Little Bushey, Hertfordshire, 14 April 1977.
A slow left-arm bowler, Melluish was given a trial as an amateur in three matches in 1926. He took the wicket of Hills of Glamorgan, and later took two wickets in the game against Derbyshire.

Educated at Haberdashers' Aske's School, he was a butcher by profession and was a celebrated club cricketer in South East England. During World War Two, he played much cricket in Northamptonshire and helped to keep the game alive in that county.

M	Inns	NOs	Runs	HS	Avge
4	3	1	18	16*	9.00

Overs	Mds	Runs	Wkts	Avge	Best
37	5	115	3	38.33	1/17

Charles Frederick MERCER

Born: Hackney, London, 28 August 1896.
Died: Basildon, 20 November 1965.
A left-handed batsman, Charles Mercer appeared as an amateur against Leicestershire at Leicester, and Derbyshire at Southend in 1929.

M	Inns	NOs	Runs	HS	Avge
2	4	-	26	8	6.50

Alexander Hubert MESTON

Born: Leyton, 1 June 1898.
Died: Illogan North, Redruth, Cornwall, 1 March 1980.
Unlike his elder brother Sam, Alexander Meston played for Essex as a professional. An all-rounder, he appeared in two matches in 1926 and in ten the following season without making his mark.

M	Inns	NOs	Runs	HS	Avge	Ct
12	17	4	143	41	11.00	9

Overs	Mds	Runs	Wkts	Avge	Best
98	16	352	4	88.00	2/18

Samuel Paul MESTON

Born: Islington, London, 19 November 1882.
Died: Vancouver, British Columbia, Canada, 9 January 1960.
Sam Meston was educated at St John's College, Lough-

ton, and at Salway College, Leyton. In 1906, living and playing in the west country, he took 9 for 27 when appearing for Bristol Bohemians at Weston-super-Mare, but it was as a batsman that he was asked to play for Gloucestershire in three matches as an amateur.

A member of the South Woodford club, he appeared in 14 matches for Essex in 1907. In the last Championship match of the season at home, versus Lancashire at Leyton, he hit 130 in three and a half hours. This was the highest score made by an Essex batsman during the season .

Unfortunately, business restricted his appearances to three in 1908, and after that he appeared only in minor matches. In 1910, he hit 228 for Essex Club and Ground against West Ham and District.

M	Inns	NOs	Runs	HS	Avge	100s	Ct
17	29	2	476	130	17.62	1	7

Overs	Mds	Runs	Wkts	Avge	Best
8.2	-	48	1	48.00	1/10

Geoffrey MILLER

Born: Chesterfield, Derbyshire, 8 September 1952.
Geoff Miller was a veteran of 34 Test matches and had spent 14 seasons with Derbyshire when Essex sur-

prisingly signed him in 1987. With the retirement of David Acfield, Essex were in need of an off-spin bowler, and Miller, with 60 Test wickets and 1213 Test runs, was obviously a very useful acquisition. He was with Essex for three seasons, and, in 1989, he played in the Benson and Hedges Cup Final, but, suffering from a back injury, he never quite did himself justice as batsman or bowler. As a fielder, he held 58 catches at slip and other close to the wicket positions.

He returned to Derbyshire in 1990 and then joined Cheshire as player-coach. He runs a successful sports outfitters, and more recently he has become a noted after-dinner speaker. He represented Derbyshire at table tennis.

M	Inns	NOs	Runs	HS	Avge	Ct
52	65	12	1094	77	20.64	58

Overs	Mds	Runs	Wkts	Avge	Best	10/m	5/inn
1005.2	250	2636	81	32.54	7/59	1	2

Sunday League

M	Inns	NOs	Runs	HS	Avge	Ct
32	20	6	339	44*	24.21	11

Overs	Mds	Runs	Wkts	Avge	Best
193.2	12	771	29	26.59	3/13

Benson and Hedges Cup

M	Inns	NOs	Runs	HS	Avge	Ct
12	7	3	49	20	12.25	7

Overs	Mds	Runs	Wkts	Avge	Best
78	10	279	7	39.86	3/37

NatWest Trophy

M	Inns	NOs	Runs	HS	Avge	Ct
6	4	-	52	21	13.00	3

Overs	Mds	Runs	Wkts	Avge	Best
41.3	5	142	5	28.40	3/23

Joseph MILNER

Born: Johannesburg, South Africa, 22 August 1937.

In June 1960, *The Cricketer* singled out Joe Milner as a prominent young player. He had become obsessed by cricket since seeing Denis Compton on the MCC's tour of South Africa, 1948-49. Milner was at that time an 11-year-old pupil at Athlone High School, Johannesburg, and he was one of those lucky enough to receive some coaching from Compton. Milner was always to retain the great man's eagerness to leave the crease to meet the ball, and perhaps he was always a little impetuous.

When Doug Insole was in South Africa, 1956-57, Milner approached him, and Insole encouraged the young right-hander to come to England in 1957. He was given a month's trial by Essex, played in the match against Oxford University at Westcliff, and the trial was extended to the season and he was put on contract.

While qualifying he made a considerable impression as a free-scoring batsman with Walthamstow. In 1959, he appeared in 17 matches for Essex, hit 729 runs, including 135 against Leicestershire at Leicester, and excelled in the field.

The most memorable of his feats in the field came in Ken Preston's Benefit Match against Gloucestershire at Leyton. The scores were level when Cook, the Gloucestershire number 11, deflected a ball from Knight to short-leg where Milner brought off a brilliant catch to tie the match.

His form fell away in 1960, but the following season, with centuries against Nottinghamshire and Hampshire, he scored 1387 runs in all matches. Perhaps surprisingly, he declined terms at the end of the season.

In South Africa, he played club cricket for Balfour Park, Johannesburg, and was a designer of men's clothing. Later he was involved in marketing Persian carpets.

M	Inns	NOs	Runs	HS	Avge	100s	Ct
66	117	12	2688	135	25.60	3	57

Overs	Mds	Runs	Wkts	Avge
2	-	14	-	-

Edward Sibley MISSEN

Born: Cambridge, 2 February 1875.
Died: Colchester, 17 November 1927.

For many years a stalwart of the Colchester and East Essex club for whom he scored a vast number of runs and took many wickets with his medium pace, Missen played for Essex against Hampshire at Colchester in 1921. In 1904, he had assisted Cambridgeshire.

M	Inns	NOs	Runs	HS	Avge
1	2	-	20	12	10.00

George Frederick MITCHELL

Born: Canning Town, 18 February 1897.

George Mitchell was a professional whose one match for Essex was against Oxford University at Chelmsford in 1926. He took the wicket of G.C.Newman, who was to be a future power in Middlesex cricket.

M	Inns	NOs	Runs	HS	Avge
1	1	-	4	4	4.00

Overs	Mds	Runs	Wkts	Avge	Best
17	3	45	1	45.00	1/25

Kenneth Francis MOORE

Born: Croydon, Surrey, 4 January 1940.

A left-arm medium-fast bowler, Ken Moore was given a trial for Essex in 1961. He performed well against Cambridge University at Fenner's and his four second innings wickets went a long way towards winning the

match. Among his victims was Mike Brearley who was bowled for 7. Moore was less successful in 2nd XI matches, however, and was not offered a contract.

M	Inns	NOs	Runs	HS	Avge	Ct
1	1	-	2	2	2.00	2

Overs	Mds	Runs	Wkts	Avge	Best
29	10	43	4	10.75	4/21

Harold Marsh MORRIS

Born: Wanstead, 16 April 1898.
Died: Brighton, Sussex, 18 November 1984.
Frank Thorogood of the *News Chronicle* wrote of 'Whiz' Morris in 1931 that he 'has done all his best work for Essex not as a leader but as an ordinary member of the team. The cares of captaincy have kept him under considerable restraint.' It came as no surprise that he resigned the captaincy the following season and concentrated on golf, a game at which he was very good and which many suspected that he enjoyed more than cricket.

Morris was in the Repton XI in 1915 and 1916, captain in his second year, but although he played first-class cricket at Cambridge, he did not get his blue. He first played for Essex in 1919 and was immediately recognised as an excellent cover point. That he was good in the field was not surprising, for he was an excellent soccer player, assisting Old Reptonians, Corinthians and Casuals.

In 1927, he hit a spectacular 166 against Hampshire at Southampton. His innings included two sixes and 22 fours, and he and Russell added 233 for the fourth wicket in under two and a half hours. Morris was dubbed *Mercurial* or *Whiz*. He was certainly a venturesome batsman, strong in cuts and drives, but he was inconsistent, probably because he was unable to play regularly.

After the close of the disastrous 1928 season, the Essex Committee, in controversial and acrimonious circumstances, relieved Johnny Douglas of the captaincy which he had held for 17 years and appointed Morris in his stead. Douglas had refused to resign on the grounds that he did not consider Morris was a good enough cricketer to succeed him, nor was Morris, in his opinion, committed to the job.

Events were to prove Douglas right although Essex's form improved.

Morris was a member of the well known firm of Protheroe and Morris in Cheapside who were garden suppliers. Either by the demands of business or by inclination, he did not make himself regularly available, often standing down at the last moment. Charles Bray tells how he was asked to lead Essex against the Australians in 1930 shortly before the start of the match although he had never captained a side before.

Morris' non-availability reached absurd lengths in his final season, 1932, when he was to appear in only two Championship matches. Worse still for the captain was that his once hard hitting batting form deserted him totally when he took on the responsibility of leadership. He was a likable, cheerful and generous man who should be best remembered for his dashing qualities.

He went to Jamaica with Lionel Tennyson's team, 1926-27, and he served as a flier in both World Wars. He was shot down in the North Sea and spent three days clinging to the wreckage before being rescued.

M	Inns	NOs	Runs	HS	Avge	100s	Ct
240	383	29	6974	166	19.70	3	78

Overs	Mds	Runs	Wkts	Avge	Best
226.5	20	839	14	59.92	2/16

Philip Edward MORRIS

Born: Kennington, London, 26 November 1877.
Died: Hove, Sussex, 6 July 1945.

Educated at Mill Hill and Bancrofts, Philip Morris was a leg-break bowler whose occasional appearances as an amateur for Essex were spread over the period from 1909 to 1924. He had his days of marked success. In 1922, against Somerset at Leyton, he took 8 for 106, and the following season, on the same ground, he took 7 for 72 in an innings of 204 by Gloucestershire.

He was later restricted to club cricket and captained Sussex Martlets.

M	Inns	NOs	Runs	HS	Avge	Ct
28	43	5	418	55*	11.00	13

Overs	Mds	Runs	Wkts	Avge	Best	10/m	5/inn
598.5	75	1848	83	22.26	8/106	1	6

William Bancroft MORRIS

Born: Kingston, Jamaica, 28 May 1917.

A right-handed batsman and leg-break bowler who converted to off-breaks for the sake of the county, Bill Morris played for Kenton CC as a youngster and became an outstanding all-rounder in club cricket. He played for the

Young Players of Surrey under Stuart Surridge, and, towards the end of World War Two, he appeared for the Club Cricket Conference in charity matches at Lord's.

Both before and after the war, he trained as a coach at the Gover and Sandham School, but

in 1946, he joined the Essex staff. He played for the county until 1950, but he was never able to command a regular place in the side, particularly when amateurs became available. There were instances when a good performance from Morris was followed by being left out of the side for several matches.

From 1948 to 1958, he ran a car delivery business, but his life has been dedicated to cricket. He was a key member of the Ilford club, coach at Berkhampstead School and later at Forest School, and played for Cambridgeshire from 1951 to 1958. He also played club cricket for Kilmarnock and was an MCC coach at Lord's in 1959 and 1960.

Bill Morris became the senior coach at the Ilford Indoor Cricket School where his influence on cricket in Essex became profound. He was particularly effective with emerging players of talent, and men like Graham Gooch, Ray East, John Lever, Nasser Hussain and Stuart Turner have never hidden their admiration for him, nor forgotten the debt they owe him. His contribution to the Essex success of recent years was immeasurable.

A strong disciplinarian who was educated in Canada, Bill Morris retired to Kilmarnock in Scotland in 1982.

M	Inns	NOs	Runs	HS	Avge	Ct
48	78	10	1219	68	17.92	18

Overs	Mds	Runs	Wkts	Avge	Best
671	156	1975	43	45.93	4/90

Harry Clive MORTLOCK

Born : Hackney, London, 13 October 1892.

Died: Brentwood, 29 March 1963.

A slow left-arm bowler and lower order batsman, Harry Mortlock was educated at both Brentwood School and Felsted. He played in three matches for Essex in 1912, and reappeared in the final fixture of the 1921 season.

In May 1912, at Leyton, he helped bowl Essex to an innings victory over Derbyshire by taking 5 for 104. It was a match in which Perrin hit a double century, and he and McGahey added 312 for the third wicket. In the wake of this brilliant batting, Mortlock's feat went practically unnoticed.

M	Inns	NOs	Runs	HS	Avge	Ct
4	4	-	32	26	8.00	6

Overs	Mds	Runs	Wkts	Avge	Best	5/inn
97	12	380	7	54.28	5/104	1

Alfred Samuel MOULE

Born: West Ham, 31 July 1894.
Died: Shoreham-on-Sea, Sussex, 5 February 1973.

A right-handed batsman, Alf Moule was on the Essex staff shortly after World War One. He made 17 appearances in the county side between 1921 and 1924, but he was better known as a soccer player with Millwall, Norwich City and Watford.

He appeared on several occasions for Devon in the Minor Counties Championship between 1931 and 1937.

M	Inns	NOs	Runs	HS	Avge	Ct
17	31	5	317	64	12.19	5

Overs	Mds	Runs	Wkts	Avge
1	-	6	-	-

W. NAYLOR

All that is known of Naylor is that he was a professional who kept wicket for Essex against the West Indian tourists at Leyton in June 1906. He batted at number 11.

M	Inns	NOs	Runs	HS	Avge	Ct
1	2	-	2	2	1.00	2

Captain Frederick William Herbert NICHOLAS

Born: Federated Malay States, 25 July 1893.
Died: Kensington, London, 20 October 1962.
Educated at Forest School, Nicholas went up to Oxford and played in the trials of 1913 and

1914 but did not get his blue. A fine wicket-keeper and great hitter, he first played for Essex in 1912, but the following year he assisted Bedfordshire.

A top class sprinter and a good footballer, he won blues for both athletics and soccer, and when he became a Regular Army officer he won renown for his athletic prowess. He returned to Essex in 1922 and kept wicket for the county when available until 1929. A hard, uncompromising man, he hit one century, a spectacular effort against Surrey at Leyton in 1926. In 160 minutes, he made 140 with two sixes and 12 fours, but he was unable to save the follow-on. In the second innings, he hit 52 in 50 minutes, but Essex still lost by an innings.

He made three overseas tours with Joel and Cahn's sides, and he played regularly for Sir Julien Cahn's side in England between 1927 and 1931. In 1929, he is said to have scored more than 2000 runs for Cahn's side.

His grandson, Mark, captained Hampshire and England 'A'.

MCC	Inns	NOs	Runs	HS	Avge	100s	Ct/st
63	101	2	2255	140	22.77	1	41/13

Morris Stanley NICHOLS

Born: Stondon Massey, 6 October 1900.
Died: Newark, Nottinghamshire, 26 January 1961.
'Never can I recollect a greater trier than Stan Nichols. No matter how long or how hot the day, he never flags, is never ruffled, always playing in high spirits and in the right spirit.

It does not seem to be realised why, though so excellent a bowler, he has never become even greater. The explanation is that he is flat-footed and, try as he has ever so hard, he can never get onto his toes at the moment of delivering the ball, thus losing just that little extra bit of nip which is so devastating. He is well aware of this himself, and has discussed this matter with me. In a county match, if I had to have one man play for me to save my life, pre-war it would have been George Hirst, post-war it would be Stan Nichols.'

The writer is Sir Home Gordon in 1939. The subject is Stan, or Morris, Nichols who did the double of 1000 runs and 100 wickets eight times. Only four players have achieved the 'double' on more occasions, and Nichols performed the feat in Essex matches alone.

He first played club cricket for Wickford at the age of 12. His father was one of the leading members of the club, but he moved his son to Chelmsford whose captain, P.Turrall, introduced the young left-handed batsman to the county club.

Batting at number nine, he scored four against Yorkshire at Hull in 1924, and three weeks later, he made 0 against Northamptonshire. He bowled three overs in the match at Hull without taking a wicket, but Perrin, who played in the match, recognised a potential in he right-arm fast bowler and concentrated on developing the talent in club and ground matches.

The following season, Nichols was close to being a regular in the side, and although his batting disappointed, he took 52 wickets at a moderate cost. In 1926 and 1927, he took more

than 100 wickets, and, in 1928, he hit the first of his 20 centuries, 112 against Hampshire at Leyton. He went with Sir Julien Cahn's team to Jamaica that winter, and the following season he completed his first 'double'.

Nichols won his first Test caps with Harold Gilligan's side in New Zealand, 1929-30, and he played in the fourth Test against Australia the following summer. In 1931, he performed the hat-trick against Yorkshire, but it was for his achievements against Yorkshire four years later that he will always be remembered. He took 4 for 17 and 7 for 37, and hit 146 as Essex beat the White Rose county by an innings at Huddersfield. It was in this season that he commenced a run of five 'doubles' which took him to the outbreak of World War Two.

In his benefit match, against Kent at Southend in 1936, he hit 110, and the same week he scored 205 against Hampshire. His left-handed batting was always aggressive as befitted a man more than six feet tall and powerfully proportioned.

Nichols was not a natural cricketer. What he achieved, he achieved through hard work and unrelenting effort. His bowling lacked the grace of movement of a natural athlete. His arms flailed, and his very large feet splayed, but, nevertheless, he was a magnificent bowler, attaining considerable pace and delivering what was, in effect, a very fast leg-break. Had he been better served in the field, he might well have taken more than 200 wickets a season. The astonishment is that he played for England only 14 times. Having appeared for England in four Tests against South Africa in 1935, he did not play again until the third and final Test against West Indies in 1939. And yet he did the 'double' in each of the intervening seasons and, in 1938, hit 1452 runs and took 171 wickets. Essex were not, at that time, recognised as a fashionable county.

In spite of his rather ungainly action, Nichols was a very neat and tidy man. His hair was accurately parted in the centre and brushed flat, never disturbed by the hours of bowling that he did. The man had immense stamina, and he also had a daintiness that belied the size of his feet. He never travelled without packing his dancing pumps alongside his cricket kit.

He was 40 shortly after the outbreak of World War Two, and it was apparent that his first-class career was at an end. He had been selected for the tour of India, 1939-40, but the trip was, of course, abandoned. He joined the Army, became a sergeant instructor and played in several charity matches at Lord's. In 1937, he had published an interesting instructional book, *Bowling*.

Always healthy looking, he son of a farmer, he played in the Birmingham League after the war and was active in the game until some three years before his death.

Nichols is among the greatest of cricketers to have played for Essex, and he is also among the very best all-rounders that the game has known.

M	Inns	NOs	Runs	HS	Avge	100s	Ct
418	664	66	15736	205	26.31	20	279

Overs	Mds	Runs	Wkts	Avge	Best	10/m	5/inn
11250.5	2218	34201	1608	21.26	9/32	22	108
629.5 (eight-ball)							

Geoffrey John NOLAN

Born: Colchester, 6 October 1937.
Geoff Nolan was a right-handed batsman with Colchester and East Essex. He often appeared for the 2nd XI, and, in July 1968, he played in the first match in Colchester week, against Derbyshire, batting at number seven.

He was a fine hockey player.

M	Inns	NOs	Runs	HS	Avge
1	2	-	14	11	7.00

George NORMAN

Born: Westminster, London, 23 August 1890.
Died: Virginia Water, Surrey, 24 November 1964.
A product of Bancroft's School, George Norman made four appearances for Essex in 1920 as a middle-order batsman.

M	Inns	NOs	Runs	HS	Avge	Ct
4	5	1	44	21	11.00	1

Overs	Mds	Runs	Wkts	Avge
3	-	18	-	-

Dr Ralph Oliver Geoffrey NORMAN

Born: Southend, 30 July 1911.
Died: Thorpe Bay, 26 July 1983.
Ralph Norman played in the Seniors Trial while up at Clare College, Cambridge, in 1932.

As the match was ruined by rain, and he neither batted nor bowled, it could hardly be called a fair test of his abilities. Three weeks later, he played for Essex against the University at Fenner's.

His later cricketing activities were limited by his work in the medical profession.

M	Inns	NOs	Runs	HS	Avge
1	2	-	20	10	10.00

Jack O'CONNOR

Born: Cambridge, 6 November 1897.
Died: Buckhurst Hill, 22 February 1977.
Jack O'Connor was Essex's greatest professional batsman in the years between the two world wars. He scored centuries against the 16 other counties and against both universities. He reached 1000 runs in a season 16 times, and as he also captured more than 550 wickets in his career and was only seven wickets short of the 'double' in 1926, it can be seen that he was a truly fine cricketer.

Cricket was his entire life. His father was a noted coach who played for Cambridgeshire and appeared nine times for Derbyshire in 1900 while his uncle was the great H.A.Carpenter of whom much is said elsewhere in this volume. Jack O'Connor made his first appearance for Essex in 1921, the year after his uncle had played his last match.

O'Connor was run out for 13 in his first match, against Worcestershire at Leyton and in his second match he was savaged by McDonald and Gregory as the Australians beat Essex by an innings. In truth, he was never at his best against fast bowling, but he was to become a master of spin as befitted a man of slight build who was very quick on his feet and an excellent driver on both sides of the wicket.

In spite of his modest beginning, O'Connor established a fairly regular place in the Essex side in 1922, hitting a maiden first-class century, against Northamptonshire, and claiming his first wickets in first-class cricket, the Derbyshire opening pair of Storer and Bowden. He bowled slow leg-breaks with the occasional off-break, and, to quote *Wisden*, 'had the advantage of looking a good deal simpler than he was.'

By 1926, he was being spoken of as a possible Test cricketer, and he played in Test trials in both 1927 and 1928. In June 1929, he was chosen to play against South Africa in the Second Test, at Lord's. He made 0 and 11, and he did not bowl. He did not appear in a Test match in England again although he had another trial in 1932.

As chance would have it, England sent two parties abroad in the winter of 1929-30, one to New Zealand and one to West Indies. Jack O'Connor was in the side that went to the Caribbean under Freddie Calthorpe. He played in three of the four Tests, and, in what was to be his last Test, at Kingston, Jamaica, he made 51. Forty years later, he was still to talk of that trip with pride and joy, but for the remaining decade of his career he was to be nothing more than a very good county cricketer.

Interestingly, he had twice been to Jamaica with private tours, Tennyson, 1926-27, and Cahn, 1928-29, before his official trip with MCC.

If his days with England ended in 1930, his run-scoring for Essex was prolific. He hit 2350 runs in 1934, averaged just under 56, made his single appearance for the Players ag-ainst the Gentle-men at Lord's, and scored 248 against Surrey at Brentwood. It was in this season that he established a record for the county by scoring nine centuries. The record still stands although it has been equalled by Doug Insole.

Although 1934 was the fourth and last season in which O'Connor reached 2000 runs in all matches, he maintained excellent form right up until the outbreak of World War Two, which brought an end to his first-class career. He bowled less, but he still scored more runs than any other Essex player and 'showed his old power in hitting the ball picked for punishment'. When the curtain came down O'Connor was 54 not out as Essex beat Northamptonshire by 210 runs at Clacton. That last season, 1939, had brought him four centuries, the final one against Hampshire at Brentwood in June, and this made his total for Essex, 71. No other Essex batsmen had approached this number, and the record was not beaten until Gooch passed it in 1993.

O'Connor played many times for the London Counties in wartime charity matches, and he became the county coach in 1946, a position he held for three seasons. This did not stop him from playing for Buckinghamshire in 1946 and 1947.

Cricket was his life, and he coached at Eton for 15 years. His wife wanted to move back to Essex so he 'retired' and coached at Chigwell School with occasional sessions on Saturday morning at the Ilford Indoor Cricket School.

M	Inns	NOs	Runs	HS	Avge	100s	Ct/st
516	866	76	27819	248	35.21	71	215/1

Overs	Mds	Runs	Wkts	Avge	Best	10/m	5/inn
6330.1	1212	17523	537	32.63	7/52	2	17
3.2 (eight-ball)							

Major Charles Edward Linton ORMAN

Born: Roorkee, India, 6 September 1859.
Died: Epping, 11 February 1927.
Most of Charles Orman's cricket was played for Bedfordshire between 1891 and 1900, but in 1896, in the second week in May, he played two matches for Essex. The first was against Leicestershire at Leyton when he opened the innings; and the second was against MCC at Lord's. He was an Old Felstedian.

Orman was a Regular Army officer.

M	Inns	NOs	Runs	HS	Avge	Ct
2	2	-	16	12	8.00	1

Hugh Glendwr Palmer OWEN

Born: Bath, Somerset, 19 May 1859.
Died: Landwick, Dengie, 20 October 1912.
Hugh Owen was qualified to play for three counties: Somerset by birth; Derbyshire by residence; and Essex through the family home. He chose to play only for Essex in county cricket.

His association with Essex began in 1880, and he was the first batsman to score a century for the new county club, but, like so many other of his fine deeds, this was before first-class status was obtained.

Owen was privately educated and went up to Corpus Christi College, Cambridge, where he did well at cricket. He was given only one chance for the university side, against MCC in 1882, however, and he did not get his blue.

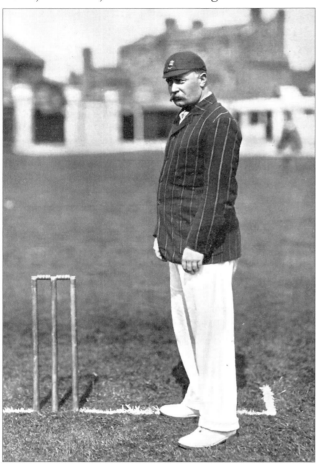

He was in the Essex side for the inaugural first-class match, against Leicestershire, in 1894, and hit 76 in the second innings so becoming the first batsman to hit a first-class 50 for the county. Some weeks later, he became the county's first centurion, hitting 109 and 86 not out against Oxford University at Leyton. This was the county's only 100 of the season.

A steady, sound batsman, Owen was large and heavy of build and sported a moustache. He often led the side when Lucas was absent, and in 1895, Essex's first year in the Championship, he took over the captaincy and retained it until his retirement in 1902.

Owen scored many valuable runs for Essex and often opened the innings, but it was as a captain that he most proved his worth. He was tactically sound, genial and popular. He played cricket with a smile, and people responded to him.

In minor cricket, he made some huge scores, and in 1887, for Trent College in Derbyshire where he was a master, he hit five centuries and scored 1809 runs. He also played for Bradwell and Tillingham, and for Notts Forest Amateurs, and he was a capable soccer player with Notts County.

M	Inns	NOs	Runs	HS	Avge	100s	Ct
133	222	17	4459	134	21.75	3	38

Overs	Mds	Runs	Wkts	Avge	Best
114.3	26	321	9	35.66	2/37

(five-ball)

Hugh Ashton PAGE

Born: Salisbury, Rhodesia, 3 July 1962.

Hugh Page arrived in England to play for Essex on a two-year contract with an excellent reputation as a right-arm quick bowler and a useful lower-order left-handed batsman. He had played for Staffordshire in 1985 and for South Africa in unofficial 'Test' matches. Unfortunately, he had little success for Essex in 1987 with his rhythm seemingly lost at the delivery stride. It was discovered that he had a knee injury, and he ended the season on crutches.

He returned to South Africa after his one shortened season for Essex, and although he played for Transvaal again, he was never able to recapture the form of his early years.

M	Inns	NOs	Runs	HS	Avge	Ct
15	20	4	266	60	16.62	5

Overs	Mds	Runs	Wkts	Avge	Best	5/inn
340.2	52	1172	35	33.48	5/26	1

Eric John PALMER

Born: Romford, 16 June 1931.
A right-arm fast medium pace bowler and left-handed batsman, Eric Palmer played for Romford Brewery and for Romford. In 1957, he appeared in four matches for the county. A bespectacled cricketer, he made his debut against Gloucestershire on his home ground, took two wickets and, according to *Wisden*, 'bowled some splendid overs'.

He had considerable success for the 2nd XI, but he did not appear in county cricket after 1957.

M	Inns	NOs	Runs	HS	Avge	Ct
4	6	5	39	11*	39.00	1

Overs	Mds	Runs	Wkts	Avge	Best
72	20	225	7	32.14	2/35

Harold James PALMER

Born: Epping, 30 August 1890.
Died: Bexhill-on-Sea, Sussex, 12 February 1967.
A medium-pace leg-break bowler, Harold Palmer was renowned in club cricket circles in Essex and assisted the county as an amateur between 1924 and 1932. Educated at Loughton School, he went to King's College, London University. He played his cricket for Epping, Loughton, Wanstead, Woodford Wells and Incogniti. For Woodford Wells in 1927, he took all ten Loughton wick-

ets at a cost of 16 runs. In his first season for the county, he played a significant part in the victory over Sussex at Eastbourne, one of only two matches the county won during the season, but his outstanding achievement came against the Australians at Leyton in May 1930. He took 5 for 40 in 20.4 overs, bowling the 'unbowlable' Woodfull and having McCabe caught at slip. Later, he knocked back the middle stumps of Fairfax and a'Beckett in the same over. Unfortunately, he was able to play in only three other matches that season, and, like so many talented amateurs, he was lost to business.

M	Inns	NOs	Runs	HS	Avge	Ct
53	65	23	257	25*	6.11	19

Overs	Mds	Runs	Wkts	Avge	Best	5/inn
1189.4	233	3477	142	24.48	6/68	19

Leonard Frederick PARSLOW

Born: Islington, London, 11 November 1909.
Died: Rochford, 6 August 1963.
Educated at the Central Foundation School, Whitechapel, Len Parslow was a fine right-handed batsman with Chingford. He served with the Royal Air Force in North Africa during World War Two, but returned home in 1943 for a brief period and hit a sparkling century for London Counties against Stork CC at Purfleet. In the early part of the war, he had been an outstanding player with British Empire XI, scoring several centuries and being described by *Wisden* as 'an opening batsman of immaculate style'.
A very fine hockey player, he played one game for Essex CCC in 1946.

M	Inns	NOs	Runs	HS	Avge
1	2	-	9	5	4.50

Charles Henry PASCOE

Born: Haggerston, London, 23 December 1876.
Died: Walthamstow, 26 January 1957.
A professional slow left-arm bowler, Pascoe played one match for Essex, in 1909.

M	Inns	NOs	Runs	HS	Avge
1	1	1	3	3*	-

Overs	Mds	Runs	Wkts	Avge
7	3	16	-	-

Robert Fraser Troutbeck PATERSON

Born: Stansted, 8 September 1916.
Died: Edinburgh, Scotland, 29 May 1980.
Educated at Brighton College where he headed the batting averages in 1933 and 1934, Robert Paterson played for the Public Schools at Lord's in his last season at the college. He came to Essex on leaving the RAF at the recommendation of Peter Smith who had played with him in Egypt. He was the complete all-round cricketer in that he was a forceful batsman, a useful medium-pace bowler and a capable wicket-keeper.

He appeared for Essex as an amateur in 1946, holding a regular place in the side, but the following year he succeeded Brian Castor as secretary, and his duties prevented him from playing for the county again although he did appear in a couple of matches for MCC. He and his wife lived in a caravan on the Essex grounds during the summer months, and the caravan was towed by an ageing Rolls-Royce. In 1951, he resigned and moved to Scotland where he coached and played with success at the West of Scotland and Stenhousemuir clubs. He died after a long and crippling illness.

M	Inns	NOs	Runs	HS	Avge	Ct/st
25	40	5	680	80	19.42	12/3

Overs	Mds	Runs	Wkts	Avge	Best
118	9	464	13	35.69	4/98

John Hanbury PAWLE

Born: Widford, Hertfordshire, 18 May 1915.
John Pawle played for Hertfordshire in 1933, his last year at Harrow. He went up to Cambridge, and although he played for the university in 1935, he did not get his blue until 1936. In 1937, he hit three centuries for Cambridge, but he 'bagged a pair' in the Varsity Match.

His debut for Essex was against his own university at Westcliff in 1935, and in 1939, he was offered the position of joint captain, but declined and did not appear that season.

An amateur rackets champion, he last appeared in first-class cricket for Free Foresters in 1947. He was a stylish right-handed batsman.

M	Inns	NOs	Runs	HS	Avge	Ct
6	11	-	194	68	17.63	4

Thomas Neill PEARCE

Born: Stoke Newington, London, 3 November 1905.
Died: Worthing, 10 April 1994.
For well over 60 years, Tom Pearce was associated with Essex County Cricket Club, as batsman, captain, chairman and president. No man has been more respected, nor more loved. He was the father-figure of Essex cricket, and his warmth, geniality and insistence that the game must be enjoyed and the spectators entertained permeated the seasons of success that the club has enjoyed for the past 15 years.

Educated at Christ's Hospital School for whom he opened the innings, bowled medium pace and hit a magnificent century against Lancing in 1922, Tom Pearce went into banking and became a prolific run-scorer in London club cricket. He played for Private Banks, United Banks and Southgate, the club of which his brother-in-law Cyril Hawker was captain for some years.

In 1929, Pearce made his debut for Essex, playing in the match against Sussex at Leyton. He opened with Cutmore, was stumped for six, and, most notably, with Nichols injured, he was pressed into sending down 22 overs which cost him 122 runs and did not bring a wicket.

He played in four matches for Essex the following season and was in the Club Cricket Conference side which met the Australians at Lord's in September. Trayton Grinter was also in the side, and it was he who lured Pearce from the bank into the wine trade and who was to make it possible for him to play more first-class cricket.

Appearing in six Championship matches in 1931, Tom Pearce hit a maiden first-class century, 152 against Lancashire at Clacton, and finished top of the county batting averages. He was far less successful in his six games the following season, but he did take his first first-class wickets, capturing 4 for 12 as Worcestershire lost their last six wickets for 31 runs at Leyton.

The Essex captain from 1929 to 1932 was H.M.Morris, but by 1932, he was scarcely able to play at all, and, for 1933, Essex appointed Pearce and Denys Wilcox as joint captains. Wilcox was to take over after the season at Cambridge was over.

The system was surprisingly successful. Playing only in the first half of the season, Pearce scored 1000 runs in 1935, and repeated the feat in 1936 when he was first chosen for the Gentlemen. In 1938, Wilcox led for the first half of the season, reversing the previous

arrangement, and Tom Pearce played at Scarborough for the first time. He was later to become closely associated with the Festival.

He headed the county batting averages in 1938, but he could not play at all in the last season before World War Two because he was serving with the Territorial Army. He was commissioned as a major and played occasionally in matches at Lord's towards the end of the war.

A fine all-round sportsman, Tom Pearce was an excellent rugby forward as captain of Old Blues, and he was an international referee with an outstanding reputation.

In 1946, he became sole captain of Essex and had the difficult task of trying to revive the county's fortunes with limited bowling resources. As a batsman he prospered, and in 1948, he hit his only double century, against Leicestershire, at Westcliff. He scored 1826 runs that season, and, as he later remarked with dry humour, he captained the only county side that bowled Bradman's Australians out in a day. The Australians scored 721 on that first day at Southend.

The previous season, Pearce had been approached by Sir Pelham Warner to captain the England side that was to tour West Indies. He made the necessary arrangements to take leave from work for the winter months only to read in an evening paper that 'Gubby' Allen had been named as captain of the party.

Pearce himself was a Test selector in 1949 and 1950 which was his last season with Essex. He felt that now was the time to hand over to Insole as captain, and this he did in mid-season. His last match for the county was, coincidentally, against Sussex at Clacton at the end of July, beginning of August. He made six and 26 not out, and, with Sussex needing nine runs for a ten-wicket victory, he bowled one over for four runs.

Following his retirement from the wine trade, he retired to Findon Valley, near Worthing, but his commitment to cricket, and to Essex in particular, continued unabated. He was a man of the utmost dignity and charm. He had the courtesy and good humour of a true gentleman, and the county club has been enriched by his presence.

M	Inns	NOs	Runs	HS	Avge	100s	Ct
231	376	48	11139	211*	33.96	20	144

Overs	Mds	Runs	Wkts	Avge	Best
232.2	38	927	15	61.80	4/12

Richard Michael PEARSON

Born: Batley, Yorkshire, 27 January 1972.
A tall off-break bowler who was educated at Batley Grammar School, Richard Pearson went up to St John's College, Cambridge, and won his blue in three successive seasons, 1991 to 1993. He also played for Northamptonshire, but he was not offered a contract on leaving university and joined Essex on a three-month trial. He bowled so impressively in 2nd XI matches that he was given a contract with the county with two months of his 'trial' period still to run. He made his first-team debut in the match against Gloucestershire at Chelmsford at the beginning of June 1994, when Such was on Test duty, and acquitted himself admirably.

NatWest Trophy

M	Inns	NOs	Runs	HS	Avge	Ct
3	4	-	45	20	11.25	2

Overs	Mds	Runs	Wkts	Avge	Best
74	17	226	4	56.50	1/39

Sunday League

M	Inns	NOs	Runs	HS	Avge
9	6	5	23	7	23.00

Overs	Mds	Runs	Wkts	Avge	Best
55.2	2	259	8	32.37	2/33

Percival Albert PERRIN

Born: Abney Park, Stoke Newington, London, 26 May 1876.
Died: Hickling, Norfolk, 20 November 1945.
A 'curiously original individual, for not only is he a sportsman in every instinct as well as shrewd and humorous with a portentously retentive memory, but he is *quite a character* and supremely lacking in self-consciousness, whilst destitute of the prevalent craze for self-advertisement. Gaunt, tall, indifferent to what he wears, with enormous reserved charm, he has a remarkable faculty for listening, saying little in discussion and yet getting his own way - because it is the wisest.' - so wrote Sir Home Gordon, Bart., of his friend 'Peter' Perrin, one of Essex's greatest batsmen and personalities whom spectators watched with interest and the warmest admiration.

From the time of his first school, Heath Brow at Boxmoor, Perrin showed a rare natural talent as a batsman, and the ability

was nurtured at Margate College where he was coached by the father of Jack O'Connor who played for Cambridgeshire and had a few games for Derbyshire. Perrin played for Tottenham in club cricket and was spotted by George Cashford of the Dalston Alberts club who recommended him to C.E.Green, the great patron of Essex cricket.

Green had just engaged the Surrey professionals Bobby Abel and Maurice Read to coach the Essex county players prior to the start of the 1896 season, and he immediately sent for Perrin to join the group of players who were being coached. Perrin later said, 'At first I could make very little of the bowling, which in its length and spin was very different from anything to which I had been accustomed.' Nevertheless, he was included in the Essex side for the first match of the season, and in the next four years he did not miss a match. It was the beginning of a career which was to see him appear in 525 matches for Essex, the first when he was 19, the last when he was 52.

He had made a century for Tottenham against Herne Hill in 1895, and at the beginning of the following season he was batting against the great Surrey side of the period and scoring 1 and 51. At the end of the same week, he hit 35 and 20 against the touring Australians. In July, he hit 139 in the match with Warwickshire, at Birmingham. It was the first of 65 centuries he scored for Essex.

From the start, he batted at number three with Charlie McGahey, another six footer, at number four. The pair became known as the Essex Twins. Perrin was at home on any wicket, and he was ever eager for runs although a certain caution tempered his approach as he matured. C.B.Fry called him a scientific batsman who had modelled himself on the great professionals. Certainly, he was studious and perceptive, with strong back play and supple wrists. His height gave added strength to his forward play.

In 1898, he hit 1000 runs in the season for Essex, and he was to achieve that feat in the ten seasons that followed, and in 17 seasons in all. He had grace and style, and perhaps his popularity sprang in part from the fact that there was an ease about him, the ease of one who regarded batting as not the most important thing in the world. He was to say in middle age that when he was young he would rather have had a day's fishing than play in a county match, and all his life he was a keen ornithologist.

He hit six centuries in 1899 to establish an Essex record which lasted until 1922, and he was a prolific scorer in the early part of this century. Between 1903 and 1919, he hit a century in each innings on four occasions, and,

at Chesterfield, in 1904, he hit 343 not out, in an innings of 597 against Derbyshire. Remarkably, there were 68 fours in this brilliant knock, full of magnificent drives. It remains the highest innings ever played for Essex who lost the match.

A shyness had made Perrin a trifle rough in his early days, but he quickly developed a dry wit and a quiet charm, helped, no doubt, by his shrewd successes on the stock market. Threatened with consumption when he was young, he was sent on a liner to Australia by C.E.Green, and the illness was averted. He was confronted by a crisis of a different kind in 1911 when, by seniority and judgment, it seemed that he must be captain of Essex. The honour passed instead to Johnny Douglas, and, after a brief hesitation, Perrin agreed to play on and served Douglas loyally, captaining the side himself on occasions.

He possessed a keen knowledge of the game, and his judgment was respected by all. He was a Test selector in 1926, and from 1931 to 1939 when he was chairman. Jardine said of him, 'Perrin, perhaps alone, was fitted to choose an England side.' He was the first selector to travel all over the country to watch cricketers of interest, and the first to advocate that the selector's occupation was a full time job.

He scored 1000 runs in 1925, but virtually disappeared from cricket the following year. He reappeared for Essex in 1928, captaining the side against Oxford University in the absence of Douglas and scoring 51. He played in the next match and hit 7 and 44 against Northamptonshire, at Kettering. Then he came back for the last game of the season, against Sussex, at Leyton, and was caught and bowled by James Langridge for 0. That was the end of a career which had spanned 32 years.

Peter Perrin was one of the great batsmen of his time, yet he never played for England, nor did he appear for the Gentlemen against the Players. The reason was not hard to find, 'a remarkable incapacity for fielding.' There was no lack of enthusiasm or endeavour. He simply could not cover ground quickly in an athletic manner. He accepted the humour of the situation, and once, when asked if he had really stopped one of Hobbs' boundaries down Vauxhall way, replied, 'Oh, yes. Mind you, they ran eight.'

Dry wit, good humour, good sense, Percy Perrin was a tower of Essex cricket.

M	Inns	NOs	Runs	HS	Avge	100s	Ct
525	894	88	29172	343*	36.19	65	284

Overs	Mds	Runs	Wkts	Avge	Best
183.4	40	740	16	46.25	3/13
33 (five-ball)					

Patrick John PHELAN

Born: Chingford, 9 February 1938.

'Paddy' Phelan was educated at Newport Grammar School and played for Bishop's Stortford when Essex tried him as an off-break bowler and left-handed batsman in the 2nd XI in 1956 and 1957. He turned professional after his first team debut against Gloucestershire at Bristol, May 1958. He began promisingly, capturing the wickets of Milton and Nicholls, and he finished the season with 50 wickets to his credit.

National Service in the RAF robbed him of much county cricket in 1959 and 1960, and he was never quite to fulfil the promise of that first season. His career coincided with that of two other off-spinners, Hurd and Laker, and from the latter, Phelan learned much.

His best season was 1964 when he captured 66 wickets, which included an outstanding performance against Kent at Blackheath. He took 8 for 109 as Kent were bowled out for 258. Unfortunately, Essex were bowled out twice on the second day, for 51 and 101.

With a qualification in mechanical engineering, Phelan retired from cricket at the end of the 1965 season and joined a civil engineering company. He moved to Cementation as contracts manager in their tunnelling division in 1972. He worked for several companies in tunnelling before setting up his own firm, MTC Well Systems. He played cricket for Rotherham, Worksop, where he now lives, and Bridon, and, in 1986, at the age of 48, he played two matches for Cambridgeshire in the Minor Counties Championship. By then, he was playing for Grasshoppers, but a year later he retired and decided to concentrate on classic motor cycle racing.

M	Inns	NOs	Runs	HS	Avge	Ct
154	192	70	1505	63	12.33	67

Overs	Mds	Runs	Wkts	Avge	Best	10/m5/inn	
2960	731	8510	300	28.36	8/109	2	17

Gillette Cup

M	Inns	NOs	Runs	HS	Avge	Ct
1	1	-	4	4	4.00	1

Norbert PHILLIP

Born: Bioche, Dominica, 12 June 1948.

Contrary to general belief, Norbert Phillip was a very experienced cricketer when he joined Essex in 1978, succeeding Keith Boyce as a fast bowler and a hard-hitting middle order batsman. He had played for the Saints club and took 4 for 23 in a 50-overs game against the Duke of Norfolk's XI in 1970. A few weeks later, he made his first-class debut, hitting 96

and taking 2 for 45 against Glamorgan. He was run out for 99 when playing for Combined Islands against Guyana 1972, and the following year he had figures of 5 for 90 and 3 for 35 for Windward Islands against the Australian tourists.

In 1974, Les Ames said that Phillip was the

fastest bowler encountered by D.H.Robins' XI on their tour of the West Indies. Phillip had scored 1000 first-class runs and taken more than 100 first-class wickets before Essex registered him, and he had also enjoyed a season with Colne in the Lancashire League, hitting 747 runs and taking 83 wickets.

If Norbert Phillip did not quite capture the public imagination as Boyce had done - he was a quieter, more introvert personality - his contribution to the first golden age of Essex cricket was immeasurable, and there are those who believe, with justification, that it was his arrival that transformed Essex from near-missers into winners. Boyce, crippled by injury, had been struggling for pace towards the end of his career; Phillip could be very quick, and he proved to be the ideal foil for John Lever who had just reached the peak of his form.

Phillip's batting was violence founded on correct method, and he hit 134 against Gloucestershire in his first season, 1978. He also took 65 Championship wickets and immediately gave evidence of his value. He became a Test player, winning nine caps for West Indies, and he thrived in the Essex 'double' year of 1979.

Few will forget his innings of 80 not out, five sixes and two fours, from 18 overs at The Oval in 1981 in the match that clinched the Sunday League for the first time, nor his 6 for 4 as he and Foster bowled out the same county for 14 at Chelmsford in 1983.

Norbert Phillip left Essex at the end of the 1985 season and returned to Dominica.

M	Inns	NOs	Runs	HS	Avge	100s	Ct
144	201	22	3784	134	21.13	1	45

Overs	Mds	Runs	Wkts	Avge	Best	10/m5/inn	
3477.1	645	10638	423	25.14	6/4	1	18

Sunday League

M	Inns	NOs	Runs	HS	Avge	Ct
111	98	19	1515	95	19.17	20

Overs	Mds	Runs	Wkts	Avge	Best	5/inn
719	46	2879	134	21.48	6/13	1

Benson and Hedges Cup

M	Inns	NOs	Runs	HS	Avge	Ct
32	20	7	232	33*	17.84	2

Overs	Mds	Runs	Wkts	Avge	Best
306.4	39	1113	44	25.29	4/32

Gillette Cup / NatWest Trophy

M	Inns	NOs	Runs	HS	Avge	Ct
15	15	2	201	45	15.46	12

Overs	Mds	Runs	Wkts	Avge	Best
129	16	473	21	22.52	4/26

Leslie Jack PHILLIPS

Born: Leyton, 2 December 1881.
Died: Woodford Wells, 22 April 1979.
A useful batsman and a slow left-arm bowler who learned his cricket at Forest School, Leslie Phillips was one of the many amateurs who appeared for Essex shortly after World War One. He made his debut in the last match of the 1919 season, against Surrey at Leyton. He played in one match in each of the next three seasons, the last being against Dublin University at Brentwood in 1922.

M	Inns	NOs	Runs	HS	Avge
4	5	1	38	19	9.50

Overs	Mds	Runs	Wkts	Avge
4.2	-	31	-	-

Harry Gordon PICKERING

Born: Hackney, London, 18 January 1917.
Died: Seaford, Sussex, 4 March 1984.
A colourful character who played three times for Essex in 1938, Harry Pickering was a customs officer in the Civil Service who would accumulate the leave due to him so that he could play cricket throughout the summer. He was a right-handed batsman who opened the innings in club cricket where he also took a vast number of wickets with his leg-breaks.

He played for very many clubs and sides during the course of a season, and it is claimed that he scored more than 3000 runs in 1937. He had played for Finchley before joining Ilford, and there is a story that he asked Ilford if they wanted to buy some cricket balls from him. The club agreed and then told him that the balls would do in place of the subscription which he had failed to pay.

His successes for Ilford led him to being invited to play three games for Essex as an amateur in 1938. After the war, in which he served in the Army and played cricket, he appeared for Leicestershire. In his role with Customs and Excise, he had been moved to Leicestershire, and he hit three half centuries in his five games for the county. There was talk of his becoming county secretary, but he was later moved to Gatwick and played for the Eastbourne club.

M	Inns	NOs	Runs	HS	Avge
3	6	-	62	17	10.33

Henry PICKETT

Born: Stratford, 26 March 1862.
Died: Aberavon, Glamorgan, 3 October 1907.
Harry Pickett was one of the first of the *great* professional bowlers of Essex County Cricket Club. One does not use the term 'great' lightly, for Pickett must stand alongside men like John Lever, Walter Mead, Ray Smith and others in his unflagging efforts on behalf of the side. If his final record looks meagre when compared to the records of bowlers like Peter Smith and Morris Nichols, it is because he played 13 years for Essex before the county attained first-class status.

He was stocky, strong, of average height, and he bowled quickly off about eight yards, 12 short strides. In his own words, 'An amateur can manage to take a long run without hurting himself, but a professional who has to bowl day after day at the nets as well as in matches is likely to wear himself out very soon if he takes a long run.' One cannot even begin to conjecture how many balls Pickett sent down in the course of his short life.

In 1878, at the age of 16, he took 80 wickets for the Forest Gate Alliance. He moved to the Victoria club and caused a sensation when he took 7 for 15 against the strong Barking side. He became a professional with the Beckton club, a very strong organisation upon whom Essex were to draw heavily for the best part of 30 years.

In 1881, playing for Beckton against Brentwood on what was then the county ground, he took 7 for 1. This was a performance which the county club could not ignore. He was included in the Essex side for the next match and was a regular until the end of the season by which time he had captured 48 wickets. For Beckton, in the same season, he had claimed 110 wickets at just over three runs each.

Engaged by Liverpool CC for the 1882 season, Pickett still played for Essex. He thrived under C.E.Green's leadership, and the next year was back with Beckton. His achievements for Essex drew the attention of

MCC who engaged him in 1884, and he made his first-class debut against Sussex in the opening match of that season. It was to be another ten years before he played a first-class game for Essex, and by then he was 32 and putting on weight.

Harry Pickett was in the Essex side for the match against Leicestershire at Leyton in 1894 although Kortright and Mead were now the main strike bowlers. Kortright had 32 wickets in the season, Mead 54, and Pickett 11. Just as Essex were beginning the most important stage of their history, the career of

one of those who had worked so hard to bring the county first-class status was drawing to a close, and yet his greatest moment was still to come.

Pickett did not begin the first Championship season, 1895, with any hint of good form. He did not capture a wicket until the third match, against MCC, but at the beginning of June came the sensation. On the first day of the match against Leicestershire at Leyton, he opened the bowling, bowled unchanged and took all 10 wickets for 32 runs. This is the longest standing Essex record, and Pickett's figures have been bettered by only six bowlers in the history of the game. 'Though helped by the ground,' wrote *Cricket,* 'which was very fast and somewhat fiery, Pickett's success was due to grand bowling. He kept a splendid length throughout. A collection made for him on the ground realised nearly £20.'

In 1897, he was granted the match against Hampshire at Leyton as a benefit. He was now overweight and was not chosen for the Essex team in his own benefit match. It rained, and the takings were restricted to £150, but 'he was presented with a handsome timepiece, the result of a penny subscription by the schoolboys of Essex, and with a miniature set of stumps, bats and ball in gold and silver, purchased with the proceeds of a halfpenny subscription from the boys of Leyton, West Ham etc.'

Harry Pickett was much loved, and he symbolised all that was good in the county game. He was the honest workman, the bread and butter cricketer upon whom any success has to be founded.

His career ended with that benefit match. His last first-class wicket had come three weeks earlier, appropriately enough against Leicestershire. From 1899 to 1901, he was a first-class umpire, and he coached at Clifton College. He had loved Essex, 'the best little county in the world to play for.'

By 1907, he was penniless, and with a wife and children to support. On 27 September, he walked into the sea off Aberavon. His body was found a week later, but it was not identified until the end of December when some articles of clothing were recognised as being his. His wife died within six months, and there was no provision for the children.

M	Inns	NOs	Runs	HS	Avge	Ct
52	80	34	387	35	8.41	19

Overs	Mds	Runs	Wkts	Avge	Best	10/m5/inn	
1230.4	377	2780	114	24.38	10/32	1	4

Stephen George PLUMB

Born: Wimblish, Essex, 17 January 1954.
Educated at Cranleigh and at Writtle Agricultural College, Stephen Plumb played club cricket for Ilford, Chingford and Saffron Walden and made his debut for Essex 2nd XI and Essex Under-25 XI in 1973. The following year he joined the staff. He played against Cambridge University at Fenner's in both 1975 and 1977, but he was not re-engaged after the 1977 season.

A right-handed batsman who sometimes opened and a medium-pace right-arm bowler, he has played for Norfolk since 1978 and captained the county from 1987 to 1990. He has also led the Minor Counties representative XI. He hit 204 not out against Cumberland in 1988. A farmer in Norfolk, he plays hockey for Cambridgeshire.

M	Inns	NOs	Runs	HS	Avge
2	3	1	68	37*	34.00

Overs	Mds	Runs	Wkts	Avge	Best
14	3	47	2	23.50	2/47

Sunday League

M	Inns	NOs	Runs	HS	Avge
2	2	1	4	2*	4.00

Ian Leslie PONT

Born: Brentwood, 28 August 1961.
Like his brother Keith, Ian Pont was coached by his father and gained rich experience with Hutton. He also spent his last years in education at Brentwood School. He was on the Essex staff for two years before joining Nottinghamshire on a three-year contract in 1982. Released after the end of the 1984 season, he rejoined Essex.

A fast-medium bowler and middle-order batsman, he was renowned for his magnificent throw. He was a late replacement for Neil Foster in the NatWest Cup Final of 1985, Neil having gone down with glandular fever, and Pont's throw from the boundary to run out Chris Broad was one of the turning points of the match. Ironically, this was the only NatWest Trophy match in which Pont appeared.

In 1987, he had his best first-class bowling performance against Lancashire at Chelmsford, and he took five wickets against Surrey at The Oval and made his first 50 in first-class cricket, against Cambridge University, but he was not retained at the end of the season.

For one so young, he has had a remarkably varied career. He coached at Stowe School, played for Buckinghamshire in 1983 and 1984, for Northumberland in 1989 and for Lincolnshire in 1990 and 1991. He played for Natal in 1985-86 and went to the United States to try, unsuccessfully, to win a contract as a baseball pitcher.

When he left Essex he went into business primarily concerned with the marketing of shirts allied to sports teams. He is now in partnership with his brother Keith.

M	Inns	NOs	Runs	HS	Avge	Ct
23	26	9	356	68	20.94	4

Overs	Mds	Runs	Wkts	Avge	Best	5/inn
569.1	70	2141	65	32.94	5/73	3

Sunday League

M	Inns	NOs	Runs	HS	Avge
13	7	3	111	36	27.75

Overs	Mds	Runs	Wkts	Avge	Best
84.2	1	360	14	25.71	2/16

Benson and Hedges Cup

M	Inns	NOs	Runs	HS	Avge
1	-	-	-	-	-

Overs	Mds	Runs	Wkts	Avge
7	-	44	-	-

NatWest Trophy

M	Inns	NOs	Runs	HS	Avge
1	-	-	-	-	-

Overs	Mds	Runs	Wkts	Avge	Best
12	-	54	1	54.00	1/54

Keith Rupert PONT

Born: Wanstead, 16 January 1953.
One of three cricketing brothers who were coached by their father Doug and who graduated through school and club cricket for Hutton, Keith Pont made his debut for Essex in 1970, scoring five and failing to take a wicket in the rain-ruined match against a Jamaican XI. A hard-hitting batsman and a medium-pace bowler, he was of immense value in one-day cricket in particular. Few will forget his all-round performance in the Benson and Hedges Cup semi-final, 1979, when his disciplined cricket against Yorkshire won him the Gold Award and took Essex into their first Final.

Keith Pont was an unlucky cricketer who, perhaps, did not quite fulfil his potential. The arrival of players like Foster, Pringle and Prichard gave Essex a wealth of talent, and Pont was often omitted from the side. On two occasions he was left out immediately after hitting a century.

A man of sharp wit, he was a great asset to the dressing-room, and he shared in all of the county's early triumphs.

He went into business on retirement and has done some broadcasting on local radio. He went into partnership with his brother Ian and was then appointed by the National Cricket Association as organiser for the Greater London area.

M	Inns	NOs	Runs	HS	Avge	100s	Ct
198	305	44	6558	125*	25.12	7	92

Overs	Mds	Runs	Wkts	Avge	Best	5/inn
1088.3	217	3189	96	33.21	5/17	2

Sunday League

M	Inns	NOs	Runs	HS	Avge	Ct
168	142	31	1968	55*	17.72	32

Overs	Mds	Runs	Wkts	Avge	Best
551.4	38	2533	96	26.38	4/22

Benson and Hedges Cup

M	Inns	NOs	Runs	HS	Avge	Ct
55	41	10	648	60*	20.90	11

Overs	Mds	Runs	Wkts	Avge	Best
227.2	19	878	33	26.60	4/60

Gillette Cup / NatWest Trophy

M	Inns	NOs	Runs	HS	Avge	Ct
23	22	2	265	39	13.25	2

Overs	Mds	Runs	Wkts	Avge	Best
88.5	10	338	12	28.16	2/18

Neil Robert POOK

Born: Rainham, 9 February 1967.
A right-handed middle-order batsman and a medium pace bowler, Robert Pook enjoyed successful seasons in the 2nd XI, but he could find no regular place in the first team and left the staff at the end of the 1989 season. Educated at Chafford School, he learned his cricket at the Ilford Cricket School where he later coached for a time before taking up an appointment

in the City. He played for the Ilford club and for Essex Schools' sides, and his one first-class game for Essex was against Cambridge University in 1988 when he held three catches.

He was at one time on the MCC groundstaff, and he played one match for Glamorgan in 1990.

M	Inns	NOs	Runs	HS	Avge	Ct
1	1	-	6	6	6.00	3

Dudley Fairbridge POPE

Born: Barnes, London, 28 October 1906.
Died: Writtle, 8 September 1934.

A right-handed opening batsman with exceptional defensive qualities, Dudley Pope played in 11 matches for Gloucestershire between 1925 and 1927 without ever establishing a regular place in the side. He qualified for Essex by residence and made his debut for the county in 1930, scoring more than 1000 runs in his first season and generally opening the innings with Roy Sheffield.

Educated at Clark's College, Ealing, he had first played for Ealing Dean, but he assisted various clubs while qualifying for Essex and hit 29 centuries in all matches in 1929. A personal friend of Fred Perry, the great tennis player, he went into business with Peter Smith and established a sports outfitters in Chelmsford, a firm which thrives to this day.

He completed 1000 runs in 1932, 1933 and 1934, hitting 690 runs in the last nine matches of the last of the seasons. In the final match of the season, at the end of August he scored 23 and 108 against his former county, Gloucestershire. A week later, he was killed in a road accident. He and Peter Smith had planned to spend a week-end in Walton-on-Naze, and Smith had driven on ahead. Smith heard a crash and returned to find that Pope had died instantly when the car he was driving had collided with a motor lorry near Writtle. One of their colleagues learned that Pope had hired the car he was driving, and that when he put his foot on the brake nothing had happened.

M	Inns	NOs	Runs	HS	Avge	100s	Ct
148	248	14	6443	161	27.53	7	35

Overs	Mds	Runs	Wkts	Avge	Best
58	3	272	4	68.00	1/11

Adam Gordon POWELL

Born: Boxted, 17 August 1912.
Died: Sandwich, Kent, 7 June 1982.

A first-rate wicket-keeper who was in the Charterhouse XI for three years, Adam Powell went up to Magdalene College, Cambridge, but, to the surprise of the majority, he did not get his blue until his third year, 1934. By then, he had already made his debut for Essex, which came in 1932.

Coached by Herbert Strudwick, Powell was neat and clean in all that he did and stood up to all but the very fastest of bowlers. He was a capable late order batsman and played a significant part in Essex's innings victory over Yorkshire at Southend in 1934. He toured Australia and New Zealand in the MCC's goodwill tour, 1935-36, and also made three tours of Egypt and two of Canada when no first-class matches were played.

He last played for Essex in 1937 after which the doctors forbade him to play serious first-class cricket. He continued to play club cricket and assisted Suffolk from 1938 to 1953. He captained the side when they won the Minor Counties Championship in 1946.

M	Inns	NOs	Runs	HS	Avge	Ct/st
23	35	7	495	62*	17.67	30/8

Henry Charles PREECE

Born: Wembley, Middlesex, 27 October 1867.
Died: Highgate, Middlesex, 17 September 1937.

A stylish right-handed batsman, Henry Preece played for Cheshire in 1893, and, after scoring heavily for Bees CC, he was brought into the Essex side in 1895. Burns was omitted to accommodate him in the game against Hampshire at Leyton which Essex won, Preece scoring 49 in the second innings. He played in the next match, against Yorkshire, made 0 and 6 and was not seen again.

He worked in the India office and, tragically, lost his sight at an early age. He became lecturer in History at King's College, London University, and he worked assiduously on behalf of the blind.

M	Inns	NOs	Runs	HS	Avge
2	4	-	74	49	18.50

Edward Robert PRESLAND

Born: High Beech, 27 March 1943.
Brought up in East Ham, Eddie Presland first played club cricket for Romford, but later moved to Orsett and Thurrock. He joined the Essex staff in 1962 and made his debut against Nottinghamshire at Trent Bridge when he batted number nine and scored 23. A right-handed batsman and off-break bowler, he made occasional appearan-

ces until the end of the 1965 season when he was not re-engaged. It was agreed, however, that he would play on a match to match basis.

He did this until the end of the 1970 season, making his last first-class appearances that year, but he played in Sunday League matches until 1972.

Presland was a very fine fielder as befits a man who was a professional footballer with West Ham United, Crystal Palace and Colchester United. A full-back, he made 61 appearances for Crystal Palace.

M	Inns	NOs	Runs	HS	Avge	Ct
30	41	4	625	51	16.89	24

Overs	Mds	Runs	Wkts	Avge	Best
295.1	61	761	13	58.53	2/19

Sunday League

M	Inns	NOs	Runs	HS	Avge	Ct
19	15	4	149	38	13.55	6

Overs	Mds	Runs	Wkts	Avge
1	-	4	-	-

Gillette Cup

M	Inns	NOs	Runs	HS	Avge	Ct
5	5	1	38	17	9.50	3

Overs	Mds	Runs	Wkts	Avge	Best
41	4	148	3	49.33	1/2

Kenneth Charles PRESTON

Born: Goodmayes, 22 August 1925.
The arrival of Ken Preston from Romford in 1948 seemed to have given Essex a strike bowler of pace and of international potential. He was not only quick, but he was hostile, willing to hit the ball hard late in the order and an excellent fielder who held some fine catches close to the wicket.

'Casey' had played for the 2nd XI against Sussex in 1947 and had taken 0 for 71, but on his first-class debut, against Glamorgan at Cardiff, May, 1948, he captured the wicket of Clift in his third over. He took 5 for 85 against Worcestershire in his debut season which gave every sign of future greatness, but in the winter of 1948-49, he broke a leg playing football. The injury was more serious than it would be today, perhaps, and Ken missed the whole of the 1949 season.

Dogged, determined, cheerful, he eased his way back into the game in 1950. He shortened his run and reduced his pace, but he was still a most effective fast medium pace bowler with a lethal leg-cutter. He was selected for the Players against the Gentlemen at Scarborough in 1951, which was the nearest he came to international honours, but for Essex he was a constant source of strength. He looked like a farmer, open and bluff, and he was a man of the utmost perseverance and determination. He was an immense favourite with the crowd, not least because he had an appetite for hitting sixes.

Like the best wine, he improved with age. In 1956, he took 7 for 55 against Northamptonshire at Peterborough, and the following season he captured 140 wickets at 20.35 runs each. In 1959, he hit 70 against Derbyshire, and three years later, he returned his best match analysis, 12 for 85 against Lancashire at Leyton.

In 1955, he became secretary/organiser of the Essex Supporters' Club, and he worked hard to raise much money for the county club at a period when the economic situation of the club was uncertain. His last game for Essex was against Leicestershire at Grace Road at the end of the 1964 season. By now, he was no longer opening the bowling, but in six matches in his farewell season, he took 15 wickets and finished second to Trevor Bailey in the bowling averages.

He took up a position at Brentwood School as cricket coach and manager of the school shop, with emphasis on the latter in the years before his retirement. He still enjoys an occasional game of golf.

M	Inns	NOs	Runs	HS	Avge	Ct
391	460	165	3024	70	10.25	344

Overs	Mds	Runs	Wkts	Avge	Best	10/m	5/inn
11453	2482	30288	1155	26.22	7/55	2	37

Gillette Cup

M	Inns	NOs	Runs	HS	Avge	Ct
2	2	1	6	4*	6.00	1

Overs	Mds	Runs	Wkts	Avge	Best
28	1	110	2	55.00	2/39

Eric James PRICE

Born: Middleton, Lancashire, 27 October 1918.
Eric Price was a cricketer who did not fulfil his promise. He joined the Lancashire staff in 1939 and made his debut after World War Two. He topped the county's bowling averages,

took 82 wickets and was selected for a Test Trial at Canterbury. He seemed to be out of favour at Old Trafford the following season, 1947, where Ken Cranston had taken over as captain from Fallows, and appeared in only nine matches. He left the staff at the end of the season and joined Essex.

After a moderate first season, 1948, he fared better for his new county in his second year, taking 8 for 125 against Worcestershire at New Road. At the end of the season, he expressed the desire to return north and was released. He joined Middleton in the Central Lancashire League, the club with whom he had previously been associated, and he also assisted St Anne's and Kearsley.

M	Inns	NOs	Runs	HS	Avge	Ct
43	56	16	214	26*	5.35	24

Overs	Mds	Runs	Wkts	Avge	Best	5/inn
1031.3	238	3013	92	32.75	8/125	4

Paul John PRICHARD

Born: Billericay, 7 January 1965.
Paul Prichard first played for Essex Schools at the age of nine, and he was immediately recognisable as a batsman of elegance and style. He had been nurtured at the Hutton club where his father was a noted player and had been much helped by Doug Pont. He graduated through the Essex Schools' sides to England Schools and England Youth sides and joined the Orsett and Thurrock club.

He was on the Essex staff by the age of 16 and made his first-class debut in 1984. Called into the side at the end of May, he went to the wicket against Worcestershire at Worcester with his side on 22 for 4. He hit an immaculate 86 and remained in the side for the rest of the season. His maiden first-class century came against Lancashire at Old Trafford. In style and temperament, there was more than a hint of Keith Fletcher.

As a schoolboy, Prichard had kept wicket,

but in the county side he quickly won praise for his outstanding catching close to the wicket. A golden future was predicted for Prichard, but his career suffered a dreadful setback early in 1987 when he had a finger shattered by a ball from the South African pace man Allan Donald. Both physically and mentally, it took the Essex batsman a long time to recover.

In 1990, he proved his rehabilitation was complete with an innings of 245 against Leicestershire at Chelmsford. He and Gooch put on 403 for the second wicket, a record partnership for the county for any wicket. Two years later, Prichard hit 1485 runs and was named as Britannic Assurance Player of the Season. He was also selected for the England 'A' tour of Australia. In 1993, he was vice-captain of Essex, leading the side on many occasions in Gooch's absence.

He is a batsman in the classical mould, full of delicate cuts and exquisite drives. Even in the limited-over dash for runs, he never profanes the beauty of his style. No batsman in England gives more aesthetic pleasure.

Prichard has played grade cricket in Australia for some winters and coaches at the Chelmsford Indoor School.

M	Inns	NOs	Runs	HS	Avge	100s	Ct
224	359	43	11498	245	36.38	23	146

Overs	Mds	Runs	Wkts	Avge	Best
48.1	1	497	2	248.50	1/28

Sunday League

M	Inns	NOs	Runs	HS	Avge	100s	Ct
126	108	9	2507	107	25.32	2	27

Benson and Hedges Cup

M	Inns	NOs	Runs	HS	Avge	100s	Ct
41	39	8	929	107	29.96	1	10

NatWest Trophy

M	Inns	NOs	Runs	HS	Avge	Ct
21	20	2	675	94	37.50	10

Derek Raymond PRINGLE

Born: Nairobi, Kenya, 18 September 1958.

Derek Pringle was born into cricket. His father, Don, played for East Africa in the first World Cup, 1975. Derek excelled at Felsted and went up to Cambridge where he won his blue as a freshman, 1979, and in the two succeeding years. He was elected captain in 1982, but he took the unprecedented step of missing the Varsity match in order to play for England. He went to Australia with the England side the following winter, and it seemed that a long test career had begun. In fact, his appearances at international level were to be spasmodic although he became an invaluable member of the one-day side and appeared in the World Cup Final, 1992.

He first played for Essex shortly after leaving Felsted, 1978, and he was to play a major part in the triumphs of the 1980s. Tall, bespectacled, later to adopt contact lenses, strong, he had a languidity in his movement and a proneness to bizarre injury which caused him to be regarded as something of a comic figure in his earlier days. His mighty hitting and relentlessly accurate fast medium pace bowling which would nip off the pitch with unexpected venom converted the critics, and 'Del Boy' became one of the most popular of cricketers, held in the warmest affection by the Essex crowd and cheered at international level.

Derek Pringle became a character with his enormous boots in which a hole was cut to accommodate the big toe. He was also a top class all-rounder, and his bowling brought him 94 wickets at modest cost in 1989. In limited-over cricket, he would invariably bowl the closing overs, for his captains had the utmost trust in his control. He proved his worth with his ultimate victory over Derek Randall in the NatWest Bank Trophy Final of 1985.

A man of intelligence, wit and genial humour, he displayed his capabilities as a journalist with periodical articles on cricket in *The Daily Telegraph* which were refreshing in their honesty and unashamed criticism of the establishment of the game. They brought him some fines from the TCCB, but they gave immense pleasure to their readers. It was sad, but no surprise, when he decided to retire at

the end of the 1993 season to take up an appointment as cricket correspondent of *The Independent on Sunday*.

M	Inns	NOs	Runs	HS	Avge	100s	Ct
213	280	55	6325	128	28.12	5	115

Overs	Mds	Runs	Wkts	Avge	Best	10/m	5/inn
5300.3	1297	14365	566	25.38	7/18	2	20

Sunday League

M	Inns	NOs	Runs	HS	Avge	Ct
151	115	25	2315	81*	25.72	42

Overs	Mds	Runs	Wkts	Avge	Best	5/inn
1016.5	59	4747	177	26.81	5/41	1

Benson and Hedges Cup

M	Inns	NOs	Runs	HS	Avge	Ct
59	47	13	1028	77*	30.23	16

Overs	Mds	Runs	Wkts	Avge	Best	5/inn
570.4	74	2003	92	21.77	5/35	2

NatWest Trophy

M	Inns	NOs	Runs	HS	Avge	Ct
34	30	6	541	80*	22.54	11

Overs	Mds	Runs	Wkts	Avge	Best	5/inn
334.5	55	1102	41	26.87	5/12	2

Graham Charles PRITCHARD

Born: Farnborough, Hampshire, 14 January 1942.

Educated at King's School, Canterbury, where his fast bowling gave the school one of their most successful periods, Pritchard played for Kent 2nd XI before going up to Cambridge. He disappointed in his first two seasons at university and did not get his blue until 1964. He had pace and stamina, but he failed to maintain a consistent length.

He appeared in seven matches for Essex in 1965 and took 4 for 24 against Warwickshire at Coventry, but after three more games the following season, he decided to return to teaching.

M	Inns	NOs	Runs	HS	Avge	Ct
10	11	2	19	8	2.11	3

Overs	Mds	Runs	Wkts	Avge	Best
129	20	406	7	58.00	4/24

Stanley PROFITT

Born: Oldham, Lancashire, 8 October 1910.

Stan Profitt played his club cricket for Clayhall before joining the Essex staff. He had played for Lancashire 2nd XI at the age of 17, and he joined Essex in 1936. A left-handed opening batsman and a left-arm spinner, he appeared in seven matches in 1937, but he was not seen after that season.

He was far better known as a table-tennis international and Swaythling Cup player.

M	Inns	NOs	Runs	HS	Avge	Ct
7	14	-	170	39	12.14	1

Overs	Mds	Runs	Wkts	Avge
9	-	32	-	-

Sydney Charles PUDDEFOOT

Born: Limehouse, London, 17 October 1894.
Died: Rochford, 2 October 1972.
A right-handed batsman and a left-arm medium-pace bowler, Syd Puddefoot appeared in eight matches as a professional in 1922 and 1923. He captured the wicket of G.R.Jackson, the Derbyshire captain, in his first game, but thereafter had little success. He was better known as an outstanding soccer player with West Ham United, Falkirk and Blackburn Rovers. He played twice for England in 1926 and won an FA Cup winners' medal with Blackburn Rovers in 1928. When he moved from West Ham to Falkirk in 1922 he was the first player to be transferred at a fee of £5,000.

M	Inns	NOs	Runs	HS	Avge	Ct
8	8	2	101	42	16.83	2

Overs	Mds	Runs	Wkts	Avge	Best
33	6	105	1	105.00	1/34

George Richard PULLINGER

Born: Islington, London, 14 March 1920.
Died: Thurrock, 4 August 1982.
George Pullinger went to school in Chadwell St Mary and played club cricket for Aveley. A right-arm fast medium pace bowler, he did well for Essex in the Minor Counties Championship in 1948 and played 16 first team matches as an amateur in 1949

when Ken Preston was injured. Against Middlesex at Lord's, 'Pullinger made a startling debut as opening bowler for Essex. In his first spell he broke the back of the Middlesex batting by taking 4 wickets for 63, and he enjoyed the distinction of twice dismissing Denis Compton.' He took 4 for 87 in the second innings, but Essex lost.

Later that season he took 5 for 54 against Somerset at Bath, but he appeared only twice in 1950 and then disappeared from first-class cricket. He joined Orsett Cricket Club and concentrated on his work for Thames Board Mills.

M	Inns	NOs	Runs	HS	Avge	Ct
18	20	11	53	14*	5.88	14

Overs	Mds	Runs	Wkts	Avge	Best	5/inn
519.3	109	1557	41	37.97	5/54	1

James Hamilton PURVES

Born: Hemel Hempstead, Hertfordshire, 4 December 1937.
A left-handed batsman who was educated at Uppingham, James Purves played cricket for Free Foresters and MCC. In 1960, he opened for Essex against Cambridge University at Fenner's, and the following year he appeared in four matches for the county without making his mark.

M	Inns	NOs	Runs	HS	Avge	Ct
5	7	-	36	14	5.14	1

Arnold Bertram QUICK

Born: Clacton, 10 February 1915.
Died: Colchester, 23 July 1990.
Arnold Quick's prowess as a hard-hitting batsman with Frinton and Clacton for whom he once hit six sixes in an over attracted the attention of Essex, and he appeared in the last three matches of the 1936 season, making his debut

against Nottinghamshire at Clacton, his home ground.

He was never able to play regularly because of his involvement with the family firm as a newspaper publisher. He was later to become a director of IPC. He hit a maiden 50 against Nottinghamshire, at Trent Bridge 1937, but he never quite did himself justice as a batsman at county level. He was a fine fielder, distinguished by his long sweater and a very strong throw. He probably lost his best years to the war in which he served as an officer in the Royal Marines.

He reappeared for Essex in 1952, hitting 57 in his last innings, against Yorkshire, at Clacton. He did tremendous work for the county in leading the 2nd XI from 1956 to 1963 and helped to bring on several young players. He was treasurer of the county club until 1964, a trustee from 1965 to 1976, and a vice-president from 1965 until his death. He was chairman from 1972 to 1976.

M	Inns	NOs	Runs	HS	Avge	Ct
19	32	1	433	57	13.96	12

Overs	Mds	Runs	Wkts	Avge
1.5	-	10	-	-

Stanley Edgar Vivian QUIN

Born: Bishops Glen, Orange Free State, South Africa, 3 April 1896.
Died: Bishops Glen, Orange Free State, South Africa, 9 April 1970.
Stan Quin played for Essex against Middlesex in the rain-ruined match at Lord's in 1924. Returning to his native South Africa, he captained Orange Free State against Rhodesia and Griqualand West in 1930-31 season. An innings of three in the first of these matches for the Free State was his only score in five first-class innings, and he failed to take a wicket with his medium pace off-breaks.

M	Inns	NOs	Runs	HS	Avge
1	1	-	0	0	0.00

Overs	Mds	Runs	Wkts	Avge
7	1	13	-	-

Maxwell RAISON

Born: Wanstead, 7 November 1901.
Died: Theberton, Suffolk, 26 July 1988.
Max Raison was one of several amateurs who

assisted Essex in the late 1920s. His 17 matches for the county were played between 1928 and 1930. He was a middle-order right-handed batsman and a medium-pace bowler,  born in Essex and educated at Forest School. In the late 1920s, he was captain of Dulwich CC, and most of his cricket after that was played for Free Foresters and the Gentlemen of Essex.

For the county, his most notable bowling performance was against Gloucestershire at Chelmsford in 1928. He took 5 for 104 and was presented with the silver-mounted ball. One of his victims was the great Wally Hammond, bowled for 244! In fact, Raison took 13 of his 14 first-class wickets in his seven matches that first season.

He was more noted for his success in the publishing world. He was the founder of *Farmer's Weekly, The Eagle, New Scientist* and *New Society,* and was general manager of *Picture Post* from its inception.

One of his sons, Timothy, is Conservative MP for Aylesbury and held various ministerial posts in Mrs Thatcher's governments.

M	Inns	NOs	Runs	HS	Avge	Ct
17	27	2	451	57	18.04	6

Overs	Mds	Runs	Wkts	Avge	Best	5/inn
153.2	18	575	14	41.07	5/104	1

Louis Henry Roy RALPH

Born: Upton Park, 22 May 1920.
Educated at Clark's College, Ilford, Roy Ralph was a club cricketer with Hale End and Ilford, and he was 33 years old when he first played for Essex as an amateur. He was a medium pace right-arm bowler who could bowl all day, and, batting low in the order, he hit the ball hard and often.

Weakened by injuries, Essex called upon him to play against a Commonwealth XI at Romford in June 1953. He made 12, and when eight wickets were down he was brought on to bowl. He had the great Everton Weekes caught behind with his fourth delivery in first-class cricket, and in the second innings, he accounted for Frank Worrell and Ken Grieves as Essex claimed their first win of the season.

Short, stocky and supremely fit, he took 7 for 42 against Gloucestershire at Romford in 1956 and had match figures of 12 for 104 against Nottinghamshire on the same ground three years later. He was a tremendous asset to the Essex attack and, able to play regularly, he took 102 wickets in 1957. The following season, at the age of 38, he turned professional, and he continued to enjoy success until his retirement after the 1961 season.

He assisted Longton in the North Staffordshire League for two seasons, coached at Bancroft's School and returned to club cricket for Ilford. He decided not to follow his father into the tailoring business, but became coach at the Sports Centre at Oakfield School. He holds coaching diplomas in cricket, soccer, golf and archery and so was a man highly qualified for the job. Injury forced him to retire in 1979.

A capable golfer, he also played soccer for Clapton Orient Reserves for a time.

M	Inns	NOs	Runs	HS	Avge	Ct
174	262	39	3763	73	16.87	143

Overs	Mds	Runs	Wkts	Avge	Best	10/m	5/inn
4071.1	903	11053	460	24.02	7/42	3	19

Arnold Holcombe READ

Born: Snaresbrook, 24 January 1880.
Died: Englefield Green, Surrey, 20 May 1957.
Father of 'Hopper' Read, Arnold Read was a right-handed batsman and slow medium pace bowler who assisted Essex as an amateur between 1904 and 1910. His best season was in 1978 when, reappearing after two years absence, he hit 181 runs in ten completed innings and took 30 wickets. His outstanding performance was at Northampton where he bowled Essex to an innings victory by taking 7 for 75 when the home side were forced to follow-on.

He was educated at Winchester, and his passion for golf caused him to move to Surrey where he delighted in the courses.

M	Inns	NOs	Runs	HS	Avge	Ct
22	30	6	419	70	17.45	7

Overs	Mds	Runs	Wkts	Avge	Best	5/inn
360.2	77	1192	38	31.36	7/75	1

Holcombe Douglas READ

Born: Woodford Green, 28 January 1910.
The son of A.H.Read who played for Essex between 1904 and 1910 and who, enchanted by the golf course at Sunningdale, moved to Engelfield Green in Surrey at the beginning of World War One, H.D.Read was qualified to play for both Essex, by birth, and for Surrey,

by residence. He was educated at Winchester where he got the nickname 'Hopper', and he played his club cricket in Surrey for whom he appeared against both Oxford and Cambridge in 1933. A bowler of considerable pace, he was injured in those matches and did not do himself justice. Accordingly, Surrey took no further interest in him and raised no objection when Essex asked if they could play him against Lancashire in July. He did not take a wicket, but he had become one of the few cricketers to appear for two different counties in the same season.

The following season, he took his intermediate accountancy examinations and was available to assist Essex from the beginning of June onwards. He took 54 Championship wickets, claiming Jack Hobbs as his first wicket, and beginning with what was to be a career best 7 for 35.

His reputation as a pace bowler was growing at the time that England were looking for a successor to Larwood, and, in 1935, he took 74 Championship wickets. It was he and Nichols who bowled out Yorkshire for 31 and 99 at Huddersfield so shocking the cricket world. Read had match figures of 9 for 62, and three weeks later, he was in the England side for the final Test against South Africa. In a high-scoring match, he had figures of 4 for 136 and 2 for 64.

That winter, he toured Australia and New Zealand with the MCC side, a side composed mainly of amateurs who were seeking to heal the wounds caused by the Body-line tour. On his return to England, he was confronted by the senior partner of the firm for whom he worked who said simply, 'Well bowled, Mr Read. Now you've got to make up your mind whether you're going to be a professional cricketer or a professional accountant.' 'Hopper' Read never played county cricket again.

A genial man of great charm, he played club cricket, bowling at a reduced pace, until after World War Two. He lived in the same house at Engelfield Green for 63 years before moving to Chichester. He and his wife then retired to Nether Stowey, near Bridgwater, in Somerset, where they live within 100 yards of John Wilcox, son of one of 'Hopper' Read's former captains.

M	Inns	NOs	Runs	HS	Avge	Ct
32	41	15	104	17*	4.00	14

Overs	Mds	Runs	Wkts	Avge	Best	10/m	5/inn
749.5	122	2675	131	21.20	7/35	1	7

Ian REDPATH

Born: Basildon, 12 September 1965.
Ian Redpath graduated through Basildon Schools cricket, Essex and England Schools, and Benfleet, and Orsett and Thurrock Cricket clubs to the Essex staff in 1985. He was given a run in the first team in 1987, but

he was not retained at the end of the 1988 season.

A quiet and unassuming opening batsman, he had a trial for Derbyshire in 1989 and later played grade cricket in Australia. He also had a position in banking.

M	Inns	NOs	Runs	HS	Avge	Ct
7	12	1	128	46	11.63	2

Sunday League

M	Inns	NOs	Runs	HS	Avge
3	1	1	11	11*	-

Daniel REESE

Born: Christchurch, New Zealand, 27 January 1879.
Died: Christchurch, New Zealand, 12 June 1953.
Dan Reese began a distinguished career for New Zealand at the age of 19. An aggressive left-handed batsman and a slow left-arm bowler from Canterbury, he went with the New Zealand side to Australia in 1898-99 and emerged as a very successful all-rounder.

He worked in Melbourne for two years as a draughtsman and played for the Melbourne club, but returned home in time to play against Lord Hawke's team, 1902-03. While others around him fell, he hit 148 against the Englishmen who included F.L.Fane in their XI.

Reese then took a boat to England – he was an inveterate traveller – and in 1903 he assisted W.G.Grace's London County side. He also played for the Tottenham club alongside Stan Trick who appeared for Essex in five matches between 1909 and 1915. Against Essex Club and Ground, Reese hit 98, and Borradaile invited him to Leyton for a trial. In 1906, Reese appeared in eight matches for Essex and hit 20 and 70 in the game against the West Indians.

He returned to New Zealand in time to captain his country against MCC in 1906-07, and he led the side to Australia, 1913-14, when he topped both the batting and bowling averages. His international career ended when Sims' side came to New Zealand a few months later.

Dan Reese captained New Zealand in eight of his 12 appearances. He first played for Canterbury in 1895 at the age of 16, and he represented the province until 1921. He had been an apprentice engineer, a draughtsman and had worked as a marine engineer in order to come to England to play cricket. Later, he was in the timber trade, which involved much travel, and with his brother as his business partner, Reese Brothers Ltd became one of the most successful enterprises and most well-known in New Zealand.

Dan Reese was president of the Canterbury Cricket Association from 1925 until his death, and he was also a member of the management committee of the New Zealand Cricket Council and was president for many years.

In 1948, he published a fascinating autobiography, *Was It All Cricket?*, and his brother Tom compiled a two-volume history of New Zealand cricket, 1841 to 1933.

M	Inns	NOs	Runs	HS	Avge
8	15	2	198	70	15.23

Overs	Mds	Runs	Wkts	Avge	Best
43	5	165	6	27.50	4/55

William REEVES

Born: Cambridge, 22 June 1875.
Died: Hammersmith, London, 22 March 1944.
Bill Reeves was one of the great humorists of cricket, the game which was his life. He married into Essex cricket. E.C.Freeman, the head groundsman at the county ground at Leyton was his father-in-law, and E.J. Freeman his brother-in-law. Bill joined the groundstaff at Leyton and made his debut for Essex against Warwickshire at Edgbaston in May 1897. An aggressive batsman and a medium pace bowler, he scored four in his first match and did not take a wicket.

By 1904, he had developed into a good, hard-working county all-rounder, taking 106 wickets. The following season he scored over 1000 runs and hit 135 in two hours against Lancashire at Leyton. In 1906, he and Buckenham put on 163 in 70 minutes for the eighth wicket against Sussex at Leyton. Reeves scored 104. Even in his last season, 1921, he hit 71 out of 90 in 50 minutes against Yorkshire.

Perhaps his most memorable bowling performance came in 1901, inevitably at Leyton, when he took the last five Derbyshire wickets in 11 balls without conceding a run.

Figures give no indication of Bill Reeves' worth to Essex, for no man served a county better. He had bowled to Hobbs on Parker's Piece before that great batsman joined Surrey, and when his playing days were over he sent down many more overs as a member of the Lord's groundstaff and helped many a schoolboy at the Easter coaching classes.

He was better known as a first-class umpire, standing from the time of his retirement until the outbreak of World War Two. He umpired in five Test matches, the first at Edgbaston, England v South Africa, 1924, and the last at the Oval 15 years later when England and West Indies drew the last Test match to be played before war ended international cricket for six years.

Reeves' witty remarks as an umpire have passed into cricket folk lore. It was he who told the batsman who protested that he wasn't out to look in the paper the following morning, and it was Reeves who said to the bowler notorious for his appealing, 'There's only one man who appeals more than you do.' 'Who's that?' asked the bowler, 'Dr Barnado,' said Reeves.

He died following an operation.

M	Inns	NOs	Runs	HS	Avge	100s	Ct
271	422	34	6451	135	16.62	3	115

Overs	Mds	Runs	Wkts	Avge	Best	10/m	5/inn
4939.1	1085	16137	581	27.77	7/33	5	37
175.2 (five-ball)							

Robert John RICHARDS

Born: Winchester, Hampshire, 5 June 1934.
Senior coach at the Indoor Cricket School at Chelmsford, Bob Richards often kept wicket for the 2nd XI. He was brought up in Basildon and played his club cricket for Westcliff and Leigh. He appeared in the match against Jamaica at Leyton in 1970, but the game was ruined by rain.

M	Inns	NOs	Runs	HS	Avge
1	-	-	-	-	-

Charles Stewart RICHARDSON

Born: Terling, 23 March 1885.
Died: Great Totham, 5 April 1948.
C.S.Richardson was chairman of the County Club from 1928 until 1945, and he became the first post-war president in 1946.

His first task as chairman was to negotiate the sacking of Johnny Douglas, a matter which was not well handled, but he later gave the club great service and contributed much towards a successful period in the 1930s.

He played once for Essex, against Yorkshire at Headingley in 1914.

M	Inns	NOs	Runs	HS	Avge	Ct
1	1	-	15	15	15.00	1

James Vere RICHARDSON

Born: Prenton, Cheshire, 16 December 1903.
An outstanding rugby player for Oxford University and for England, James Richardson was also a very useful cricketer. A right-handed batsman and a right-arm medium pace bowler, he first played for Essex in 1924 while still at Oxford. In one of his early innings for the county, he hit a most attractive 82 in two hours against Hampshire. His innings included ten fours and gave much hope for the future.

He was awarded his blue in 1925, but he was able to play for Essex in only three matches that summer, and three more the following summer marked the end of his time with the county.

M	Inns	NOs	Runs	HS	Avge	Ct
14	18	3	300	82	20.00	8

Overs	Mds	Runs	Wkts	Avge	Best
78	11	253	7	36.14	2/55

Percy John RICHARDSON

Born: Herman Hill, Snaresbrook, 2 April 1891.
Died: Wray Park, Reigate, Surrey, 23 March 1964.
Educated at Clifton College, Percy Richardson went up to Cambridge University where he played one game for the XI in 1912. The same season he appeared in two matches for Essex, against the South Africans and against Hampshire. The second of these matches was ruined by rain, and Richardson did not bat.

M	Inns	NOs	Runs	HS	Avge	Ct
2	2	-	34	21	17.00	1

Overs	Mds	Runs	Wkts	Avge
5	-	12	-	-

Kenneth Roy RICKARDS

Born: Rollington Town, Kingston, Jamaica, 22 August 1923.
Ken Rickards played for Jamaica over a period of 13 years and went on two tours with the West Indies. He was restricted to two Test matches, but he was a highly entertaining right-handed batsman and leg-break bowler whose international career was limited because of the wealth of talent available to

West Indies. He played league cricket for Darwen and was in the Commonwealth XI v England XI at Kingston, Surrey, in 1952. The following season, he played for Essex against the Commonwealth XI at Romford.

M	Inns	NOs	Runs	HS	Avge
1	2	-	25	13	12.50

Henry Wadsworth RIDING

Born: Epping, 19 September 1899.
Died: Forest Side, Chingford, 21 May 1923.
Educated at Bancrofts, Henry Riding was a right-handed batsman who played for Essex against Lancashire in the last match of the 1921 season. He died only two years later.

M	Inns	NOs	Runs	HS	Avge
1	2	-	23	16	11.50

Gerald Vernon Newport RIDLEY

Born: Felsted, 23 October 1897.
Died: Chignal St James, 12 November 1953.
Better known as a Justice of the Peace and as a committee member of the county club from 1929 until his death, Gerald Ridley was in the XI at Marlborough and made occasional appearances for Essex between 1922 and 1926. A right-handed batsman, he hit 54 against Gloucestershire at Colchester on his one appearance in 1924.

M	Inns	NOs	Runs	HS	Avge	Ct
6	11	-	113	54	10.27	3

Frank Henry RIST

Born: Wandsworth, London, 30 March 1914.
Few people outside Essex would be able to recognise the worth of Frank Rist to cricket in the county. He joined Essex in 1932, made his debut in 1934 and played his last game against Leicestershire, at Colchester, in July 1953. During his long association with the county he appeared in only 65 matches and batted anywhere in the order. He opened the innings in the famous victory over Yorkshire at Huddersfield in 1935, and when asked to keep wicket, as he often was in 1948 when Wade was incapacitated, he generally batted as low as nine or ten. He was a cricketer whose worth could never be gauged by statistics.

For several years, particularly after World

War Two in which he served in the RAF, he was mainly concerned with the welfare and development of young players and simply played himself when required. In 1949, he became the county club's official coach, and, in the difficult financial period in the late 60s, he ran the 2nd XI and coached without receipt of any salary. The county's debt to him is incalculable.

He bowled only once in first-class cricket, and that was at Northampton in 1952 when Brookes and Barrick both hit double centuries for the home side who made 532 for 8 in reply to Essex's 428 for 9. Frank Rist's victim was the England captain, Freddie Brown.

Rist was very well known as a footballer. Clapton Orient signed him from Grays Athletic, but he spent most of his career as centre-half for Charlton Athletic. He also played for Colchester United when they were in the Southern League and for Tonbridge. In the mid-1950s, he looked after West Ham United's 'A' team.

He played a few games for Walthamstow after he left the county staff in 1968, but by then he was already a director of Arthur Sedgwick's sports goods and outfitters in Walthamstow, which always had close links with Essex CCC.

M	Inns	NOs	Runs	HS	Avge	Ct/st
65	108	9	1496	62	15.11	35/5

Overs	Mds	Runs	Wkts	Avge	Best
4.1	2	8	1	8.00	1/8

Darren David John ROBINSON

Born: Braintree, 2 March 1973.
Darren Robinson graduated to the Essex staff

from the whole layer of Essex Schools and Essex representative sides. A right-handed batsman, he was coached at the county's indoor school, and his development owed much to men like Bob Richards and Nick King, and Graham Saville and Ray East.

He joined the staff in 1992 and made an impressive first-class debut against Kent at Maidstone the following season. In his second match, against Gloucestershire at Bristol, he was the Essex top-scorer with 67.

Robinson has completed a diploma course in Building and Construction at Chelmsford College of Further Education.

M	Inns	NOs	Runs	HS	Avge	Ct
3	5	-	150	67	30.00	3

Sunday League

M	Inns	NOs	Runs	HS	Avge
1	1	-	2	2	2.00

Lieutenant-Colonel Douglas Charles ROBINSON

Born: Lawrence Weston, Bristol, Gloucestershire, 20 April 1884.
Died: Ham Court, Charlton Kings, Gloucestershire, 29 July 1963.

A member of the great Bristol paper manufacturing family, Douglas Robinson chose the Army for a career. Both his father and his brother played for Gloucestershire, and, having kept wicket for Marlborough in 1901, Robinson first played for his native county in 1905.

In 1908, with a residential qualification, he appeared for Essex in seven matches and kept with distinction. Having gained his commission, he served in World War One and was awarded the Military Cross. He returned to Gloucestershire and captained the county from 1924 to 1926.

Robinson had gone as wicket-keeper with the MCC side to South Africa, 1913-14, under the captaincy of Johnny Douglas, but he fell ill before any matches were played and took no further part in events.

M	Inns	NOs	Runs	HS	Avge	Ct/st
7	12	1	148	37	13.45	12/1

Ralf Hubert ROBINSON

Born: Stratford, 28 June 1885.
Died: Westhoek Ridge, Ypres, Belgium, 23 August 1917.

A wicket-keeper of considerable talent, Ralf Robinson played for Wanstead and was considered to be one of the best amateur 'keepers in the country although his county career was limited to four matches in 1912, a troubled year for Essex. Enlisting in the Army, he served first in the Rifle Brigade and then in the Royal Fusiliers. He won the Military Medal and was then commissioned. A second lieutenant, he was killed in action at Ypres in 1917.

M	Inns	NOs	Runs	HS	Avge	Ct/st
4	7	2	25	11*	5.00	9/4

Robert John ROLLINS

Born: Plaistow, 30 January 1974.

An England Youth wicket-keeper who began his career as a fast bowler with Essex Schools, Robert Rollins made his first-class debut in the match against Pakistan at Chelmsford in 1992. An ebullient cricketer, he made his Championship debut in 1993 with matches against Kent, Sussex and

Hampshire. He also appeared in the Sunday League for the first time.

His brother Adrian, a batsman and occasional wicket-keeper, plays for Derbyshire.

M	Inns	NOs	Runs	HS	Avge	Ct/st
5	7	1	42	13	7.00	7/3

Sunday League

M	Inns	NOs	Runs	HS	Avge	Ct/st
11	9	4	27	9*	5.40	11/4

Charles James ROUND

Born: Kensington, London, 3 September 1885.
Died: Birch, 6 October 1945.
The son of Rt Hon James Round, one of the founders of Essex County Cricket Club and the club's first captain, C.J.Round appeared in two matches in 1921. An Army officer, he played in Colchester week against Hampshire and Sussex. His one wicket was that of another Army officer, Colonel Greig of Hampshire. He was educated at both Eton and Winchester.

M	Inns	NOs	Runs	HS	Avge
2	4	-	9	8	2.25

Overs	Mds	Runs	Wkts	Avge	Best
13	1	62	1	62.00	1/49

Francis Erskine ROWE

Born: Hartford End, 30 November 1864.
Died: Littlehampton, Sussex, 17 May 1928.
Born near Felsted, Francis Rowe was in the Marlborough XI for three seasons, 1881 to 1883, and captained the side in his last two years. His father had been in the Cambridge side in 1859, but, although a sound middle order bat, Francis Rowe failed to get his blue and played no first-class cricket at university.

He first played for Essex in 1886, before the county had first-class status, and, in July 1892, he hit 129 against Surrey at Leyton. He had made his first-class debut two years earlier when, at Leyton, he had made 17 and four not out for Cambridge Past and Present against Murdoch's Australians.

His first-class games for Essex were against Leicestershire and Surrey in 1894, and against Derbyshire in the last match of the 1895 season. He made 19 against Surrey. From 1900 to 1911, he played for Berkshire.

M	Inns	NOs	Runs	HS	Avge	Ct
3	5	-	32	19	6.40	1

Sir George William ROWLEY

Born: Brabourne, Kent, 10 May 1896.
Died: Newlyn, Cornwall, 8 August 1953.
Sir George Rowley played in five matches for Essex in 1926. He had been educated at Repton, and he later played first-class cricket in India.

M	Inns	NOs	Runs	HS	Avge
5	7	1	53	23	8.83

Overs	Mds	Runs	Wkts	Avge
10	1	29	-	-

Alfred Edward RUSSELL

Born: Lewisham, London, 9 January 1875.
Died: Whipps Cross, Leytonstone, 8 September 1940.

Alf Russell succeeded his elder brother Tom as the Essex wicket-keeper. He began to appear occasionally as early as 1898, but he did not take over regularly until Tom stepped down at the end of the 1905 season.

A.E., generally recognised by his second initial and referred to as Edward, batted low in the order most of the time, but he hit 100 against Derbyshire at Chesterfield in 1901.

He played little in 1910 and when Gibson became more available in 1911 Russell dropped out of the side altogether. He later became groundsman at Valentine's Park, Ilford.

M	Inns	NOs	Runs	HS	Avge	100s	Ct/st
130	196	42	2025	100	13.14	1	163/44

Charles Albert George RUSSELL

Born: Leyton, 7 October 1887.
Died: Whipps Cross, Leytonstone, 23 March 1961.
C.A.G.Russell, more generally known as A.C.,

and more familiarly as 'Jack' was the finest of Essex professional batsmen before the arrival of Keith Fletcher. He was born close to the County Ground in Leyton and would play truant to watch his father and his uncle in the Essex side.

Finely built, nearly six feet tall, 'Jack' Russell made his first appearance for Essex against Northamptonshire at Leyton in July

1908. He played in the next match, against Gloucestershire at Bristol, and in both games

he was alongside his uncle. He did not really establish himself in the side until 1913 when he was promoted to open the innings with McIver. At Leyton, the pair began the Essex innings with a partnership of 210 against Hampshire, a record at the time, and Russell hit the first of his 71 centuries. In the last match of the season, at Old Trafford, he scored a faultless 110 and so passed 1000 runs for the first time.

'Jack' Russell had benefitted much from the coaching of 'Bob' Carpenter, and when cricket resumed after World War One he was a mature, consistent batsman with a watchful defence and a wonderful eye which enabled him to master the trickiest of wickets. In 1920, he became the first Essex batsman to reach 2000 runs in a season. He finished eighth in the national averages and won a place in the England party to go to Australia under Johnny Douglas.

He hit 156 against South Australia in his first match of the tour, but his Test debut brought him 0 and 5. He duplicated these scores in the Second Test when batting in the middle-order, but he hit 135 not out and 59 in the third match, at Adelaide, a favourite ground. Not chosen for the first three Tests against Australia in the disastrous series of 1921, he hit centuries in the Fourth and Fifth Tests. In 1922-23, at Durban, he became the first English batsman to score a century in each innings of a Test match.

Ironically, this was to be his final Test match. In ten matches, he had scored 910 runs, with five centuries, and averaged 56.87. Very few men can boast so fine an international record.

Not a great stylist, Russell was a batsman of the utmost determination with a particular strength on the on-side. He was an excellent slip fielder and a slow medium pace bowler of more than average ability. He was also a man of great resolve, evidenced by the fact that when he scored his century in each innings against South Africa he was a sick man and was defying doctor's orders.

He made his highest score, 273, against Northamptonshire, at Leyton, in 1921, and it is true to say that at this period in Essex's history, Russell and Douglas were the only batsmen to offer serious resistance to the opposition. Douglas valued Russell highly and consulted more with his senior professional than he was accustomed to do with others. Russell responded by scoring centuries against every other county and against West Indies, and for the Players against the Gentlemen. Arguably, he should have played much more for England than he did, but, in naming him one of their Five Cricketers of the Year in 1923, *Wisden*, perhaps, echoed the criticism that some outside Essex had of him.

'Judged by results since the war he is an exceptional player and yet his batting lacks the quality that fascinates. One cannot imagine people jumping into taxi-cabs and rushing off to Lord's or The Oval because they had seen on the tape that he was not out at lunch-time. A master of on-side play, he is rather too utilitarian to rank among the great ones. He has a fine off-drive at his command, but he is very sparing in the use of it. Still he must not be blamed for playing the game that pays him best.'

What the writer of this piece misses is that Essex was not a fashionable county. It was a county that faced one crisis after another, and Russell *was* the batting. Men may not have leapt into taxi cabs to see him, but they climbed on to the trams to Leyton to support 'Jack' Russell. But it must also be said that much as Douglas valued him, he was also frustrated by him, believing that he never quite realised his potential and should have practised more.

Russell could point to the fact that he topped 1000 runs in 13 seasons, and that in five of those seasons he scored more than 2000 runs. In his last season before his retirement, 1930, he hit 1536 runs, average 39.63, with four centuries. The last of them was an innings of 178 against Sussex at Hove in July.

He began to coach at Red Triangle Cement Company CC at Osterley Park; and for several years he was coach at Westminster School and later groundsman. He retired in 1954. He was also a first-class umpire in 1938 and 1939.

Russell was deeply moved when, in 1949, he was one of the 26 professionals elected as honorary life members of MCC

M	Inns	NOs	Runs	HS	Avge	100s	Ct
379	628	51	23610	273	40.91	62	280

Overs	Mds	Runs	Wkts	Avge	Best	5/inn
3210.1	741	7480	276	27.10	5/25	5

Thomas Maychurch RUSSELL

Born: Lewisham, London, 6 July 1868.
Died: Leyton, 28 February 1927.

A man of reserved disposition, Tom Russell, the father of the great C.A.G., was a popular member of the Essex side that was granted first-class status in 1894. He had first represented Essex in 1888 and had played on the Leyton ground as a boy.

He established himself as the regular wicket-keeper and was in the side for the

opening match, against Leicestershire in 1894, and the first Championship match, against Warwickshire a year later. He batted anywhere in the order and was a useful performer, averaging 23 in 1896 when he hit 110 against Surrey at Leyton. His highest score came against Derbyshire at Derby four years later.

He was a more than capable wicket-keeper, and he had 20 or more dismissals in every season from 1895 to 1903 when he began to give way more often behind the stumps to his younger brother. This record puts him among the top flight of Essex wicket-keepers as does the fact that he established a record of six dismissals in an innings, three caught and three stumped against Lancashire, 1898, and two caught and four stumped against Kent, 1901, which was not beaten until David East's eight catches at Taunton in 1985.

He kept to a most varied attack during his career – Kortright, Mead, Picket and Bull – and he missed little.

Tom Russell last played for Essex in 1905. Like the other Essex professionals of the period, he was taken on the MCC groundstaff in 1894, and he remained at Lord's until 1926. He was also a first-class umpire from 1920 to 1926 when he was forced to retire through ill health. He died a year later.

M	Inns	NOs	Runs	HS	Avge	100s	Ct/st
162	246	45	3106	139	15.45	3	246/88

Sadiq MOHAMMAD

Born: Junagadh, India, 5 May 1945.

A member of the dynasty which has represented Pakistan with such renown since their first days in Test cricket, Sadiq Mohammad was a left-handed opening batsman and leg-break bowler. He is recorded as having made his first-class debut before he was 15 years old and first played Test cricket in October 1969. The following August, he played for Essex against a Jamaica XI at  Leyton, the match in which Keith Pont made his first-class debut. Play was possible only on the second afternoon, and Sadiq 'shaped impressively while seeing his colleagues fall'. Two years later, he joined Gloucestershire. He has also played for Tasmania and was employed first by United Bank of Pakistan and then by Pakistan International Airlines.

M	Inns	NOs	Runs	HS	Avge
1	1	-	20	20	20.00

Gary Edward SAINSBURY

Born: Wanstead, 17 January 1958.

A product of Wanstead CC, Gary Sainsbury was a left-arm medium pace bowler who  seemed destined to take over from John Lever, but the consistent form and fitness of Lever meant that Sainsbury had only three first-class matches in his six years on the Essex staff. In 1983, he joined Gloucestershire and played for them until 1987, making 71 appearances.

He read Statistics at Bath University and represented the UAU, and his feats for the 2nd XI were outstanding. He made his debut for the county side against Northamptonshire in 1979, and the following year, he took 4 for 85 against Surrey at The Oval. He coached and played in Australia during the winter months.

M	Inns	NOs	Runs	HS	Avge	Ct
3	2	2	2	2*	-	1

Overs	Mds	Runs	Wkts	Avge	Best
80	12	268	8	33.50	4/85

Sunday League

M	Inns	NOs	Runs	HS	Avge
3	2	-	0	0	0.00

Overs	Mds	Runs	Wkts	Avge	Best
20	2	62	2	31.00	2/24

Norman Hunt SAINT

Born: Tollington Park, Islington, London, 22 April 1901.

Died: Whitechapel, London, 15 August 1930.

Educated at Merchant Taylors, Norman Saint batted right-handed and bowled left-arm medium pace. He appeared for Essex with some regularity in 1920 and 1921, but thereafter little was seen of him, and he played his last match in 1924.

M	Inns	NOs	Runs	HS	Avge	Ct
44	72	7	757	36	11.64	10

Overs	Mds	Runs	Wkts	Avge	Best
179.3	17	800	17	47.05	3/32

Salim MALIK

Born: Lahore, Pakistan, 16 April 1963.
Salim Malik was recognised as one of the leading batsmen in the world when he joined

Essex for the 1991 season. An exquisite stroke-maker, initially he seemed too anxious to hit every ball for four, but by the close of the season he had scored 1972 runs, more than any other Essex batsman, and had been a most vital part of a Championship-winning side.

Salim had been playing first-class cricket since he was 16 and had appeared in more than 50 Tests before he came to Essex. He added more glory in his time with the county, hitting his highest score, a brilliant 215 against Leicestershire at Ilford, and

establishing an Essex fourth wicket record of 314 with Nasser Hussain against Surrey at The Oval. He also proved to be a very effective leg-break bowler and an excellent close to the wicket fielder.

He returned to Essex in 1993, but he had suffered a loss of form in international matches, and he could never quite rekindle the spark of his first year with Essex which was memorable for a host of glorious shots bringing runs at a rapid rate.

Employed by Habib Bank, Salim was appointed captain of Pakistan in 1994.

M	Inns	NOs	Runs	HS	Avge	100s	Ct
39	63	11	2889	215	55.56	8	38

Overs	Mds	Runs	Wkts	Avge	Best	5/inn
373.3	50	1265	39	32.44	5/67	1

Sunday League

M	Inns	NOs	Runs	HS	Avge	Ct
24	24	2	756	89	34.37	10

Overs	Mds	Runs	Wkts	Avge	Best
37.2	1	163	4	40.75	3/36

Benson and Hedges Cup

M	Inns	NOs	Runs	HS	Avge	Ct
8	7	2	218	90*	43.60	1

Overs	Mds	Runs	Wkts	Avge	Best
2	-	7	1	7.00	1/7

NatWest Trophy

M	Inns	NOs	Runs	HS	Avge	Ct
5	5	1	148	74	37.00	5

Overs	Mds	Runs	Wkts	Avge	Best
12.2	-	59	4	14.75	4/25

Leslie Austin SAVILL

Born: Brentwood, 30 June 1935.
Les Savill was a sound right-handed batsman who was spotted by Frank Rist when he was playing for Essex Schools. He went to Norlington Road School, Leyton, later to play a part in Graham Gooch's formative years. Savill joined the Essex staff and made his debut in 1953 in the match against Glamorgan at Llanelli. He batted number nine, made 1 and 0, but a week later he hit a courageous 67 against Hampshire on a wet wicket at Brentwood. He was still a week short of his 18th birthday.

National Service took him out of the game for much of 1954 and 1955, but in 1956, he hit his maiden first-class century, 100 against Somerset at Brentwood. His best season was

1959 when, in spite of a broken finger, he scored 1197 runs and twice, against C a m b r i d g e University and N o r t h a m p t o n - shire, hit 115.

A placid and gentle person, Les Savill never really had enough faith in his own ability, and he left the game after the 1961 season. For a time he worked for Barc- lay's Bank, and then he took a teachers' training course at St Luke's College, Exeter. In 1964, he played for Devon.

He left teaching in 1973 to become a social worker. He completed a BA degree in 1981 and continued his studies in advanced social work. His cricket became more occasional and less competitive, but he continued to play table-tennis to a good standard.

M	Inns	NOs	Runs	HS	Avge	100s	Ct
125	200	16	3919	115	21.29	4	50

Overs	Mds	Runs	Wkts	Avge	Best
2	-	26	1	26.00	1/26

Graham John SAVILLE

Born: Leytonstone, 5 February 1944.
Graham Saville's playing career with Essex was divided into two parts. He made his debut against Sussex at Hove in August 1963, scoring 23 and 48. A right-handed opening batsman and excellent slip fielder, he appeared in four matches the following season and played more regularly in 1965 and 1966.

He was not re-engaged after the 1966 season and played for Norfolk from 1967 to 1969. Appearing for Minor Counties against West Indies in 1969, he batted with neatness

and confidence in scoring 116 and 55, and these innings attracted the attention of Essex who signed him for the 1970 season. In the words of *Wisden*, he did 'a great deal to atone for the loss of Irvine' and reached 1000 runs.

He enjoyed two good sea- sons after this, but he played little in 1973 and retired at the end of the year.

Saville be- came assist- ant secretary to Essex CCC in 1974 and played in one match that season. He did much to est- ablish strong- er links with schools and

became the first coach at the Indoor School. In 1979, he was appointed Eastern Region coach of the National Cricket Association, and he has managed and coached England youth sides at home and abroad. He has also coached Cambridge University and managed the Combined Universities' side in the Benson and Hedges Cup.

A cousin of Graham Gooch and a fervent Essex patriot, he is chairman of the Cricket Committee and has worked passionately for the club as administrator and coach since his retirement.

M	Inns	NOs	Runs	HS	Avge	100s	Ct
124	214	29	4265	126*	23.05	1	101

Overs	Mds	Runs	Wkts	Avge	Best
15	4	59	3	19.66	2/30

Sunday League

M	Inns	NOs	Runs	HS	Avge	Ct
35	29	7	328	35	14.90	15

Benson and Hedges Cup

M	Inns	NOs	Runs	HS	Avge	Ct
5	4	1	148	85*	49.33	3

Gillette Cup

M	Inns	NOs	Runs	HS	Avge	Ct
6	6	-	38	22	6.33	4

Denis SAYERS

Born: St Pancras, London, 17 March 1934.
A right-arm medium-pace bowler, Denis Sayers was educated at Haverstock Hill Grammar School and joined the MCC groundstaff. He played club cricket for Walthamstow and for Sutton, and, in August 1967, he appeared in the Championship match against Nottinghamshire at Leyton. He took the wicket of Basharat Hassan, but he did not appear in first-class cricket again.

M	Inns	NOs	Runs	HS	Avge
1	1	1	0	0*	-

Overs	Mds	Runs	Wkts	Avge	Best
21	2	64	1	64.00	1/22

Frederick John SCOULDING

Born: Bow, London, 26 August 1887.
Died: Whitechapel, London, 25 August 1928.
Fred Scoulding was a slow left-arm bowler who made his debut in the final home Championship match of the 1912 season, against Hampshire. He remained on the staff until the end of 1920, but he never commanded a regular place in the side.

He went to work in Monmouthshire and played as an amateur for that county with considerable success in 1923 and 1924.

M	Inns	NOs	Runs	HS	Avge	Ct
22	28	11	92	21	5.41	6

Overs	Mds	Runs	Wkts	Avge	Best
410.5	68	1252	32	39.12	4/50

Cyril John SEARLE

Born: Battersea, London, 12 May 1921.
Cyril Searle kept wicket for Essex against Cambridge University at Fenner's in May 1947.

M	Inns	NOs	Runs	HS	Avge	Ct/st
1	1	1	5	5*	-	1/1

Leslie Daniel SEARS

Born: Wokingham, Berkshire, 12 January 1901.
Died: Amesbury, Wiltshire, 1992.
A fine left-handed batsman and excellent slip fielder, Leslie Sears played twice for Essex as

an amateur in 1925 when he was living in and playing club cricket in East London. Both of his appearances were at Leyton in early June, the first was against Worcestershire, and the second against Derbyshire when he 'bagged a pair'. He later returned to Wokingham where he captained the town side and appeared for Berkshire in the Minor Counties competition. His son Alan also represented Berkshire, and he is now chairman of the county club.

M	Inns	NOs	Runs	HS	Avge
2	4	-	18	16	4.50

Derek John SEMMENCE

Born: Worthing, Sussex, 20 April 1938.
A much travelled professional cricketer, Semmence played for Sussex from 1956 until 1960, for Devon from 1963 until 1966, and reappeared for Sussex in 1967 and 1968. He assisted Northumberland from 1973 to 1975 and played for Cambridgeshire in 1976.

In June 1962, he played for Essex against Oxford University. Later, he became a professional with Brechin in Scotland.

M	Inns	NOs	Runs	HS	Avge
1	2	-	33	24	16.50

Overs	Mds	Runs	Wkts	Avge
8	3	31	-	-

Edward Humphrey Dalrymple SEWELL

Born: Lingsugur, India, 30 September 1872.
Died: Westbourne Park, Paddington, London, 20 September 1947.
Born in India where his father was a British Army officer, E.H.D.Sewell was a forceful right-handed batsman and a medium-pace bowler. He played for the Europeans when he was 11 years old, scoring 9 and holding two

catches. Initially coached by Lieutenant Plummer, he was educated at Bedford Grammar School, and his success in the school XI was so marked that he played five times for Bedfordshire in 1891.

The following year he returned to India as a civil servant, and his cricketing achievements became legendary. He hit two double centuries for Madras, a feat which had never before been accomplished in India, and he established another record when he hit three

centuries in succession. He sometimes played under the captaincy of Ranjitsinhji. In all, he scored nearly 8,000 runs and took more than 700 wickets in India.

He was persuaded to return to England by the Essex committee who offered him a temporary engagement as a professional. Having spent the necessary period qualifying by residence, he played for the county from 1902 until 1904, with, perhaps, not quite the degree of success that had been anticipated.

In 1904, at Edgbaston, he and 'Bob' Carpenter opened the Essex innings with a partnership of 142 in 80 minutes. Sewell, who was first out for 107, always insisted that the time was 65 minutes and added that they didn't get prizes for fast centuries in those days.

A fine rugby footballer, he played for Blackheath and Harlequins, Sewell wrote for various newspapers on rugby and cricket, and he played for W.G.Grace's London County side, for whom he made his highest score, 181, and for MCC. He was coach to Surrey from 1908 to 1910, and he then became honorary secretary of Buckinghamshire for whom he played as an amateur.

He wrote more than a dozen books on cricket, and, in *Cricket Under Fire, Well Hit! Sir* and several others, he revealed a pungent style and forthright opinions on many topics related to the game.

M	Inns	NOs	Runs	HS	Avge	100s	Ct
55	91	5	1822	107	21.18	2	45

Overs	Mds	Runs	Wkts	Avge	Best
110	19	388	7	55.42	2/79

Adam Charles Hilton SEYMOUR

Born: Royston, Hertfordshire, 7 December 1967.

A product of Millfield School where he was recognised as a left-handed opening batsman

of exceptional merit, Adam Seymour attracted the attention of Essex when his family moved to Colchester. He first played for the 2nd XI in 1984 and was a prolific run-scorer for the Colchester and East Essex club.

He hit a century in his first 2nd XI match and joined the staff as a professional in 1988. He made his first-class debut that season, scoring 33 not out at number nine against Cambridge University. Tall and purposeful, he began the 1990 season with 89 at Fenner's, and he made his Championship debut against Gloucestershire at Ilford as Gooch's deputy. Unfortunately, he suffered a broken hand when he was hit by a ball from Courtney Walsh and was forced to retire hurt.

In 1991, he played in ten first-class matches and scored his maiden first-class century, a splendid 157 against Glamorgan at Cardiff. He made 533 runs in the season, but, frustrated by the lack of opportunity, he left the county at the end of 1991 and joined Worcestershire.

M	Inns	NOs	Runs	HS	Avge	100s	Ct
14	24	4	697	157	34.85	1	8

Overs	Mds	Runs	Wkts	Avge
4	-	27	-	-

Sunday League

M	Inns	NOs	Runs	HS	Avge	Ct
5	4	-	46	25	11.50	1

NatWest Trophy

M	Inns	NOs	Runs	HS	Avge	Ct
1	1	-	0	0	0.00	1

Nadeem SHAHID

Born: Karachi, Pakistan, 23 April 1969.
Educated at Ipswich School, Nadeem Shahid played for Suffolk at all levels, experiencing Minor Counties cricket from 1986 to 1988 after which he joined Essex. He won the *Daily Telegraph School Cricket Award* for 1987, and he also assisted Copdock CC.

He made his Essex debut against Leicestershire, June 1989, impressing with his leg-breaks and claiming Potter and Winston Benjamin as his first victims in first-class cricket. At Ilford, against Hampshire, he played a significant part in Essex's victory with innings of 40 and 27 not out. He at once established himself as a batsman of sound temperament and elegant style.

His fluency continued into the 1990 season when he hit a maiden first-class century against Lancashire at Colchester and reached 1000 runs for the season. He bowled effectively on occasions and was Essex's leading fielder with 22 catches, mostly at short-leg, in Championship matches.

There was a loss of form and limited opportunities in 1991, but an innings of 132 against Kent at Chelmsford in 1992 suggested that the undoubted potential would be realised.

M	Inns	NOs	Runs	HS	Avge	100s	Ct
65	97	16	2523	132	31.14	2	64

Overs	Mds	Runs	Wkts	Avge	Best
270.3	46	1040	27	38.51	3/91

Sunday League

M	Inns	NOs	Runs	HS	Avge	Ct
43	34	3	561	64	18.09	14

M	Inns	NOs	Runs
3	-	11	-

Benson and Hedges Cup

M	Inns	NOs	Runs	HS	Avge	Ct
8	4	-	51	42	12.75	1

NatWest Trophy

M	Inns	NOs	Runs	HS	Avge	Ct
4	3	1	115	85*	57.50	3

Overs	Mds	Runs	Wkts	Avge	Best
3	3	0	1	0.00	1/0

Captain Robert Henry SHARP

Born: Doncaster, Yorkshire, 11 June 1893.
Died: Bradford-on-Avon, Wiltshire, 15 March 1961.
One of the Regular Army officers who assisted Essex while stationed in the county and therefore qualified by residence, Sharp was an all-rounder whose greatest value was his right-arm fast-medium pace bowling.

He played for the county between 1925 and 1928, and his most successful season was his first when he took 5 for 66 in Somerset's second innings at Taunton.

M	Inns	NOs	Runs	HS	Avge	Ct
16	25	7	169	36*	9.38	16

Overs	Mds	Runs	Wkts	Avge	Best	5/inn
179	15	696	16	43.50	5/66	1

James Roy SHEFFIELD

Born: Barking, 19 November 1906.
One of the richest characters ever to have played cricket for Essex and certainly the most travelled, Roy Sheffield seemed to have solved the Essex wicket-keeping problem when he made his debut against Warwickshire in June 1929. He performed admirably behind the stumps and hit 85 not out, batting at number nine.

Sheffield had played cricket in the Wanstead League and had been taken on the staff at Leyton. He was also a noted amateur footballer with Chelmsford City, and he represented the London League and Essex in county matches. He was on West Ham United's books as an amateur.

He quickly established himself as the regular Essex 'keeper and was soon being spoken of as a possible England player, but it was his winter adventures which intrigued people most. He played soccer in Malta and went motor-cycling in the Isle of Man. In the winter of 1932-33, he planned to make a canoe trip the whole length of the River Paraguay in South America. As this proved to be impracticable, he worked as a cow-puncher in Descalvados, became caught up in the war that was being waged between Paraguay and Bolivia and was arrested on suspicion of being a Bolivian spy. He was released on the intercession of a British business man, but the adventure spawned Sheffield's interesting book, *Bolivian Spy?*

The following winter saw him in South Africa where he made a two-month trek over the Drakensburg Mountains and through Basutoland accompanied only by a native guide and pack pony.

In 1934, he surprisingly lost form and favour, giving way to Wade and Powell, but he was back in the side the following season when he often opened the innings. A serious football injury in the winter of 1935-36 deeply affected his career. A week after leaving hospital, he hit the only century of his career, 108 against Sussex at Hove, but he did not sustain that form, and with Wade now regular behind the stumps, Sheffield was not retained at the end of the season.

The inveterate traveller set off for Australasia in the company of Tom Wade and met his future wife on the boat on his way. In New Zealand, he was offered a job as guide to the Chateau, Tangariro National Park which he accepted. Settled in New Zealand, he assisted Wellington 1938-39, joined the Royal New Zealand Air Force in World War Two and later worked as a physical education teacher and for the government as a community recreation officer. Other outdoor jobs followed, and he has continued to remain physically active in retirement. Canoeing is still a passion of this remarkable man.

M	Inns	NOs	Runs	HS	Avge	100s	Ct/st
177	272	40	3822	108	16.47	1	194/54

Overs	Mds	Runs	Wkts	Avge
12	2	28	-	-

Howard Richard SHERMAN

Born: Seven Kings, 15 June 1943.

A good amateur soccer player with Clapton and Barkingside, Howard Sherman was

educated at Chigwell School and played for the Ilford club. A right-handed batsman, he made his county debut against Nottinghamshire at Leyton in 1967 when he hit 66. This was part of the county policy of the period of calling upon leading club cricketers from time to time. Sherman responded admirably, finishing second in the batting averages with 288 runs in seven matches. He appeared in six more matches in the next two seasons.

M	Inns	NOs	Runs	HS	Avge	Ct
13	21	3	448	66	24.88	4

Overs	Mds	Runs	Wkts	Avge
7	1	23	-	-

Sunday League

M	Inns	NOs	Runs	HS	Avge
1	1	-	2	2	2.00

Richard Nicholas SHORTER

Born: Loughton, 26 July 1906.
Died: Drogheda, County Meath, Ireland, 20 January 1984.
A tall medium pace bowler, Richard Shorter was a noted club cricketer with Loughton,

Incogniti and Cryptics. He made his debut for Essex against Nottinghamshire at Trent Bridge in 1927. He was bowled by Larwood and not given a turn with the ball. In all, he played in ten matches that season and took five wickets. His career extended until 1929, but he was unable to repeat at county level the success he enjoyed at club level. He played as an amateur.

M	Inns	NOs	Runs	HS	Avge	Ct
23	29	11	104	21	5.77	12

Overs	Mds	Runs	Wkts	Avge	Best
259.4	55	695	15	46.33	3/14

Ivor John SKINNER

Born: Walthamstow, 1 April 1928.
Ivor Skinner's services were not retained after he had appeared in 13 matches in 1950. He was a right-arm fast medium pace bowler who made his debut against Glamorgan in May, and against Warwickshire in his second match, he took 4 for 56.

Following his days with Essex, he moved to Cornwall and assisted that county for four seasons, 1956-59.

M	Inns	NOs	Runs	HS	Avge	Ct
13	21	7	28	7*	2.00	5

Overs	Mds	Runs	Wkts	Avge	Best
243	37	808	21	38.47	4/56

Geoffrey John SMITH

Born: Braintree, 2 April 1935.
Educated at Braintree County High School, Geoff Smith made his debut in 1955, batting initially at number ten and failing to take a wicket with his off-breaks. By 1958, he had forced his way to number three in the order and hit a maiden first-class century, against Hampshire, at Clacton. In 1960, he succeeded Les Savill as Gordon Barker's opening partner

and hit 1000 runs in a season for the first time. He was capped the same season.

In all, he scored 1000 runs in a season four times. He appeared in only two Championship matches in 1966, the last against Kent at Dartford, and retired at the end of the season. He assisted Hertfordshire for three seasons and became a director of Pope and Smith, the sports retailers. He had special responsibility for the wholesale side of the business. In 1977, he established his own sports clothing company which specialised in swimwear.

He captained Braintree and has become a most capable golfer.

M	Inns	NOs	Runs	HS	Avge	100s	Ct
239	412	30	8519	148	22.30	4	(3)

Overs	Mds	Runs	Wkts	Avge	Best	5/inn
367.4	112	913	33	27.66	5/39	1

Gillette Cup

M	Inns	NOs	Runs	HS	Avge	Ct
4	4	-	134	63	33.50	1

George William Oswald SMITH

Born: Halstead, 7 March 1906.
Died: Worthing, Sussex, 25 November 1989.
A wicket-keeper and batsman at Bishop's Stortford College, George Smith had a good record before going up to Cambridge. He played in the Seniors' Match in his second year, but he did not appear in any first-class matches. He was given an extended run of nine matches for Essex in 1929 as a batsman, hitting 30 as an opener at Derby and making 39 not out lower down the order at Northampton. He played once in 1930.

He played club cricket for Halstead, Frinton

and the Gentlemen of Essex, and he assisted Suffolk in 1937 and 1938, playing alongside H.P.Waugh.

M	Inns	NOs	Runs	HS	Avge	Ct
10	18	3	206	39*	13.73	2

Harry Thomas Oliver SMITH

Born: Warley, 5 March 1906.
When he was available Tom Smith was a most valuable addition to the Essex attack in the 1930s. A right-arm fast medium pace bowler, a good fielder and a useful late order batsman, he was the son of a keen cricketer who had a close association with Hounslow CC. Tom himself played for Hounslow, and at the age of 17, in 1923, he became the first winner of the Rouse Spoon. He remains the youngest winner of this trophy which was given in honour of the founder of the club and which is awarded to the outstanding performer of the season.

Tom Smith took up a position with the Midland Bank and played for both Hounslow and for the Midland Bank side at week-ends. His achievements in club cricket drew the attention of Essex, and, in late summer, 1929, he played in five matches for the county. He caused a tremendous stir in the match at Lord's when he bowled three Middlesex batsmen, Freddie Mann, Denis Russell and Walter Robins, within the space of four balls.

Available for two Championship matches the following season, both at Leyton, he took 6 for 56 against Derbyshire in the second and finished top of the Essex bowling averages.

It was in this season, 1930, that he made two appearances against the Australians. The first was for Essex at Leyton when he had Woodfull caught at slip, and the second was for the Club Cricket Conference at Lord's. This was the penultimate match of the Australian tour, and the Test series had been completed. Smith bowled splendidly, took 4 for 70, and had Bradman dropped second ball by Nazeer Ali who was later to claim the great man after he had hit 70 in 75 minutes. Tom Pearce and Trayton Grinter played in this game, and there is a feeling that had Smith captured Bradman second ball, and had the game been earlier in the season, the young quick bowler may well have been set for a Test career, but his life in cricket was to be full of what might have been.

He was never to be available for more than five matches in a season, and in 1934, he could play only in the game against the Australians at Chelmsford. Bill Ponsford came to the match with two double centuries in his two previous innings, but Tom Smith had him caught at slip for 0.

In 1935, he bowled well for the Club Cricket Conference against the South African tourists, but he was available for only two Essex Championship matches and captured only two wickets. These were his last for the county. He played for Levenson-Gower's XI in 1936, but thereafter he concentrated on club cricket and on becoming a manager with the Midland Bank.

There was always a sense of the dramatic when H.T.O.Smith bowled. In his famous feat against Middlesex in 1929, he had broken a stump when he bowled Walter Robins; and playing for Hounslow against Dulwich Hamlet he broke four stumps while taking 6 for 30. Against Barnet Wanderers shortly before World War Two he took two wickets with the last two balls of the match to bring about a tie.

He played alongside his two brothers for Hounslow and for the Club Cricket Conference, and he became captain of Hounslow in 1950. One can only wonder what he might have achieved had he been able to give himself fully to first-class cricket.

M	Inns	NOs	Runs	HS	Avge	Ct
23	36	5	361	38	11.64	19

Overs	Mds	Runs	Wkts	Avge	Best	5/inn
539.1	100	1618	61	26.52	6/56	3

Harry William SMITH

Born: Mile End, London, 6 September 1890. Harry Smith was a right-arm fast medium pace bowler who played one match for Essex in 1912, two in 1914 and reappeared in 1920. He took 22 Championship wickets in 1921, and in the match against Somerset at Southend, he took 3 for 47 and 5 for 59. Nothing was seen of him after 1922, and no trace of his death has yet been discovered.

M	Inns	NOs	Runs	HS	Avge	Ct
20	31	12	195	22	10.26	12

Overs	Mds	Runs	Wkts	Avge	Best	5/inn
323.5	53	1055	35	30.14	5/59	1

Neil SMITH

Born: Ossett, Yorkshire, 1 April 1949.
For two seasons, 1979-80, Neil Smith had no superior in England as a wicket-keeper. His keeping day in and day out in the county Championship was as consistent as it was masterly. He had kept wicket for Yorkshire in eight matches in two seasons, 1970 and 1971, and in 1972 had kept for the Minor Counties against the Aust-

ralians. The advent of David Bairstow had allowed York-shire to release Smith although there were those in the White Rose County who were of the opinion that the wrong man was allowed to leave.

He joined Essex in 1973, and he succeeded Brian Taylor in the side when the captain retired. A forceful batsman, he drove the first ball he received to the off-side boundary to bring victory over Yorkshire in the Benson and Hedges Cup semi-final, 1979, and so take Essex into their first Cup Final at Lord's. In the Final itself he took a spectacular catch to account for Roger Knight who was in full flow. There were occasions when he opened the innings in Sunday League matches.

In 1981, he suddenly lost form and was replaced by David East. Smith left the staff at the end of the 1982 season. A genial man, he has not had a happy business career, neither in his wine-bar activities nor in his property dealings.

Returning north, he played for the Cheadle Hulme club and assisted Cheshire, 1987-89.

M	Inns	NOs	Runs	HS	Avge	100s	Ct/st
178	226	47	3225	126	18.01	2	381/47

Sunday League

M	Inns	NOs	Runs	HS	Avge	Ct/st
106	73	21	614	60	11.80	76/17

Benson and Hedges Cup

M	Inns	NOs	Runs	HS	Avge	Ct/st
41	20	3	170	61	10.00	34/3

Gillette Cup / NatWest Bank Trophy

M	Inns	NOs	Runs	HS	Avge	Ct/st
11	9	1	57	12	7.12	6/2

Raymond SMITH

Born: Boreham, 10 August 1914.
Frank Chester, the great Test match umpire, once wrote of Ray Smith that he was the 'torch bearer of the true spirit of cricket'. Certainly he was a cricketer who put his county first at all times. He was loyal, whole-hearted, and he walked like a guardsman with a constant air of keenness.

Ray Smith was the true all-rounder. He

would open the bowling with his medium-pace seam, and then he would put on his cap and bowl off-breaks. In the years immed-iately after the war, he and his cousin Peter car-ried the Essex attack. As a bats-man, Ray was a ferocious hitter. He made his debut in 1934, and the following season he hit 54 out of 58 in 25 minutes against Gloucestershire at Southend. In 1939, he scored 91 in 100 minutes against Yorkshire at Sheffield, and in 1947, he made three lightning 50s against Gloucestershire. This was the season in which he completed the first of his three 'doubles'.

In 1948, he hit a century in 63 minutes against Derbyshire at Colchester; in 1951, in 65 minutes against the South Africans at

Ilford; and in 1955, in 73 minutes against Northamptonshire at Wellingborough. On each of these occasions, these centuries were the fastest of the season. When one considers the amount of bowling that he had to do, these were astonishing performances. Four times he hit 1000 runs in a season, and seven times he captured 100 wickets. He would often joke that his 125 wickets at 37.26 runs each in 1947 was the most expensive 100-wicket haul in the history of English cricket, but he worked phenomenally hard for them.

His highest score was made when he hit the fastest century against the South Africans in 1951, and his best bowling performance came four years later when he took 8 for 63 against Glamorgan at Pontypridd.

It would be true to say that he was at his peak during the war when he captained the British Empire XI in their one-day charity matches. He captured 335 wickets in this period, an average of more than three an innings.

The closest he came to representative honours was when he toured India, Ceylon and Pakistan with the Commonwealth team, 1949-50.

Ray Smith retired at the end of the 1956 season, but he ended on a high note. Essex were playing Yorkshire at Southend and needed seven from the last over of the match to win. Ray Smith got them with a ball to spare by hooking and cutting Fred Trueman.

For a time after he left cricket, he was in the broiler chicken business, and he was also coach at Felsted School. He then ran a restaurant in Warwickshire with his two sons before retiring to tend his garden.

He was a true and faithful servant at the county club.

M	Inns	NOs	Runs	HS	Avge	100s	Ct
419	646	81	11125	147	19.69	6	179

Overs	Mds	Runs	Wkts	Avge	Best	10/m	5/inn
13358.3	2964	39817	1317	30.23	8/63	10	73
394.5 (eight ball)							

Thomas Peter Bromley SMITH

Born: Ipswich, Suffolk, 30 October 1908.
Died: Hyeres, France, 4 August 1967.
Peter Smith was one of the great Essex cricketers, a handsome man who appeared in films as an extra and who broadcast as a commentator in India when he was a member of Lord Tennyson's team in 1937-38. He was educated first at Chelmsford Grammar School and then at Highfield College, Leigh-on-Sea, where he was a boarder. He played for Boreham as a batsman and a somewhat erratic fast bowler and later joined Chelmsford. The depression in the late 1920s left him no scope to follow a career in farming, and he worked for two years as a Post Office electrical engineer. Seeking more excitement, he enlisted for the Rhodesian Mounted Police and was due to sail to Africa in June 1929, but his mother became seriously ill, and his

departure was postponed for six months.

With a summer free for cricket, he asked for a trial as a batsman with Essex who had sent Nichols and O'Connor on a talent-spotting trip. He was rejected as a batsman, but O'Connor spotted his potential to bowl leg-breaks. He was given an extended trial of a month and responded to the coaching of McGahey so well that he was engaged for the rest of the 1929 season. He made his debut against Derbyshire at the beginning of July, but in five county matches in 1929, he took the wicket of Jupp with a full toss at the cost of 233 runs, and in seven innings, he mustered only 42 runs.

Nevertheless, he decided not to go to Rhodesia, went instead to the Faulkner Cricket School at Walham Green and was re-engaged by Essex. Realising he was unable to pay for lessons, Aubrey Faulkner offered him free coaching, expenses and £1 a week if he would act as a net bowler at the school. He opened the bowling in the first match of the 1930 season and bowled Holmes and Mitchell. At Whitsun, at Leyton, he bowled his leg-breaks for the first time, captured 12 wickets in the match and was awarded his county cap. From that time on, he concentrated on spin bowling although he opened the bowling on occasions and bowled seamers.

In 1930, he took 89 wickets for Essex, and in 1933, he captured 100 wickets in the season for the first time. He was spoken of as a potential England bowler, and he was in a Chelmsford cinema on the eve of the third Test match against West Indies in 1933 when a message was flashed on the screen that he was to leave immediately. He was told that he had been picked for the Test match, but on arrival at The Oval, he discovered that it had been a cruel hoax, and he was to wait another 13 years for his Test debut.

In 1936, he hit the first of his eight first-class centuries. It came against Hampshire in 80 minutes and was the second fastest of the season. By now, he was considered an all-rounder and went with Sir Julien Cahn's team to New Zealand in 1938-39, and with Lord Tennyson's team to India in 1937-38.

In 1938, at Chelmsford, he scored 1 and 101 and took 2 for 69 and 8 for 99 against Middlesex so becoming one of the few cricketers to score a century and take ten wickets in the same match. It will surprise no Essex supporter to know that Middlesex won by one wicket. The following year, he was at last chosen as a member of an England touring party. It was for the tour of India, 1939-40, but the outbreak of war brought the cancellation of the tour.

Smith had enlisted in the Army on 1 September 1939, and he was commissioned in June the following year. He became a captain in the Essex Regiment, was posted to Egypt in May 1943, and was staff-captain of Combined Operations and Troop Movements at Alexandria. He was also able to play some cricket, captaining the Middle-East Army side that played against the Central Mediterranean Forces in Rome.

In the years immediately after the war, he and his cousin Ray Smith shouldered the whole burden of the Essex attack, sending down 2,000 overs between them in 1946. Peter Smith was picked for the Second Test against India at Old Trafford, but was unable to play through injury. His Test debut came in the rain-ruined match at The Oval when he bowled Rudi Modi. He was chosen to go to Australia and New Zealand with Wally Hammond's side, took a record 9 for 121 against New South Wales, but met with little success in the three Tests in which he played. He was not selected for England again, for, in

spite of doing the 'double' for the first time in 1947, he was by then nearing his 39th birthday.

He took 16 wickets in the match against Middlesex at Colchester, including his career best 9 for 77, and, against Derbyshire at Chesterfield, he hit a career best 163, an innings all the more remarkable in that he was batting at number 11. This is the highest score ever made by a batsman going in last, and his partnership of 218 in two and a half hours with Frank Vigar remains an Essex record for the tenth wicket.

His 172 wickets in that 1947 season also remains an Essex record, and with nine-wicket hauls against Nottinghamshire and Kent in 1948, he moved towards becoming the highest wicket-taker in Essex history. He captured wickets consistently until the end of his career which came with retirement at the end of the 1951 season. By then, he had taken 1610 wickets, two more than Nichols, and sent down nearly 150,000 overs. He had every right to feel tired.

In 1933, he had set up the sports firm of Pope & Smith with his friend Dudley Pope who was killed in a car crash a year later.

Peter Smith died on holiday in France. He had a fall and suffered a brain haemorrhage. In the annals of Essex cricket, he will live for ever.

M	Inns	NOs	Runs	HS	Avge	100s	Ct
434	647	115	9652	163	18.14	8	330

Overs	Mds	Runs	Wkts	Avge	Best	10/m	5/inn
14263.4	2935	42314	1610	26.28	9/77	27	117

541.4 (eight-ball)

Walter Gordon SPENCER

Born: Chingford, 2 August 1912.
Died: Chelmsford, 20 July 1971.
A short, smart man with a good business sense, 'Don' Spencer played his club cricket for Chingford and captained the side. He was educated at Bancroft's and batted right-handed, but bowled slow left-arm. He played for Suffolk in 1936, but in 1938, he appeared for Essex against Somerset and Middlesex at Chelmsford in June.

During World War Two, he made occasional appearances for the British Empire XI and for Ray Smith's Essex XI, and, in June 1948, he appeared for Essex in the match against

Middlesex at Brentwood, scoring 25 and capturing the wicket of Syd Brown.

Spencer's contribution to Essex cricket cannot be measured by his achievements in his three first-class matches, however, for in the years after World War Two, he did excellent work as captain of the 2nd XI and helped in the development of many young cricketers.

He was a partner in the sports outfitters, Pope & Smith.

M	Inns	NOs	Runs	HS	Avge
3	5	1	52	25	13.00

Overs	Mds	Runs	Wkts	Avge	Best
3	-	8	1	8.00	1/8

Peter Alfred SPICER

Born: Ilford, 11 May 1939.
Died: Hainault, 18 August 1969.
Peter Spicer was a left-handed batsman and a slow left-arm bowler who lacked the self-discipline that would have enabled him to reach the very highest level. He certainly possessed the ability to become an outstanding professional cricketer.

He played club cricket for Ilford, Clayhill and Wanstead, and, in 1962, he made his debut for Essex. It came at the beginning of May, against Somerset at Taunton. The first ball he received he hit into the pavilion for six, and he finished with 80 in 75 minutes, an innings which included one more six and nine fours.

Later in the season, he hit a splendid 86 against the Pakistan tourists after Essex had lost their first five wickets for 96 runs. He seemed set for a glittering career, but the following season he played in only two matches, and then never again. He lacked the temperament necessary for the first-class game, often seemingly unwilling to accept authority or advice.

He joined the Fire Service, and he coached in Holland. In August 1969, he was killed in a road accident. In every way, he was one of the tragedies of Essex cricket.

M	Inns	NOs	Runs	HS	Avge	Ct
17	29	2	526	86	19.48	4

Overs	Mds	Runs	Wkts	Avge	Best
11.1	-	55	2	27.50	2/1

Gillette Cup

M	Inns	NOs	Runs	HS	Avge
1	1	-	6	6	6.00

Overs	Mds	Runs	Wkts	Avge	Best
0.2	-	1	1	1.00	1/1

Edward Frederick SPINKS

Born: Bermuda, 3 August 1902.
Died: Orsett, 19 October 1982.
A bowler on the Essex groundstaff in the 1920s, Fred Spinks appeared in two Championship matches in 1926 without success.

M	Inns	NOs	Runs	HS	Avge	Ct
2	3	1	2	2	1.00	1

Overs	Mds	Runs	Wkts	Avge
20	-	81	-	-

Harold SPURR

Born: Leytonstone, 17 June 1889.
Died: Dunmow, 21 December 1962.
Educated at Merchant Taylor's School, Harold Spurr played for Essex against the West Indians at Ilford in 1923.

M	Inns	NOs	Runs	HS	Avge
1	2	-	13	9	6.50

Ernest Arthur William STANLEY

Born: Leyton, 27 September 1926.
A right-handed batsman and off-break bowler, Ernest Stanley was on the Essex staff from

1950 to 1952, but he failed to establish a regular place in the side. He played club cricket for Walthamstow. For several years, he was on the Arsenal staff. An inside-forward, he played for the most part in the London Combination side.

M	Inns	NOs	Runs	HS	Avge	Ct
13	21	3	226	35	12.55	2

Overs	Mds	Runs	Wkts	Avge
0.3	-	8	-	-

Anthony Roy STANYARD

Born: Plaistow, 5 April 1938.
A right-handed batsman who played for Loughton, Stanyard made his debut for Essex against Kent at Ilford in May 1960. He impressed with a brisk 26 and appeared in the next match, against the South Africans, but he was not re-engaged at the end of the season.

M	Inns	NOs	Runs	HS	Avge
2	3	-	47	26	15.66

John Patrick STEPHENSON

Born: Stebbing, 14 March 1965.
John Stephenson has every right to be considered now as an all-rounder. A right-handed opening batsman of aggressive character, he has developed his medium pace bowling to such an extent that he took 41 wickets in 1993 and finished close to John Childs in the averages.

A prominent cricketer at Felsted, he went to Durham University where he captained the XI and led the Combined Universities in the Benson and Hedges Cup in 1987 with considerable distinction. He had made his debut for Essex in 1985, and his progress was rapid once he became Gooch's opening partner.

Stephenson played for Boland in South Africa, 1988-89, was awarded his county cap the following summer and played for England against Australia at The Oval. Since then, rather unluckily, his international career has been restricted to 'A' tours of Zimbabwe and West Indies.

In 1990, at Bath, he hit 202 not out, but he is a cricketer who has thrived in all forms of competition, a fine fielder in any position.

An intelligent, sensitive and a courteous young man, John Stephenson has played grade cricket in Australia and has travelled to Honduras. He is an exciting batsman who lacks only a little confidence and self-belief to lift him to the highest level.

M	Inns	NOs	Runs	HS	Avge	100s	Ct
171	293	29	9383	202*	35.54	16	104

Overs	Mds	Runs	Wkts	Avge	Best	5/inn
1258.5	260	4296	112	38.35	6/54	3

Sunday League

M	Inns	NOs	Runs	HS	Avge	100s	Ct
110	96	13	2548	109	30.69	3	42

Overs	Mds	Runs	Wkts	Avge	Best	5/inn
472.1	19	2098	85	24.68	5/58	1

Benson and Hedges Cup

M	Inns	NOs	Runs	HS	Avge	100s	Ct
25	21	3	724	142	40.22	1	6

Overs	Mds	Runs	Wkts	Avge	Best
109.2	8	438	18	24.33	3/22

NatWest Trophy

M	Inns	NOs	Runs	HS	Avge	Ct
17	16	1	593	90	39.53	6

Overs	Mds	Runs	Wkts	Avge	Best
81.5	5	437	8	54.62	3/78

Lt.-Colonel John William Arthur STEPHENSON

Born: Hong Kong, 1 August 1907.
Died: Pulborough, Sussex, 20 May 1982.
'For here is a cricketer to whom the game was the best thing in life; who kicked cynicism and smugness violently aside; who evidently and unashamedly thought cricket "fit to employ all the heart and the soul and the senses for ever

in joy"; who could and would bowl all day with a sort of ferocious accuracy; who danced with delight when he flattened a stump, slapped umpires on the back, ran three when the book said two, and was probably known by his first name to the sparrows in the deep-field.' So wrote R.C.Robertson-Glasgow of Stephenson in 1943, and three years later, Dudley Carew confirmed, 'He did really tear his hair, he did really leap off the ground like some figure in a mad Frederick Ashton cricketing *ballet.*'

Undoubtedly, Stephenson was an all-round cricketer of such zest that it was said that had there been more cricketers like him, there would have been fewer empty grounds.

His first cricket was for Buckinghamshire, and he made his first-class debut for Europeans in 1928 when he was with the Middlesex Regiment in India. He also played for Madras. He first played for Essex in 1934, and the following season he was awarded his county cap when he took 4 for 92 against Yorkshire at Colchester. He also bowled well against the touring South Africans, but his Army duties always prevented him from appearing regularly.

He produced a sensational performance for the Gentlemen against the Players at Lord's in 1936 when he took 9 for 46, and he was very close to winning a place in the side that went to Australia the following winter. He did play in a Test trial in 1937, but he strained a tendon hurdling for his battalion at Aldershot and was out for the rest of the season.

One of Essex's triumvirate of captains in 1939, he played more often than before, but World War Two virtually brought an end to his career although he did play one match for Worcestershire in 1947.

An inspiring leader of men, he commanded the 1/7 Battalion of the Middlesex Regiment from 1942 to 1945. He fought in North Africa, Sicily and Italy, and he was awarded the DSO in 1944 for action in Tunisia.

After the war he joined *Picture Post* and *Life* and became director of *Life International*. He retired to Pulborough where he played much golf and became renowned for his one-handed, back-handed putting.

M	Inns	NOs	Runs	HS	Avge	Ct
61	93	21	1050	65	14.58	30

Overs	Mds	Runs	Wkts	Avge	Best	10/m	5/inn
1023.5	236	4156	174	23.88	8/46	1	10

297.3 (eight-ball)

Exley Anthony Whiteford STEWARD

Born: Durban, South Africa, 27 June 1941.
Steward came from South Africa to try his luck as a professional cricketer with Essex. In four seasons in the 2nd XI, 1962-65, he scored 2164 runs, but he could never repeat that form in his matches in the county side in 1964 and 1965.

Educated at Maritzburg College, he was a right-handed batsman, leg-break bowler and wicket-keeper. He also played polo, tennis and hockey. He developed his cricket with Durban Collegians, and when he came to England he played for Buckhurst Hill.

He hit 47 against Middlesex at Westcliff in one of his early matches for the county, 1964, but he played little the following season and returned to South Africa in 1966. He appeared in three matches for Natal 'B' in the 1967-68 season, but he was not seen after that. He restricted himself to club cricket and to his work as a farmer.

M	Inns	NOs	Runs	HS	Avge	Ct
15	23	2	272	47	12.95	17

Frank STREET

Born: Kensington, London, 31 May 1870.
Died: Ovilliers la Boiselle, France, 7 July 1916.
'A good bat with an extremely pretty style', Frank Street was in the Westminster XI in 1888 and 1889, being captain in his second year. He went up to Oxford and won his blue for soccer but played no first-class cricket while at University. He appeared for Essex against Surrey, Leicestershire, Warwickshire and Derbyshire early in 1898, and in five

matches the following season, he averaged 30.66, hitting 76 against Leicestershire at Leicester, and 60 against Hampshire at Southampton. Thereafter, he disappeared into business. At school, he had been recognised as a steady medium-pace bowler.

Commissioned in the Royal Fusiliers at the outbreak of World War One, Lieutenant Street was killed in action on the Western Front in 1916.

M	Inns	NOs	Runs	HS	Avge	Ct
9	11	-	246	76	22.36	4

Overs	Mds	Runs	Wkts	Avge
2	-	14	-	-

(five-ball overs)

Benjamin Thomas STRUTTON

Born: 1892.
Died: Southwark, London, 9 February 1968.
A professional slow left-arm bowler whose career was disrupted by World War One, Strutton appeared in 1914 and 1919, but he failed to take a wicket in his four matches.

M	Inns	NOs	Runs	HS	Avge	Ct
4	6	1	64	19	12.80	1

Overs	Mds	Runs	Wkts	Avge
49	4	197	-	-

Peter Mark SUCH

Born: Helensburgh, Dumbartonshire, Scotland, 12 June 1964.
Born in Scotland, Peter Such moved to East Leake, Nottinghamshire, when young. He played cricket at both primary and secondary school and won a place in the Nottinghamshire School sides. He played for Nottinghamshire 2nd XI while still at school, and, in spite of academic successes, he chose cricket as a professional career. He was with Nottinghamshire from 1982 to 1986, and he benefited greatly from playing alongside Rice and Hadlee, and learned much from Hemmings and Bob White, but he was frustrated from lack of opportunity and moved to Leicestershire in 1987.

He enjoyed a good first season with Leicestershire, but the attitudes within the county were not totally conducive to off-spin bowling, and he declined a new contract at the end of the 1989 season.

Peter Such moved to Essex in 1990 and after a 'probationary' first season, he established a spin partnership with John Childs that had no superior in the country. Both his fielding and his batting, still limited in technique, developed, and his bowling matured intelligently.

He underwent knee surgery at the end of the 1992 season but then had a highly successful tour of Australia with the England 'A' team. A splendid start to the 1993 season won him a place in the Test side against Australia, and his 16 wickets in the series made him England's leading wicket-taker. He finished the season with 76 wickets, but England's decision not to take an off-spinner to the Caribbean was a disappointment. He responded by again bowling well for the 'A' team on their tour of South Africa.

M	Inns	NOs	Runs	HS	Avge	Ct
71	62	13	509	54	10.38	26

Overs	Mds	Runs	Wkts	Avge	Best	10/m	5/inn
2164.5	570	5742	205	28.00	7/66	3	14

Sunday League

M	Inns	NOs	Runs	HS	Avge	Ct
54	22	11	97	19*	8.18	13

Overs	Mds	Runs	Wkts	Avge	Best	5/inn
388.2	19	1670	56	29.82	5/32	2

Benson and Hedges Cup

M	Inns	NOs	Runs	HS	Avge	Ct
13	6	2	12	4	3.00	2

Overs	Mds	Runs	Wkts	Avge	Best
106	8	404	12	33.66	4/22

NatWest Trophy

M	Inns	NOs	Runs	HS	Avge	Ct
10	3	2	6	6	6.00	1

Overs	Mds	Runs	Wkts	Avge	Best
98	9	317	9	35.22	2/29

George Thomas SUTTON

Born: West Ham, 1 October 1887.
Died: Penge, Kent, 16 January 1949.
George Thomas Sutton was a professional right-handed batsman who played for Essex against Yorkshire at Huddersfield in June 1912. He batted at number ten and was the second victim in a hat-trick performed by the left-arm medium pacer Alonzo Drake.

M	Inns	NOs	Runs	HS	Avge
1	1	-	0	0	0.00

Charles Frederick SWANN

Born: Leyton, 6 August 1883.
Died: Harrow Green, Leytonstone, 7 March 1960.
Like Sutton, Swan was a professional batsman whose only game for Essex was against Yorkshire at Huddersfield in 1912. He batted at number eight in the rain-affected match in which Alonzo Drake finished the Essex innings by taking 6 for 7 in 43 balls. The last five wickets went down at 103, and Swann was one of Drake's victims.

M	Inns	NOs	Runs	HS	Avge
1	1	-	0	0	0.00

Basil James SWYER

Born: West Ham, 6 June 1898.
Died: Sherwood, Nottingham, 7 July 1964.
Educated at Bancroft's School, Basil Swyer was a medium-pace bowler who played for Essex against Kent at Leyton in June 1923.

M	Inns	NOs	Runs	HS	Avge
1	2	-	12	7	6.00

Overs	Mds	Runs	Wkts	Avge
13	1	56	-	-

Captain Alfred George TAYLOR

Born: West Ham, 29 December 1891.
A Regular Army officer who played for Essex against Derbyshire at Chesterfield, and against Surrey at Leyton, in 1923. He batted low in the order and was second or third change bowler. He took the wicket of Morton of Derbyshire.

M	Inns	NOs	Runs	HS	Avge
2	3	-	7	7	2.33

Overs	Mds	Runs	Wkts	Avge	Best
19	4	77	1	77.00	1/40

Brian TAYLOR

Born: West Ham, 19 June 1932.
One of the very great men in Essex cricket history, Brian Taylor played for the county over a period of five decades, captained the side from 1967 to 1973, appeared in 301 consecutive Championship matches between 1961 and 1972, instilled fitness and discipline into a small band of players and brought them to the point of greatness. That he never shared in the final triumphs is one of the sadnesses of Essex cricket.

Educated at Central Park School, East Ham, he was strongly influenced by his teacher, Leslie Fielding, who recognised his all round talent as a sportsman. Taylor captained Essex Schools at cricket, and he was one of those selected for the *Evening News Colts* scheme, an admirable project which coached and encouraged talented young cricketers. Alan Moss, the Middlesex and England fast bowler, and Malcolm Heath, the Hampshire bowler, were among its beneficiaries.

A left-handed batsman and wicket-keeper, he made his debut for Essex against Cambridge University, at Fenner's, in May 1949. This was the occasion when Dewes and Doggart shared an unbroken second wicket stand of 429 in five hours for Cambridge. Taylor batted number ten, scored 2 and did not claim a wicket. He could play only the occasional game over the next two seasons because of National Service.

With the retirement of Wade, Essex had engaged Paul Gibb from Yorkshire as wicket-keeper, and this restricted Taylor's opportunities, but a pre-season injury to Gibb in 1954 gave Taylor his chance, and he impressed to such an extent, with his aggressive batting as well as with his keeping, that he was retained in the side for his batting when Gibb was fit again. By 1956, he had established himself as the regular Essex wicket-keeper.

In that season, he hit his first first-class century, was named as *Young Cricketer of the Year* by the Cricket Writers' Club and was chosen for the tour of South Africa as Godfrey Evans' understudy. It was the nearest he was to come to Test selection.

In 1962, he established an Essex record with 89 dismissals in the season, and by the end of his career, he had taken 1083 catches and made 211 stumpings. His 1294 dismissals place him sixth in the list of all time wicket-keepers, and it is unlikely that he will ever be ousted from that position.

His belligerence as a batsman earned him the nickname of *Tonker,* and he became a favourite with the crowd. Nevertheless, it came as something of a surprise when he was appointed captain of Essex in succession to Trevor Bailey. This was a difficult time. The staff was small, and the debts were great. Everyone on the staff worked hard, and Brian Taylor drilled his men with a fitness campaign that had a military stamp about it. As one of those players has said, 'We were the first county that ever seriously considered physical fitness.'

If the limited playing resources realistically placed the Championship beyond the scope of Essex, Taylor recognised that the style and character of his side would allow them to thrive in the new Sunday League. In the first four years of its existence, they did not finish outside the top four, and once they were cruelly deprived of the title by a decimal point. More than anything at this stage, Essex's success was founded on some outstanding fielding, the reward for their physical fitness campaign, and on the fact that they played for each other.

Taylor had always kept himself in peak condition. He had been a professional footballer with Brentford, Bexley United, whom he managed, and Dover. He was an uncompromising left-back, hard and honest.

His honours in cricket were to be restricted to an appearance for the Players against the Gentlemen in 1957, a place as one of *Wisden's* Five Cricketers of the Year in 1972, and to be on the Test selectors panel in 1973 and 1974.

He appeared in only 11 matches in 1973, his last season, and his final match for Essex was against Nottinghamshire, at Chelmsford, at the end of August when he led his side to a nine-wicket victory. He made five and had six dismissals in the match, the last being when he stumped Stead off Acfield. Two days later, he was unbeaten for 10 as Essex beat Warwickshire in their last Sunday League game of the season.

For a period, he coached and captained the 2nd XI. He also ran the sports outfitters in Romford which had formerly been owned by Ted Ditchburn, the former Tottenham Hotspur and England goalkeeper. He also worked for a public relations company and for one selling provisions, and he was coach to Cambridge University CC. More recently, he has returned to Essex and works with Alan Lilley in liaising with schools cricket and in coaching and developing young players.

Brian Taylor is a monumental figure in the history of Essex cricket. Fiercely fit, transparently honest, he was devoted to his wife, his mother and to Essex cricket. The game and the county owe him much.

M	Inns	NOs	Runs	HS	Avge	100s	Ct/st
539	901	69	18240	135	21.92	9	1040/191

Overs	Mds	Runs	Wkts	Avge	Best
8.3	2	21	1	21.00	1/16

Sunday League

M	Inns	NOs	Runs	HS	Avge	100s	Ct/st
78	77	3	1540	100	20.81	1	62/19

Benson and Hedges Cup

M	Inns	NOs	Runs	HS	Avge	Ct
10	7	-	76	30	10.85	11

Gillette Cup

M	Inns	NOs	Runs	HS	Avge	Ct/st
19	17	-	221	31	13.00	20/3

John Frederick TAYLOR

Born: West Ham, 9 June 1937.

John Taylor's bad luck with Essex was that he was on the staff at a time when the county had

too many wicket-keepers available. He was engaged in 1958, having impressed as a wicket-keeper and batsman with Wanstead, but he did not make his debut until 1960 when he took over behind the stumps from Brian Taylor who had lost form.

He began the 1961 season as the county wicket-keeper, but Brian Taylor recaptured his form and took over again as wicket-keeper. John Taylor played occasionally as a batsman, and was not keeping wicket when he made his highest score, 86 against Somerset at Westcliff. Sensing a lack of future opportunities, he accepted a business appointment that was offered to him and left first-class cricket although he did appear for MCC in 1967, performing admirably against Cambridge University at Lord's.

Taylor had a highly successful career with Moseley in the Birmingham League where he was a great favourite. He was a fine amateur soccer player with Grays Athletic.

M	Inns	NOs	Runs	HS	Avge	Ct/st
14	23	6	436	86	25.64	19/3

Reginald Minshall TAYLOR

Born: Southend, 30 November 1909.
Died: Johannesburg, South Africa, 7 January 1984.
Reginald Taylor was a stylish right-handed

batsman and a slow left-arm bowler who played one match in 1931, against Sussex, at Chelmsford, when he did not score a run and did not take a wicket. Educated at Southend High School and a regular member of the Southend club, he established a place in the county side in 1932 when he hit an impressive century against Yorkshire, at Scarborough. The following season, he scored 1000 runs for the first time, but, in 1935, he did not play at all due to injury, and it was not until 1938 that he began to bowl with any regularity. In the last season before the war, he took 55 wickets.

His chinaman and googly were very effective on his day, but, as a batsman, his compulsive hooking often cost him his wicket.

He joined the Royal Air Force at the outbreak of war, was commissioned and was awarded the DFC for his outstanding work as an observer with Bomber Command. He was the first professional cricketer to win the DFC in World War Two, and, the award came when he was serving with a Lysander Squadron during the Dunkirk evacuation.

Taylor returned to Essex in 1946 and played for one season as an amateur. He scored freely, but, in spite of returning his best bowling figures in the match at Taunton, he was less successful as a bowler. He went into business and emigrated to South Africa where he joined the Wanderers club of which he later became captain. He was a popular man of great charm.

At Southend, in August 1946, when Essex were in danger of being forced to follow-on against Warwickshire, he and Denys Wilcox added 263 for the eighth wicket, and Essex went on to win by an innings. This remains an eighth wicket record stand for the county.

M	Inns	NOs	Runs	HS	Avge	100s	Ct
206	349	21	6755	193	20.59	5	185

Overs	Mds	Runs	Wkts	Avge	Best	10/m	5/inn
415.5	66	2933	92	31.88	7/99	-	3
272.3 (eight-ball)							

Ernest Cranfield TEDDER

Born: Woodford Green, 5 September 1915.
Died: Ipswich, Suffolk, 9 September 1972.
Tedder was a distinguished club cricketer, captain of Woodford Wells, and known as a great character with a zest for life. He had a fine record at Chigwell School before going into the family printing business.

In 1946, he appeared in eight matches for Essex, and, at Ilford, against Sussex, 'Tedder, a Woodford Wells amateur, drove delightfully in helping Essex gain a first innings lead,' said *Wisden*.

Like many of his generation, Tedder's best formative years were lost to the war, and he was destined to be a top class club cricketer.

A great golfing enthusiast, he opened a hotel in Aldeburgh on the Suffolk coast.

M	Inns	NOs	Runs	HS	Avge	Ct
8	14	-	208	55	14.85	3

Kevin Oliver THOMAS

Born: Mile End, London, 20 June 1963.
Kevin Thomas enjoyed considerable success  for Ilford CC before being released from his work at the Post Office temporarily for a one-year engagement with Essex in 1990. A right-arm fast medium pace bowler, he was already 26 years old when he joined the staff, and he appeared in only one game, against the New Zealand tourists.

He has assisted Cambridgeshire in a few matches since being released by Essex.

M	Inns	NOs	Runs	HS	Avge
1	1	-	2	2	2.00

Overs	Mds	Runs	Wkts	Avge
18.2	3	81	-	-

Eddie Clarke THOMPSON

Born: Leyton, 27 February 1907.
Died: Torquay, Devon, 18 March 1982.
Eddie Thompson was a slow left-arm who could spin the ball prodigiously, but he lacked the necessary control to earn him a regular place in county cricket. He played for Essex from 1926 until 1929, his debut coming at Trent Bridge against Nottinghamshire. He was bowled for 0 and failed to take a wicket in the three overs he was given.

A stylish left-handed batsman, he left Essex after the 1929 season and disappeared from cricket circles. His death at the age of 75 went unrecorded in *Wisden* and the cricketing press.

M	Inns	NOs	Runs	H.S	Avge	Ct
44	61	17	696	45*	15.81	10

Overs	Mds	Runs	Wkts	Avge	Best
291.4	45	938	17	55.17	2/12

Hubert Wethered THORN

Born: Tiptree, 21 April 1909.
Died: Colchester, 20 May 1982.
An all-rounder, Hubert Thorn played for Essex against Northamptonshire at Leyton in July 1928. An amateur, he did not appear again in first-class cricket.

M	Inns	NOs	Runs	HS	Avge
1	2	-	12	7	6.00

Overs	Mds	Runs	Wkts	Avge	Best
10	-	42	1	42.00	1/42

Percy TOONE

Born: Colchester, 27 July 1883.
Died: Isleworth, Middlesex, 4 February 1955.
A right-arm quick bowler whose career with Essex lasted from 1912 to 1922, Percy Toone could never command a regular place in the side. He had come somewhat late to professional cricket, and the bulk of his wickets were taken in 1920 and 1921 when he was 38 years old.

Tall, he used his height well, but he did not always command a length. He performed the hat-trick against Kent at Leyton in 1920 when he dismissed Collins, Seymour and Woolley with the first three balls he bowled in the match. The first two were taken by Russell at

slip, and Woolley played on. Toone became a first-class umpire in 1930.

M	Inns	NOs	Runs	HS	Avge	Ct
29	42	13	215	24	7.41	23

Overs	Mds	Runs	Wkts	Avge	Best	10/m	5/inn
484.3	47	1954	62	31.51	6/51	1	2

Thomas Donald TOPLEY

Born: Canterbury, Kent, 25 February 1964.
Few cricketers have had such a varied career as Don Topley, a hard-hitting right-handed batsman and a right-arm medium-fast bowler. He played for Norfolk in 1984 and 1985 and was on the MCC groundstaff in 1984 when, fielding as substitute for England in the Test match against West Indies at Lord's, he took a spectacular one-handed catch on the boundary off a hit from Malcolm Marshall. Unfortunately, he had one foot over the rope, and Marshall was credited with six.

In 1985, Topley played for Surrey against Cambridge University at Fenner's in June, but he had no contract with the South London county, and a month later he was taking five wickets for Essex against Gloucestershire at Southend.

He played for Griqualand West, 1987-88, and took 7 for 75 against Derbyshire at Chesterfield in the England season that followed. In 1989, he took 77 wickets, proving himself to be a most valuable county all-rounder.

Topley coached in Zimbabwe and was coach to the national side for the World Cup in 1991-92. He drew great satisfaction from the fact that Zimbabwe beat England.

More recently, he has returned to his old school, the Royal Hospital School, Holbrook in Suffolk, as a physical education teacher. He left the Essex staff at the end of 1994.

M	Inns	NOs	Runs	HS	Avge	Ct
113	127	26	1520	66	15.04	65

Overs	Mds	Runs	Wkts	Avge	Best	10/m	5/inn
2988.4	605	9431	336	28.06	7/75	1	12

Sunday League

M	Inns	NOs	Runs	HS	Avge	Ct
111	58	19	309	38*	7.92	22

Overs	Mds	Runs	Wkts	Avge	Best	5/inn
774.5	41	3536	126	28.08	6/33	2

Benson and Hedges Cup

M	Inns	NOs	Runs	HS	Avge	Ct
26	7	4	35	10*	11.66	7

Overs	Mds	Runs	Wkts	Avge	Best
248	36	836	36	23.19	4/22

NatWest Trophy

M	Inns	NOs	Runs	HS	Avge	Ct
15	6	2	65	19*	16.25	3

Overs	Mds	Runs	Wkts	Avge	Best
155.2	18	582	27	21.55	4/21

Gilbert TOSETTI

Born: Bromley, Kent, 1 August 1879.
Died: Plateau, Eldoret, Kenya, 16 April 1923.

A right-handed batsman and right-arm medium pace bowler, Tosetti was educated at Bancroft's School and played club cricket for Woodford Wells. He played for Essex between 1898 and 1905, and, in 1902, at Old Trafford, he hit 132 not out in three and three-quarter hours.

M	Inns	NOs	Runs	HS	Avge	Ct
41	63	6	1054	132*	18.49	15

Overs	Mds	Runs	Wkts	Avge	Best
256.3	60	891	16	55.68	3/67

45 (five-ball)

Evelyn Murraugh O'Brien TOULMIN

Born: Hatfield Peverel, 13 August 1877.
Died: Paris, France, 7 January 1945.

A left-handed batsman and slow right-arm bowler, Toulmin was an excellent all-rounder at King's School, Canterbury, but failed to win a place in the Oxford side when he went up to Magdalen College. He made two appearances for Essex, the first in 1899, and the second in 1912. His run and his wickets came in the first match.

M	Inns	NOs	Runs	HS	Avge	Ct
2	2	-	1	1	0.50	2

Overs	Mds	Runs	Wkts	Avge	Best
5	10	57	2	28.50	2/16

24 (five-ball)

Arthur Fenton Miles TOWNSEND

Born: Clifton, Bristol, 1 August 1885.
Died: Brompton, Kensington, London, 24 August 1948.

Miles Townsend made one rather bizarre appearance for Essex in 1910. He was in the side that played Worcestershire at Bourneville at the beginning of July. Only three hours play was possible, and that was on the second day. Townsend neither batted nor bowled.

He was a member of the famous Gloucestershire family, four generations of whom played cricket for that county. Perhaps the most famous member of the family was C.L. who played for England in 1899, but D.C.H., a nephew of Miles Townsend, played for England in 1934-35. His county cricket was for Durham, and he is the last cricketer to have played for England without having played in the County Championship.

Miles Townsend played nine matches for Gloucestershire between 1903 and 1906.

M	Inns	NOs	Runs	HS	Avge
1	-	-	-	-	

Lieutenant-Colonel Claude Jesse Helby TREGLOWN

Born: Herne Bay, Kent, 13 February 1893.
Died: Worthing, Sussex, 7 May 1980.
A Regular Army officer, Claude Treglown was educated at Norwich School and played for Norfolk between 1910 and 1913. He won the Military Cross in World War One.

He also appeared for Sussex 2nd XI, and his career for Essex was restricted to his availability between 1922 and 1928. A right-handed batsman, he opened the innings on occasions and was also used as a wicket-keeper in an emergency.

M	Inns	NOs	Runs	HS	Avge	Ct
34	55	3	792	77	15.23	11

Bert TREMLIN

Born: Bristol, Gloucestershire, 18 September 1877.
Died: 12 April 1936.
Bert Tremlin was unfortunate in that his career coincided with that of Walter Mead and that his opportunities for bowling his accurate, medium pace off-breaks were limited. He first played for Essex in 1900, but he made only casual appearances until 1905 when he took 99 wickets in all first-class matches. This was the season when, at Leyton, he took 9 for 126 against Derbyshire.

A late order batsman, he caused something of a sensation by hitting 160 for an Essex XI against Carmarthen at Llanelli in 1906, but, unable to agree terms, he left the county the

following season and went into the Lancashire League. Returning in 1910, he played until the outbreak of World War One, and he enjoyed his best season in 1914 when he took 101 wickets.

He appeared in 1919, but he was then 42 years old, and his 20 wickets cost 36.55 runs each.

Tremlin proved to be a good coach, and he stood as a first-class umpire in 1923 and 1924. Pelham Warner paid tribute to him for the work he did as a practice bowler when Warner was living in Kent.

M	Inns	NOs	Runs	HS	Avge	Ct
132	193	63	1776	61	13.66	62

Overs	Mds	Runs	Wkts	Avge	Best	10/m	5/inn
3650.3	706	11734	452	25.96	9/126	4	23

Stanley Arthur TRICK

Born: Stoke Newington, London, 3 June 1884.
Died: Worcester Park, Surrey, 11 February 1958.
Educated at Merchant Taylor's School, Stanley Trick was the uncle of the Glamorgan all-rounder of the immediate post-war period. A right-handed middle order batsman, Stanley Trick played five games for Essex in 1905 as an amateur without much success.

M	Inns	NOs	Runs	HS	Avge	Ct
5	9	-	69	26	7.66	1

Brigadier Arthur Jervois TURNER

Born: Mussorie, India, 10 June 1878.
Died: Graffham, Sussex, 8 September 1952.
Had A.J.Turner devoted his life to cricket rather than to the Army, he would

unquestionably have been a player of the very highest quality. C.B.Fry was one of many who held that opinion. As it is, there are thousands of cricketers who would envy Turner his record in the first-class game.

A right-handed batsman, elegant and forceful, a right-arm medium-pace lob bowler, an accomplished wicket-keeper and an outstanding fielder, he was born in India where his father was serving as a Major. Major Turner encouraged his sons to play cricket, a game he loved passionately, and 'Johnny' and his brother Walter were both to play for Essex while a third brother, J.T., played for the Europeans in India.

Tragically, Major Turner was drowned in 1892 along with the other members of the Hong Kong cricket team when returning from a match against Shanghai. The *Bokhara*, the boat on which they were sailing, sank.

'Johnny' Turner was educated at Bedford Modern School where he was in the XI for four years from the age of 13, captaining the side in his last year and being eminently successful. He played for Bedfordshire, and, still a cadet at the Royal Military Academy, Woolwich, he made his debut for Essex against Hampshire, at Southampton, in 1897, and hit 33 in an innings victory. In the same week, he hit 61

and 26 not out as Derbyshire were beaten at Leyton, and, within a month, he had hit a maiden first-class century, 111 against the mighty Yorkshire, at Huddersfield, in a match which Essex won by one run. By the end of the season, he was top of the county batting averages and ninth in the first-class averages for the country. He was 19 years old.

He played for the Gentlemen against the Players at The Oval in 1898 and caught and bowled the great Arthur Shrewsbury for one of his three wickets in the match. He was invited to play in the Lord's fixture the following season, but he was unable to appear because of his military duties. He made the highest of his 11 centuries that season, 124 against Warwickshire, at Edgbaston, when he and his brother Walter saved Essex. He also shared big partnerships with Perrin and McGahey in 1899 and played an important part in the victory over the Australians. He finished the season with 751 runs, average 46.93, but for much of the time afterwards, his demands as an Army officer claimed him.

He served with the Royal Artillery in the South African War and was wounded at Ladysmith. He could play no first-class cricket in 1900, nor, indeed, in 1902, 03, 06 or 07, but he had the wonderful capacity for being able to return to county cricket after a long absence and bat immediately with skill and confidence against the strongest of opposition. The fact that he scored a century in each of his first-class seasons, limited as his appearances were, is testimony to this.

He last played for Essex in 1910, finishing with 34 and 4 not out against his old enemy Yorkshire. He was able to play in only five Championship matches in this season, but he still managed one of the two centuries hit by an Essex batsman during the campaign, 111 not out against Nottinghamshire, at Trent Bridge. He finished second in the batting averages.

A fine rugby player, he played for Blackheath and Kent, 'Johnny' Turner ended his first-class career with a game for the Free Foresters in 1914. He was on the staff of the GHQ in France in World War One and was four times mentioned in dispatches. He was made a Companion of the Order of St Michael and St George, won the Distinguished Service Order and, significantly, the Croix de Guerre.

In every respect, this was a career of rich achievement.

M	Inns	NOs	Runs	HS	Avge	100s	Ct/st
68	116	12	3730	124	35.86	11	26/2

Overs	Mds	Runs	Wkts	Avge	Best
24	25	438	12	36.50	3/47

115.3 (five-ball)

Stuart TURNER

Born: Chester, Cheshire, 18 July 1943.

It has been said that Stuart Turner epitomised the spirit of Essex cricket which, after years of near misses, eventually brought glory. It could also be said that his career was almost a parallel of those years of endeavour which culminated in the period between 1979 and 1985 when three Championships, three Sunday League titles, and both knock-out competitions were won. Stuart Turner played a vital part in all of those triumphs, but before those years he had tasted the bad as well as the good.

It was his passion for the game that transformed Turner from a club cricketer into a first-class cricketer with an all-round record of which any player would be proud. His achievements for Buckhurst Hill brought him to the notice of Essex, and he made his debut, against Yorkshire at Bradford, July 1965. He was nearly knocked out by Freddie Trueman, was leg before to Hutton for one and did not take a wicket. In fact, it was not until his third match that he did take a wicket, that of Reynolds of Northamptonshire. In all, he appeared in nine Championship matches, and he was released at the end of the season. The horror was that, through an oversight, no-one had thought to tell him that his contract had not been renewed.

He found himself in the spring of 1966, newly-married, jobless and somewhat embittered. He found a job at Ford's, led his departmental cricket team to unparalleled heights, scored runs and took wickets for Buckhurst Hill and was re-engaged by Essex for the 1968 season. At the beginning of June, he and Hobbs put on 192 in two hours for the eighth wicket against Glamorgan at Ilford. Both men hit maiden first-class centuries. Two years later, he hit 121 against Somerset at Taunton and was awarded his county cap. A dream had been realised.

In 1971, he did the hat-trick against Surrey at The Oval, but it was not until 1974 that he reached his peak form. With 963 runs and 73 wickets, he was the outstanding all-rounder in

English cricket, and he became the second Essex player to win the Wetherall Award. He came very close to being selected for the England side to go to Australia under Denness, but the ultimate accolade just eluded him. The struggle for success had made him an abrasive character in his early years, one who did not suffer fools gladly, and an occasional clash with authority told against him. He mellowed, but he should have certainly played in one-day internationals for there was no better English limited-over cricketer. He bowled a brisk medium pace, naggingly just short of a length, and he hit belligerently and often. His fielding was dynamic, anywhere.

In 1978, he became the first player to take a total of 200 wickets in the Sunday League, and later the same season he became the first to the 'double' of 200 wickets and 2000 runs in that competition. Seven years later, in his penultimate season, he became the first and only player to score 3,000 runs and to take 300 wickets in the League. It was not just that he took wickets, he was miserly in giving away runs.

He played with a deep sense of loyalty to his county and to his colleagues, and his intense emotional involvement tended to make him suffer the disappointments of the late 1970s more than most. It was all the more gratifying that he should share in the team triumphs of

1979, his Benefit Year. The crowd always recognised his commitment, and he was the greatest of favourites. The strength of that commitment, the passion, physical and mental, touched chords in supporters and evoked memories of aspirations past. He was lightning as he ran between the wickets, and if he was never the stylist with bat or ball, he set the pulse throbbing.

He went to South Africa with D.H.Robins' side in 1974-75 and spent two seasons with Natal, sharing in their successes in the Currie Cup and Datsun Shield. At other times he coached at the Ilford Indoor School.

With the advent of Pringle and Foster, his opportunities in the Championship side became more limited, but the remained a force in the one-day game until his retirement at the end of the 1986 season. It had always seemed that he would go on for ever, but he finally called it a day at the age of 43. Not that he was finished with cricket. He took up a post as Games Master at Forest School and played for Cambridgeshire. In his first season in the Minor Counties, he took all ten wickets for 11 runs against Cumberland so establishing a record for the Minor Counties Championship.

His will shows no sign of weakening, and he served on the Essex Committee for a period.

M	Inns	NOs	Runs	HS	Avge	100s	Ct
354	503	98	9264	121	22.87	4	215

Overs	Mds	Runs	Wkts	Avge	Best	10/m	5/inn
8778.1	2249	20987	810	25.90	6/26	1	27

Sunday League

M	Inns	NOs	Runs	HS	Avge	Ct
255	205	44	3165	87	19.65	82

Overs	Mds	Runs	Wkts	Avge	Best	5/inn
1766.5	168	7231	303	23.86	5/35	1

Benson and Hedges Cup

M	Inns	NOs	Runs	HS	Avge	Ct
76	56	17	651	55*	16.69	16

Overs	Mds	Runs	Wkts	Avge	Best
770.2	132	2222	107	20.76	4/19

Gillette Cup / NatWest Trophy

M	Inns	NOs	Runs	HS	Avge	Ct
36	29	4	449	50*	17.96	5

Overs	Mds	Runs	Wkts	Avge	Best
354.5	71	1027	50	20.54	4/23

Lieutenant-Colonel Walter Martin Fitzherbert TURNER

Born: Meerut, India, 4 April 1881.
Died: Roxeth, Harrow, Middlesex, 1 February 1948.

The younger brother of Arthur Turner, and, like A.J., a Regular Army officer, Walter Turner was 'a punishing bat, possessed of plenty of nerve, and making his runs by a variety of strokes'. He captained Wellington in 1897 and first played for Essex two years later. He was not able to play sufficiently to give himself a chance to establish himself in first-class cricket, and it was not until 1906, when he hit 923 runs, that he was able to assist the county with any regularity. It was in that season that he hit 104 not out against Derbyshire at Leyton.

He played some excellent innings for Essex, and he was particularly noted for his rearguard actions, but he was lost to the county in 1910-11 when he served in India and played for the Europeans.

He did play occasional games for Essex until the end of the 1926 season so that his career with the county spanned 27 years. Memorably, in 1919, the first season after the war, he scored 172 out of 255 in two and three-quarter hours against Middlesex at Leyton. He will remain one of those of whom one will perpetually ask the question – what if he had been able to play regularly?

M	Inns	NOs	Runs	HS	Avge	100s	Ct
48	81	7	2004	172	27.08	2	58

Overs	Mds	Runs	Wkts	Avge	Best
21	10	180	3	60.00	2/12
30 (five-ball)					

Percy Wakeford TURRALL

Born: Brentford, 16 June 1883.
Died: Chelmsford, 17 May 1941.

Percy Turrall played club cricket for Chelmsford and opened the Essex innings with Jim Cutmore against Oxford University at Chelmsford, in June 1927. The pair put on 91, and Turrell batted impressively, but he was not seen in first-class cricket again.

M	Inns	NOs	Runs	HS	Avge
1	1	-	45	45	45.00

Lieutenant-Colonel Ernest James UNWIN

Born: Birdbrook, 18 September 1912.
Like his elder brother George, Ernest Unwin was educated at Haileybury. He appeared very occasionally for Essex between 1932 and 1939, but he was much better known as a rugby player. A winger, he played for Rosslyn Park and England, and he toured South Africa with the British Lions in 1938.

A Regular Army officer, he played cricket for Suffolk from 1951 until 1956.

M	Inns	NOs	Runs	HS	Avge	Ct
7	14	-	152	48	10.85	2

Overs	Mds	Runs	Wkts	Avge
30	3	103	-	-

Frederick St George UNWIN

Born: Baythorne Hall, Halstead, Suffolk, 23 April 1911.
Died: Braintree, 4 October 1990.
A tall right-handed batsman, Unwin was a positive hitter of the ball who first played for Essex in 1932. Educated at Haileybury, he was never regularly available because of his business involvement as a leading seed merchant, but he did captain Essex from 17 June until Denys Wilcox was available in mid-July 1939. He led the side most ably, but his impetuosity did not allow him to do himself justice as a batsman.

He reappeared in a few matches after

World War Two and made his highest score of 60 against Kent at Colchester in 1946, an innings which helped to save the game. He last played for Essex in 1950.

He appeared for Suffolk in 1933 and toured Egypt with Martineau's side in 1938, but he was probably better known as a rugby player for Rosslyn Park and Eastern Counties as was his brother Ernest.

M	Inns	NOs	Runs	HS	Avge	Ct
52	85	8	1125	60	14.61	33

Overs	Mds	Runs	Wkts	Avge
12	1	41	-	-

James VALIANT

Born: Wavertree, Liverpool, Lancashire, 17 July 1884.
Died: Gaza, Palestine, 28 October 1917.
A professional, Valiant played for Essex against Northamptonshire, at Northampton, in June 1912. He batted at number 11 and was first change bowler in a side that lost by an innings.

Killed in World War One, his death went unrecorded at the time.

M	Inns	NOs	Runs	HS	Avge
1	2	1	3	3	3.00

Overs	Mds	Runs	Wkts	Avge
4	-	20	-	-

Lieutenant-Colonel Henry Hamilton VAN STRAUBENZEE

Born: Parktown, Johannesburg, South Africa, 7 March 1914.
A slow left-arm bowler and right-handed batsman educated at Winchester, Van Straubenzee played first-class cricket for the Army and played for Essex against Sussex at Colchester where he was stationed at the time in July 1938.

M	Inns	NOs	Runs	HS	Avge
1	1	1	4	4*	-

Overs	Mds	Runs	Wkts	Avge
6	1	12	-	-

Dr Nicholas VERE HODGE

Born: Woodford Green, 31 October 1912.

A successful cricketer at Uppingham, Nicholas Vere Hodge did not appear in any first-class matches while he was up at Cambridge. He first played for Essex in 1936, scoring 77 on his debut against Kent at Southend in Nichols' Benefit Match. An upright batsman, he finished second in the batting averages although he appeared in only four matches and confirmed the good form he had shown in club cricket with Woodford Wells.

Making himself available for 11 matches in 1937, Vere Hodge hit 100 not out against Middlesex at Lord's in May, and 108 against Nottinghamshire at Trent Bridge in August.

Certainly he could have been a county player of considerable merit, but by 1938, he had qualified as a doctor. He played much less, and his form fell away. He appeared in only one match in 1939.

He served as a squadron-leader in the RAF in World War Two.

M	Inns	NOs	Runs	HS	Avge	100s	Ct
23	38	6	713	108	22.28	2	11

Frank Henry VIGAR

Born: Bruton, Somerset, 14 July 1917.
Engaged at the end of the 1937 season, Frank Vigar made his debut for Essex against Glamorgan at Swansea in May 1938, a game which was ruined by rain and which saw him neither bat nor bowl. A right-handed batsman and leg-break bowler, he played with some regularity as a middle-order batsman in 1939 and hit 121 against Gloucestershire at Westcliff.

Capped in 1946, Vigar enjoyed a spectacular season the following year when, in all matches, he hit 1735 runs and took 64 wickets. His four centuries all came in away matches, and, at Chesterfield, he hit 114 not out against Derbyshire and shared a last wicket stand of 218 in two and a half hours with Peter Smith, an Essex record and the seventh highest last wicket stand in cricket history.

Vigar's best bowling performance had come

against Leicestershire at Clacton the previous season, and, surprisingly, his highest first-class score was 145 for Middlesex and Essex against Kent and Surrey at Kingston-upon-Thames, 1947, his only first-class match that was not for his county.

His bowling was used less as time passed, and he bowled only 87 overs in the Championship in his last season, 1954. His final game was against Sussex at Hove.

He assisted West of Scotland as coach and player for three seasons before returning to Chadwell Heath in 1957. He took up an appointment with Bergers Paints as groundsman and coach, and he was later secretary of the sports club. When he retired he was working in the laboratory on inspection work. He now lives in Dorset.

M	Inns	NOs	Runs	HS	Avge	100s	Ct
256	397	62	8660	144	25.58	11	195

Overs	Mds	Runs	Wkts	Avge	Best	5/inn
2463.2	359	8958	236	37.95	8/128	8

51 (eight-ball)

John Ernest Walter WADDINGTON

Born: Woodford Green, 22 May 1910.
A right-handed batsman, John Waddington appeared in the last match of the 1931 season, against Leicestershire at Leyton. He captained Chigwell School in 1928 and topped the batting averages.

M	Inns	NOs	Runs	HS	Avge
1	1	-	8	8	8.00

Thomas Henry WADE

Born: Maldon, 24 November 1910.
Died: Colchester, 25 July 1987.

Educated at Maldon Grammar School, Tom Wade joined the Essex staff as a professional shortly after leaving school. He made his debut against Middlesex, at Leyton, in 1929, but, although batting at number ten and being played for his off-breaks, he did not bowl in spite of the fact that Middlesex scored 486 and Jack Hearne hit 285 not out. In his second match, against Surrey, at The Oval, he took 3 for 19 and followed this with 4 for 11 against Nottinghamshire in a friendly at Colchester. He finished the season with 33 first-class wickets at 25.57 runs each, and it was believed that Essex had found a first-rate off-spinner who also gave indication that he would become a most capable left-handed batsman.

A shoulder injury prevented him from playing at all in 1930, and when he returned in 1931 he bowled little. By 1933, he had begun to keep wicket. In June 1934, he displaced Sheffield who had been the regular 'keeper, and when Sheffield re-turned to the side it was as a batsman and slip fielder. Tom Wade was to be the Essex wicket-keeper for the rest of his career, only giving way on occasions to amateur 'keepers of the standard of A.G.Powell.

A soccer player, at centre half, for Leytonstone, Chel-msford and Southend United, Tom Wade was a quiet, witty, cheerful man who became most popular and was something of a character with his high-pitched appeal and his 'parcel-wrapping' mannerism while awaiting the bowler's delivery. Although he opened the innings on occasions, his batting never fulfilled his early promise, and he was most effective when he scored useful runs late in the order. His highest score was to be his 96 against Oxford University in 1932.

He went on a private trip to Australia in the winter of 1936-37 when G.O.Allen's side was touring there. Injuries to Ames and Duckworth left the party short of a wicket-keeper, and Wade was called upon to keep in the matches against South Australia and Victoria, stumping fast bowler McCormick in the second match to claim his single victim. He performed so capably, however, and was so popular that he was honoured by the award of an MCC touring cap.

A broken leg in 1946, sustained while playing football, left him with a noticeable limp, and he retired at the end of the 1950 season when he became troubled by fibrositis. He had enjoyed a benefit of £4,000 which was an Essex record at the time.

He set up as a poultry farmer at East Hanningfield, but his stock of birds was wiped out by fowl pest in 1973.

M	Inns	NOs	Runs	HS	Avge	Ct/st
318	472	135	4972	96	14.75	413/177

Overs	Mds	Runs	Wkts	Avge	Best	5/inn
452	72	1391	47	29.59	5/64	1

Hugh WAGSTAFF

Born: Romford, 15 October 1895.
Died: Hornchurch, 2 March 1970.
A right-arm medium pace bowler, Hugh Wagstaff appeared for Essex as a professional in 1920 and 1921. He had little success and was not seen after his second season.

M	Inns	NOs	Runs	HS	Avge
5	6	4	19	17*	9.50

Overs	Mds	Runs	Wkts	Avge	Best
33	5	135	2	67.50	1/19

Kenneth William WALLACE

Born: Romford, 27 August 1936.
A right-handed batsman, generally an opener, Ken Wallace has been one of the most prolific run-scorers in club cricket in South East England, initially with Romford, but more recently with Leigh-on-Sea.

Having worked for most of his life in the building industry, Wallace played for Essex 2nd XI over a number of years and led the side on many occasions. His matches for the county side were spread between 1967 and 1972 when he was invariably drafted in as a late replacement for a batsman who was injured. He never let the side down, and one has the feeling that had he played regularly, he would have been a very useful county cricketer.

Typical of Wallace's experiences were being called up for one John Player League game in 1970, and, in 1972, being brought in as a late replacement for the injured Keith Fletcher in the third round Gillette Cup match against Kent at Leyton. Kent were bowled out for 137, and Wallace and Edmeades started the Essex innings with 55 in 25 overs, only to see the rest of the batting collapse and Essex lose by ten runs.

M	Inns	NOs	Runs	HS	Avge	Ct
19	16	-	219	55	13.68	2

Sunday League

M	Inns	NOs	Runs	HS	Avge
1	1	-	1	1	1.00

Gillette Cup

M	Inns	NOs	Runs	HS	Avge
1	1	-	25	25	25.00

Brian WARD

Born: Chelmsford, 28 February 1944.
A somewhat dour right-handed batsman who generally batted in the middle-order but opened the innings on occasions, Brian Ward was educated at Chelmsford Technical High School and played for Chelmsford CC. He was on the groundstaff at Lord's from 1961 to 1966, and he played 20 games for Derbyshire 2nd XI during his last two seasons at Lord's. He had already appeared for Essex 2nd XI as early as 1963, and, in spite of hitting a century while assisting Derbyshire 2nd XI, he joined the Essex staff in 1967.

He quickly won a place in the side at what was an unsettled period in the club's history, and he hit his first century, against Middlesex, at Lord's, in August 1967. The following year, he blossomed, hitting 948 runs, and he was capped in 1970. His highest aggregate was in 1971 when he scored 968 runs. The 101 he made against Bedfordshire the same year was

the first century hit by an Essex batsman in the Gillette Cup.

He left the staff after the 1973 season and went to Argentina where his wife was born. He appeared for that country in the ICC Trophy in 1979, batting with customary caution. He coached in Argentina and was in business, but, following the Falklands conflict, he separated from his wife, the daughter of an Army officer, and now runs an electrical store in Uruguay.

M	Inns	NOs	Runs	HS	Avge	100s	Ct
128	222	19	4779	164*	23.64	4	60

Overs	Mds	Runs	Wkts	Avge	Best
24.4	4	68	5	13.60	2/5

Benson and Hedges Cup

M	Inns	NOs	Runs	HS	Avge
5	5	-	62	17	12.40

Sunday League

M	Inns	NOs	Runs	HS	Avge	Ct
56	54	3	1138	99	22.31	17

Gillette Cup

M	Inns	NOs	Runs	HS	Avge	100s	Ct
9	9	1	243	101	30.37	1	3

Geoffrey Hubert WARD

Born: Rainham, Kent, 22 November 1926.
Educated at King's School, Rochester, and Sutton Valence School where he shone as a batsman and a bowler in 1943, Geoff Ward was on the Kent staff as a wicket-keeper and played in two matches in 1949. The following season, he kept wicket for Essex against the Combined Services at Chelmsford. He did not appear in first-class cricket again.

M	Inns	NOs	Runs	HS	Avge	Ct
1	2	-	4	2	2.00	1

Brian WARSOP

Born: Willesden, Middlesex, 12 January 1904.
The grandson of the famous bat manufacturer who had a business in Chelmsford, Brian Warsop was a left-arm bowler and a right-handed batsman. He played against Northamptonshire at Northampton in July 1931, batting low in the order and bowling one maiden over. The following season, he appeared in the *away* matches against Derbyshire, Leicestershire, Nottinghamshire and Warwickshire, scoring 51 at Edgbaston, but he did not appear again.

He was assistant coach at the Aubrey Faulkner School of Cricket.

M	Inns	NOs	Runs	HS	Avge	Ct
5	10	2	128	51	16.00	1

Overs	Mds	Runs	Wkts	Avge
6	1	18	-	-

Alfred George WATERMAN

Born: Walthamstow, 13 May 1911.
Chairman of Essex CCC from 1978 to 1984, and a tireless worker for the club for many years, 'Tiny' Waterman was also a very fine cricketer, a fast- medium pace bowler and a hard-hitting batsman. As a youngster, he was coached by Johnny Douglas, a man for whom he had the greatest admiration, and he played

alongside W.G.Spencer in the Bancroft's side, topping the bowling averages in 1928.

Tall, well built, and at times genuinely quick, he played club cricket for Woodford Wells, and, taking leave from his work in the timber trade, he made his debut for Essex against Yorkshire, at Ilford in June 1937. On his first day in county cricket, he took the wickets of Hutton, Leyland, Sellers and Smailes at a personal cost of 79 runs, an extraordinarily fine debut.

He was never to be quite so successful with the ball again in county cricket, but at Chelmsford, in 1938, he hit 70 not out against Somerset with some fierce driving, added 109 for the ninth wicket with Ray Smith, and took his side to first innings points. In the return match at Bath, he hit 14 fours in an innings of 103 which was marked by some fine off-drives. He was awarded his county cap, but the first-class game was to see him no more.

He was commissioned in the Army in World War Two, and moved into the building supply industry when peace returned.

Blessed with a sense of history and motivated by a passion for the county club, 'Tiny' Waterman played a major part in the rise and success of Essex cricket, and he will ever be remembered for his contribution to those first golden years.

M	Inns	NOs	Runs	HS	Avge	100s	Ct
10	15	1	380	103	27.14	1	7

Overs	Mds	Runs	Wkts	Avge	Best
93	9	348	1	31.63	4/79

David WATKINS

Born: St Albans, Hertfordshire, 18 August 1928.
A fine all-rounder with the Southend club, whom he captained for several seasons, David Watkins bowled fast medium and was a stylish right-handed batsman. He was educated at Westcliff County High School and

was later to do a year's course at Reading University. He first played for the county side in 1949, taking three wickets in the match against Northamptonshire at Westcliff. He was not seen again until 1953 when, with Trevor Bailey on Test duty, he appeared in six Championship matches. His final appearances came the following season.

Watkins continued to play club cricket for Southend until he was 60, and he runs his own business, Thames Estuary Plastics in Benfleet.

M	Inns	NOs	Runs	HS	Avge	Ct
12	17	4	210	32	16.15	5

Overs	Mds	Runs	Wkts	Avge	Best
115.3	20	421	8	52.62	2/45

Lieutenant-Colonel Arthur Campbell WATSON

Born: Henfold, Newdigate, Surrey, 17 March 1884.
Died: Shermanbury , Partridge Green, Sussex, 16 January 1952.
'At his best he was one of the hardest hitters of

all time but he possessed little defence and was therefore inconsistent,' so wrote *The Cricketer* when Watson died in 1952. He was in the Uppingham XI in 1901 and went straight from school into the Army, fighting in the South African War of 1902 as a young officer.

In 1913 and 1914, he played for Essex, scoring 16 and 37 against Derbyshire at Derby in the first year, and 24 and 12 against Leicestershire at Leicester in the second.

He served in India and Egypt during World War One and was awarded the Distinguished Service Order. He had played for Norfolk in 1906, and between 1922 and 1928 he played quite regularly for Sussex. In his first season

with Sussex, batting at number ten, he hit 111 not out in 85 minutes against Northamptonshire at Hove.

M	Inns	NOs	Runs	HS	Avge	Ct
2	4	-	89	37	22.25	2

Charles John Manning WATTS

Born: Kislingbury, Northampton, 30 September 1905.
Died: Northampton, 8 February 1985.
Charles Watts was a Regular Army officer in the Northamptonshire Regiment who had been in the XI at Repton and had played for the RMC Sandhurst before playing in eight matches for Essex in 1928, generally as a wicket-keeper. He hit 41 in the second innings of the match against Kent at Leyton.

He served with the Suffolk Regiment in World War Two and was mentioned in dispatches while with the British Expeditionary Force in France in 1940 and again while in action in Malaya in 1942. He was one of several cricketers to be taken prisoner when Singapore fell in February 1942.

M	Inns	NOs	Runs	HS	Avge	Ct/st
8	11	-	119	41	10.81	2/2

Overs	Mds	Runs	Wkts	Avge
0.2	-	4	-	-

Hubert Percy WAUGH

Born: West Ham, 24 December 1898.
Died: Dollis Hill, Middlesex, 13 December 1954.
Captain of cricket at Forest School, H.P.Waugh was a right-handed opening batsman an a right-arm medium pace bowler. In 1919, he made his debut for Essex, playing against the Australian Imperial Forces and in the subsequent county matches against Lancashire and Surrey. His appearances for the county were to be very limited, but in 1928, he hit 128 against Glamorgan at Leyton. Strong in the cut, he batted for over four hours and put on 161 for the first wicket with Cutmore. *Wisden* said that there was only one false stroke to mar a splendid innings, but legend has it that Johnny Douglas, in his last year as captain, was uncomplimentary about Waugh's knock.

Waugh last played for Essex in 1929, but he was renowned in club cricket in Essex and

London, excelling with the Buckhurst Hill club and playing for the Club Cricket Conference.

In 1933, he moved to Felixstowe and became captain of the local club. He first played for Suffolk the following year, and he captained the county from 1935 until the outbreak of World War Two. He was a tower of strength as batsman and new-ball bowler.

He moved to Bournemouth and died following an operation shortly before his 56th birthday.

M	Inns	NOs	Runs	HS	Avge	100s	Ct
8	14	-	213	128	15.21	1	8

Overs	Mds	Runs	Wkts	Avge	Best
44	7	135	3	45.00	1/6

Mark Edward WAUGH

Born: Canterbury, Sydney, New South Wales, Australia, 2 June 1965.

When Allan Border returned to Australia in August 1988, in order to prepare for his country's tour of Pakistan Mark Waugh, recommended by Border, replaced him as Essex's overseas player. Waugh's first appearance was in the Sunday League match against Nottinghamshire at Colchester. He hit 103, took the wickets at Robinson and Randall at a personal cost of 16 runs, and Essex had a new hero.

In three Championship matches before the end of the season, he averaged 44.50, and the 1989 season was eagerly anticipated. He did not disappoint. He finished 1989 as Essex's leading run-scorer, and he complemented his batting with some beautifully athletic fielding and some brilliant catching in the gully.

Mark Waugh, whose twin brother Stephen won a place in the Australian side in 1985-86, the same year in which Mark himself first played for New South Wales, won immediate acclaim as a glorious clean striker of the ball. Somewhat retiring and modest by nature, he expressed himself in extrovert fashion with the bat. There was that air of arrogance which only the truly great possess, the dismissal of the bowler. In 1990, he became a Test player, and in his first Test match against England he scored a brilliant century.

More than 2000 runs in 1990, including eight Championship centuries, two of them double centuries, placed Waugh fifth in the national averages. He missed the 1991 season

because he was on duty with Australia, but he returned in 1992 in all his ease and glory. He topped the national averages, only Salim Malik of Pakistan bettering his 77.29, and his medium pace bowling brought him 21 Championship wickets.

There were moments of unforgettable brilliance. In Southend Week, Gloucestershire set Essex a target of 335 in 61 overs. At 181 for 5, the cause seemed lost, but Waugh reached his century off 93 balls. He and Foster added 116 in 16 overs, and Waugh finished unbeaten on 125 as Essex won with 13 balls to spare. Sussex were the next visitors, and they made 429 by the second morning. On the last afternoon, with Gooch making his second century of the match, Waugh hit 85 not out off 79 balls, and Essex won with ease.

At the end of July, he played against Gloucestershire in the NatWest Trophy victory at Cheltenham, and then he was gone. Australia needed him. He left behind a memory of dazzling strokes of classical beauty and immense power. Like the very greatest of actors, he left the scene with his audience hungry for more.

His Test match triumphs continue, and, in 1992-93, he averaged over 100 for New South

Wales. In 1990-91, the Waugh twins added an unbroken 464 for New South Wales' fifth wicket against Western Australia in Perth, the highest stand for any wicket in Australia.

M	Inns	NOs	Runs	HS	Avge	100s	Ct
65	100	17	5101	219*	61.46	16	78

Overs	Mds	Runs	Wkts	Avge	Best	5/inn
505	83	1932	48	40.25	5/37	1

Sunday League

M	Inns	NOs	Runs	HS	Avge	100s	Ct
47	45	11	1738	112*	51.12	4	16

Overs	Mds	Runs	Wkts	Avge	Best
135.4	4	772	25	30.88	3/26

Benson and Hedges Cup

M	Inns	NOs	Runs	HS	Avge	100s	Ct
16	14	1	438	100	33.69	1	5

Overs	Mds	Runs	Wkts	Avge	Best
15.5	-	76	4	19.00	3/31

NatWest Trophy

M	Inns	NOs	Runs	HS	Avge	Ct
6	5	-	105	47	21.00	1

Overs	Mds	Runs	Wkts	Avge	Best
19	2	81	1	81.00	1/51

Gordon Harry Sinclair WEST

Born: Upton Park, 7 August 1923.
Gordon West was a highly successful club cricketer, a dominant batsman with Southend. At the beginning of the 1949 season, he opened the Essex innings against Cambridge University at Fenner's and was run out for 55 in the first innings. Four years later, at Romford, he opened the innings against a strong Commonwealth XI. These were his only two appearances in first-class cricket.

West ran a highly successful family wholesale greengrocery business, and he now lives in Switzerland.

M	Inns	NOs	Runs	HS	Avge
2	4	-	79	55	19.75

Leslie Harold WEST

Born: Leytonstone, 24 January 1905.
Died: Leytonstone, 12 November 1982.
A stylish right-handed batsman, Leslie West scored heavily in club cricket for Ilford and Wanstead, and he did an immense amount of good work when in charge of the youth coaching at Wanstead.

He was given a trial for Essex as a professional in 1928. He made 0 on his debut against Northamptonshire at Kettering, and a month later he played against Glamorgan and Northamptonshire at Leyton, hitting 30 in the first of these matches. For a man who gave his life to cricket, it was, perhaps, appropriate that he should die at a club supper.

M	Inns	NOs	Runs	HS	Avge
3	5	-	33	30	6.60

Henry Maurice WHITCOMBE

Born: Hardwick, Buckinghamshire, 15 August 1900.
Died: Ware, Hertfordshire, 2 April 1984.
Brother of P.S.Whitcombe, Henry Whitcombe was a left-arm fast-medium pace bowler who played three matches for Essex in 1922 as an amateur.

Educated at Haileybury, Whitcombe's debut for Essex was at Tonbridge where Kent got 621 for 6, and he was one of four Essex bowlers to reach the 100 mark. His one wicket came early in his second match when he dismissed the Sussex opener Street, but another blank against Cambridge University a week later marked the end of his first-class career.

M	Inns	NOs	Runs	HS	Avge	Ct
3	4	2	13	7*	6.50	1

Overs	Mds	Runs	Wkts	Avge	Best
40	5	199	1	199.00	1/34

Major-General Philip Sidney WHITCOMBE

Born: Windsor, Berkshire, 3 October 1893.
Died: Hindhead, Surrey, 9 September 1989.
Six feet five inches tall, P.S.Whitcombe was a Regular Army officer, one of the 'Old Contemptibles' who fought in France throughout World War One. He was an upright, right-handed batsman whose one first-class game for Essex was in 1922 against Somerset at Leyton. He made five and four and did not take a wicket with his fast-medium pace.

A member of MCC for 68 years, he played

much club and Army cricket, and he assisted Berkshire, when available, between 1925 and 1933. He played first-class cricket in India for the Europeans, and, in a distinguished career, was awarded the OBE and the Companion of the Order of the Bath. His brother Henry played a few games for Essex in 1922, and his son, Philip Arthur, got his blue at Oxford, 1947-49, and assisted Middlesex as a fast bowler in 1948.

M	Inns	NOs	Runs	HS	Avge
1	2	-	9	5	4.50

Overs	Mds	Runs	Wkts	Avge
4	1	22	-	-

Denys Robert WILCOX

Born: Westcliff-on-Sea, 4 June 1910.
Died: Westcliff-on-Sea, 6 February 1953.
An outstanding all-rounder at Dulwich College from 1926 until 1929, Denys Wilcox scored a record number of runs for the school and first played for Essex in 1928, two years before he went up to Cambridge. He was in the Cambridge side in all his three years at the university, hitting 157 in his second Varsity match, 1932, and captaining the XI the following season.

Although his off-break bowling was virtually abandoned after his school days, he remained a stylish right-handed batsman of the highest class. He was joint captain of Essex from 1933 until 1939, but he was never able to play regularly because of his duties as

Headmaster of Alleyn Court, a preparatory school in the Southend area which still belongs to the Wilcox family.

In 1938, there was great speculation that he would lead England against Australia, and he captained The Rest against England in the Test trial at Lord's, but he failed to do himself justice, and his chance of an England cap really disappeared when Hammond decided to play as an amateur.

He enlisted in the Army at the outbreak of war and reached the rank of lieutenant, but he was invalided out in 1941. He played ten innings in 1946 and topped the Championship averages, but six matches in the following season were his last for the county.

He continued to do splendid work for Essex and for cricket. He arranged one of the first coaching seminars to be run in this country, and one of his early charges, T.E.Bailey, followed him to Dulwich, Cambridge and Essex. Tragically, Denys Wilcox died of leukaemia at the age of 42. One of his sons, John, also played for Essex.

M	Inns	NOs	Runs	HS	Avge	100s	Ct
118	186	8	5482	142	30.79	8	88

Overs	Mds	Runs	Wkts	Avge	Best
18.5	1	117	1	117.00	1/46

John Warren Theodore WILCOX

Born: Newton Abbot, Devon, 16 August 1940.
Son of the Essex captain of the 1930s Denys

Wilcox, John Wilcox was educated at Malvern and went up to Cambridge where he played first-class cricket in 1961 and 1962. He was unlucky not to get his blue. A capable right-handed batsman and a good fielder, he was able to play for Essex only occasionally as, like his father, he became Head of Alleyn Court School. John Wilcox came in to the county side during the school holidays in 1964, played in ten matches and finished first among Essex batsmen in the national averages. He played a significant part in Essex's first victory over the Australians since 1905.

He could play in only five matches and a Gillette Cup match at the beginning of the 1965 season when he hit 87 against Worcestershire. He did not appear in 1966, and four matches in 1967 marked the end of his first-class career.

John Wilcox captained Westcliff for a period, and, while still retaining a family interest in Alleyn Court School, he relinquished the headship and moved to Nether Stowey in Somerset where he runs an art gallery that specialises in 19th and 20th-century paintings. The gallery is in the same street as the home of 'Hopper' Read.

John Wilcox's brother Michael is the noted playwright.

M	Inns	NOs	Runs	HS	Avge	Ct
19	30	5	596	87	23.84	11

Gillette Cup

M	Inns	NOs	Runs	HS	Avge
1	1	-	2	2	2.00

Charles Cuthbert Powell WILLIAMS, Lord Williams of Elvel

Born: Oxford, 9 February 1933.

A very talented middle-order batsman who captained Oxford University in 1955, Charles Williams became lost to Essex cricket because of the demands of business and politics. Welsh in ancestry, Charles Williams is the son of a Doctor of Divinity and was educated at Westminster School. He was in the school XI for four years, captain in his last, and was awarded Public Schools' caps in 1950 and 1951. While at school he made his debut for Oxfordshire and played for them for three seasons.

In spite of his feats as a youngster, he failed to get his blue as a freshman, but he was in the side for three years and exceeded 1000 runs in all matches in his last two seasons. He made his debut for Essex against Leicestershire at Chelmsford in 1954, and he was to play for the county on an irregular basis over the next five years.

In all, he appeared in 40 matches for Essex and hit 119 against Leicestershire at Leicester in 1955. His last match was against Gloucestershire at Leyton in 1959. Had he been able to play more regularly, Charles

Williams would have been a batsman of real quality. As it was, he was of immense value whenever available.

He went into business, working for BP, the Bank of London and Montreal and Eurofinance SA. His work took him to Rome, Brussels, Guatemala, the United States and Paris before he became managing director of Baring Brothers, the merchant bankers, 1971 to 1977. He attempted to play for local clubs wherever his travels took him.

In 1964, he stood as Labour candidate for Colchester, but he was unsuccessful, but he became chairman of the Government Prices Commission in 1977. When this was dissolved by Mrs Thatcher in 1979 he returned to banking. In 1980, he received the CBE, and in 1985, he was made a Life Peer. He is most active on the Opposition Front Bench in the House of Lords and is a heartily fit man of vigour and charm.

He is president of the Campaign for the Protection of Rural Wales, and, until recently, he was chairman of that finest of recording orchestras, the Academy of St Martins in the Fields.

M	Inns	NOs	Runs	HS	Avge	100s	Ct
40	68	3	1518	119	23.35	1	23

Overs	Mds	Runs	Wkts	Avge
2.1	1	5	-	-

Herbert Reginald Hewett WILLIAMS

Born: Hendon, Middlesex, 7 June 1900.
Died: Denmark Hill, London, 19 July 1974.
Herbert Williams was in the Charterhouse XI in 1917 and 1918 and kept wicket for Essex

occasionally in 1919 and 1920. He won the DSO in World War Two.

M	Inns	NOs	Runs	HS	Avge	Ct/st
10	12	2	67	23*	6.70	18/7

Leonard Dale WOMERSLEY

Born: Frynerning Green, Ingatestone, 10 September 1891.
Died: Chelmsford, 10 February 1971.
Dale Womersley was in the Marlborough XI but played no first-class cricket at Oxford where, however, he did represent the university against Cambridge at billiards. He played for Essex against Derbyshire at Derby in 1910 although there was some confusion as to whether it was he or his brother Aleck who appeared.

M	Inns	NOs	Runs	HS	Avge
1	2	-	9	9	4.50

Albert Edward WRIGHT

Born: Great Leighs, 11 August 1902.
Died: Great Leighs, 8 November 1984.
A right-arm fast bowler and right-handed batsman, Albert Wright played against Sussex and Glamorgan at Chelmsford in 1931. He reappeared in the match against Somerset at Colchester in 1934. He played as an amateur.

M	Inns	NOs	Runs	HS	Avge	Ct
3	5	1	45	14	11.25	1

Overs	Mds	Runs	Wkts	Avge
40	8	86	-	-

John Vaughan WRIGHT

Born: Colchester, 31 December 1935.
Educated at Colchester Royal Grammar School, John Wright captained the Colchester and East Essex club and played for Essex in the two matches in Colchester Week, 1962. He hit 40 in his first innings against Northamptonshire.

It seemed that that would be the extent of his first-class career, but he reappeared in Colchester week in 1967, playing against Middlesex and the Pakistan touring side.

M	Inns	NOs	Runs	HS	Avge	Ct
4	6	-	60	40	10.00	2

Roger Wilfrid WRIGHTSON

Born: Elescar, Yorkshire, 29 October 1939.
Died: Carlisle, Cumberland, 13 September 1986.
Roger Wrightson once said that his father, who worked for Pergamon Press, had turned his sons round when they first held a cricket bat and made them all left-handers. Roger himself was a natural sportsman, excelling at whatever he put himself to. At soccer, he would take off his spectacles before heading a cross into the net, and, when playing for Orsett and Thurrock, he was known to take a catch behind his back on occasions to show how easy it all was. He excelled, but there was no conceit in him, just fun.

He had an outstanding sporting career at Palmer's School, Grays, and went from there to Loughborough where he captained a most successful cricket XI. He often kept wicket, but then he could do most things, and he played often for Essex Club and Ground and Essex 2nd XI in the early 1960s.

Roger Wrightson became a primary teacher in Thurrock and was on the Essex staff in 1965 and was hailed as by far the most promising newcomer, hitting 84 against Warwickshire at Clacton. This was the match in which A.C.Smith did the hat-trick against Essex. Late in the season, Wrightson had two front teeth knocked out by a Freddie Trueman bouncer. Indestructible, he showed the art of drinking a pint of beer with a straw through the gap in his teeth, and a week later he was back in action.

He played little after the 1965 season, and his last two matches for the county were in 1967. He decided not to accept the terms he was offered by Essex and remained in teaching. He and his wife Audrey, an art teacher, moved to Cumbria, and Roger played for Cumberland in 1970 and 1971. He kept his links with Essex before his tragically early death at the age of 47.

M	Inns	NOs	Runs	HS	Avge	Ct
12	20	4	332	84	20.75	8

Nigel Gordon WYKES

Born: Woodford, 19 March, 1906.
Died: Bridport, Dorset, 4 December 1991.
'Tiger' Wykes was not only a most capable left-handed batsman and left-arm medium pace bowler at Oundle, he was also an outstanding scholar. He first played for Essex in 1925, appearing in the last match of the season against Leicestershire at Leyton. He was up at Cambridge the following season and was brought in to the side for the last of the home matches. It was against Nottinghamshire, and he was unfortunate to encounter a rampant Larwood.

In his one game for Cambridge the following season, he scored 145 not out against the Army, and he also hit a splendid 162 in four and a half hours for Essex against Kent at Leyton. He finally got his blue in 1928, but even then he batted at number nine rather than his usual opening spot.

He took up a teaching post at Eton, becoming a most respected housemaster, so that he was only available for Essex in the holiday period. He played until 1936 and captained the county on occasions towards the end of the 1935 season.

Nigel Wykes toured Canada with an MCC side in 1937, and his younger brother James played for Scotland in 1946. Wykes was a most cultured man, a gifted artist, gardener, lepidopterist and connoisseur of fine wine and good music.

M	Inns	NOs	Runs	HS	Avge	100s	Ct
30	42	3	879	162	22.53	1	5

Overs	Mds	Runs	Wkts	Avge
18	3	52	-	-

Harding Isaac YOUNG

Born: Leyton, 5 February 1876.
Died: Rochford, 12 December 1964.
Born at Leyton, Harding Young joined the Royal Navy and made his mark in minor cricket. C.E.Green, one of the greatest of benefactors to Essex county cricket, saw Young bowling in the nets and was so impressed by the left-arm medium pace delivered from a good height with what was later described as 'a deceptive curve' that he bought Young out of the service and enrolled him on the Essex staff. From that time on, Harding Young became 'Sailor' Young.

He first played for Essex in June 1898, against Derbyshire at Leyton where Green had spotted him. In four overs, he took the wickets of Storer and Sugg; three more wickets followed in the second innings.

The Essex side of the period was a predominantly amateur one, and Young could not command a regular place in his first season, but a return of 5 for 65 against Kent at the end of July gave some indication of what was to come.

Essex began their 1899 campaign with a match against the Australian touring side at Leyton. This side, led by Joe Darling, was, in the opinion of Jack Pollard, the Australian cricket historian, 'one of the best of all Australian teams, strong in every department'. Certainly they won the series against England, and certainly Essex bowed to them on the opening day when Hugh Trumble caused havoc and sent back eight of the first nine batsmen. When 'Sailor' Young joined former skipper A.P.Lucas, the score was 144 for nine.

Imitating what he had seen Tom Russell do, Young hit at everything. In half an hour he scored 33 and the last wicket realised 55. Rightly, the Australians viewed the pitch with suspicion, for Trumble had taken 8 for 79, and if Young was an unknown quantity, Walter Mead was established as a very fine bowler indeed. The Australian fears seemed mostly unfounded when they ended the day on 75 for 3, but on the second morning they floundered against Mead and Young, who bowled the great Victor Trumper for 0, and Essex took a first innings lead of 55.

Losing their first three wickets before lunch for eight, and their last six wickets for 43, Essex appeared to have surrendered the match. The tourists had the whole of the last day, the Saturday, in which to score 200 to win the match.

Mead and Young bowled unchanged, and, in the words of *Cricket,* 'occasionally made the ball do unconscionable things'. The Aus-

tralians panicked. *Wisden* reported later, 'Young won the match for Essex on the Saturday morning and at the same time establishing his fame as a bowler. He was practically unplayable, pitching outside the off stump and turning in six or eight inches with his arm.'

In his first season, 1898, Young had taken 19 wickets. He had begun his second season with match figures of 11 for 74. Essex's famous victory and his second innings 7 for 32 prompted a collection on the ground for the professionals, and more than £46 was raised.

Young had ten wickets against Kent at the end of May, then 7 for 100 and 8 for 54 against Warwickshire at Edgbaston in June. A week later, he was in the England side at Headingley and took 4 for 30 and 2 for 72.

For the Players against the Gentlemen at The Oval, he took seven wickets and hit 81 in 75 minutes as he and Hayward put on 135 for the last wicket. There were six wickets in the Old Trafford Test match, but he never played for England again.

He finished the 1899 season with 139 wickets in all matches. Young was not to reach 100 wickets in a season again, and the following years saw a gradual decline until, by 1907, he had ceased to play regularly although it was in that season that he became the second Essex bowler to perform the hat-trick. He accomplished the feat in the match against Leicestershire at Leyton.

'Sailor' Young went with the MCC team to West Indies, 1910-11, but in 1912, a dreadful season for Essex, he played his last match for the county.

'Sailor' Young never quite lived up to the standard that he set in 1899, but he was troubled for much of his career by muscular rheumatism, and this handicapped him greatly. He was tall, raw-boned and tough with exceptionally long arms which seemed to hang almost to his knees. He bowled his left-arm round the wicket and could pose awkward problems. A character rich in wit and never lost for words, he was on the groundstaff at Lord's for many years, and from 1921 to 1931, he was a first-class umpire. He stood in three Test matches, and he was considered to be sound if loquacious. Until late in his life he coached schoolboy cricketers.

M	Inns	NOs	Runs	HS	Avge	Ct
128	186	50	1413	44	10.38	59

Overs	Mds	Runs	Wks	Avge	Best	10/m	5/inn
2435.4	883	9092	368	24.70	8/54	3	18
1108.1 (five-ball)							

Subscribers

1	Nicholas Ridley	57	Derek Pedder	113	Kenneth W Bennett
2	David Lemmon	58	Susan Cruickshank	114	G Andrews
3	Tony Debenham	59	Robert Hannan	115	Michael Dowsett
4	Mike Marshall	60	Trevor MacDonald	116	J S Biles
5	D J Insole CBE, MA	61	Adrian & Jennifer Randall	117	Arthur Albert Scollay MM
6	Peter J Edwards	62	R D Lee	118	Robert H Williams
7	John Perry	63	E M Ring	119	Brian Copp
8	Derek Maddison	64	Derek White	120	Brian Anderson
9	G H Conroy	65	K E Radcliffe	121	Ian Smith
10	Derek Chetwin	66	Ian C McEwen	122	Mrs Joyce Traxler
11	Roy Beadle	67	Martin Broom	123	Peter Bailey
12	Robin M Hornsby	68	Andrew Morrison	124	Kenneth Thomas Bailey
13	Malcolm Jarvis	69	Bruce Morrison	125	Geoff Gilbert
14	Terence F Stevens	70	J Kearney	126	Mark Greensill
15	Michael Kerry	71	Mr Geoffrey M Painter	127	Simon Smith
16	Ivor T Hobson	72	Mr Phillip James Swarbrick	128	John M Spackman
17	Mrs Z Travers	73	Steven J Lucas	129	John M Spackman
18	Brian G Bell	74	Colin Brown	130	Michael Shea
19	Ron Ketteridge	75	Tony Tween	131	M H Clark
20	David Elliott	76	Mr W M Horder	132	Helen Groom
21	Tim Short	77	Michael J Lay	133	Alex White
22	Dennis H Bustard	78	P S I Duncan	134	Alex White
23	M K Smith	79	P S I Duncan	135	Brian Hill
24	Mr Frank R Bishop	80	David Smith	136	Philip Bragg
25	Colin Harris	81	Mr R R A Harlow	137	Dan Trueman
26	Austin Burgess	82	E J Hebdidge	138	Barrie Powell
27	Michael E Smith	83	V C Law	139	Mr Paul Staines
28	Mr David Andrew Root	84	D H W Frith	140	L Lock-Dingle
29	A W Guest	85	D H W Frith	141	Joy Wood
30	Martin & Beryl Speed	86	D H W Frith	142	J C Swankie
31	Peter David Speller	87	M T Osborne	143	Robin Woods
32	Peter Gay	88	Brian Kemp	144	Stephen Lemy Franks
33	David John Flack	89	Rowena Legg	145	John R Chalmers
34	M R Hatchard	90	Alan Stanley Quinton	146	Mrs Eileen Palmer
35	Paul Burrell	91	George Sealy	147	Toni Anderson
36	T G Penman	92	C G Russell	148	Peter Smith
37	Stephen Trump	93	Rodney Kingham	149	Richard Chapman
38	Arthur Allen	94	R Shaw	150	P J Locke
39	Andrew Long	95	Laurence Henry Castor	151	Mrs M J Shakespeare
40	Peter Collins	96	Geoffrey McGregor	152	Geoff Williams
41	R C Moseley	97	E J Bernthall	153	John Lester
42	David Ebert	98	Jeff Lewington	154	Alan Goodchild
43	Mr Stephen E Hammond	99	Stephen Kerry	155	Colin Howes
44	Peter Pushman	100	Peter C Scutton	156	Clive Le Gresley
45	Dr Turner	101	Alan Sayles	157	Thomas Douglas Clyde
46	B S Chapman	102	Old Chelmsfordians Assoc.	158	H Shelsher
47	Peter C Saunders	103	Peter J Turner	159	Ian J Sutherland
48	David Beaumont	104	R H Gooch	160	Mrs M Lanham
49	John K Bright	105	B A B Barton	161	Jonathan Coles
50	Mr J W James	106	Gregory Colbourne	162	Michael Frank Tomlin
51	John H Barelli	107	B W Tames	163	John W Deal
52	Kevin J Howlin	108	Richard H I Chown	164	Derek Roy Jenkins
53	Mr & Mrs C H Keys	109	R Jarvis	165	S E Pinnock
54	Mr M Ebsworth	110	David Newton	166	Mrs Irene Ramm
55	David Ives	111	Ronald Butteriss	167	Gerry Barnes
56	W Brown	112	Mr Tom Roast	168	Roger Jennings

169	Brian Ellis	229	Richard J Lord	289	Peter Hennem
170	Mr J P Randall	230	Mr J C Hill	290	Mr R N Pack
171	Ian Sinclair	231	Simon Brown	291	Ken Cooper
172	M D Morris	232	Ron Balls	292	Enid Fordham
173	M C Lazell & Co Ltd	233	Richard Turbet	293	Richard Tye
174	Andrew Morea	234	David Gordon Kilburn	294	Dr David Beckitt
175	Duncan Sheekey	235	Malcolm F Hyde	295	Len Tarling
176	C R Walne	236	Professor Brian Goodey	296	Jim Kendrick
177	D B Rundle	237	S B Albiston	297	Nick Hammond
178	John Barter	238	Mr C J D Green	298	Chris Missing
179	Steve Peacock	239	Mr W H Green	299	F E M Allen
180	Paul E Knight	240	H A Faragher	300	F E M Allen
181	John Jeffrey Stentiford	241	H A Faragher	301	V C Fitzpatrick
182	D E Williams	242	L A Farrow	302	Anthony W Mallinson
183	Bryan E Herman	243	Alan Viney	303	Paul Cockburn
184	Robert H Smith	244	Brian Fitzgerald	304	Denis Crapnell
185	P N H Russell	245	David Lord	305	John House
186	Les Hockley	246	John Lord	306	Roy W R Titterrell
187	Martin Renshaw	247	Mrs Jean Black	307	Alan Watkins
188	Robert Bowden	248	Mrs Lorna M Piper	308	D J Rayner
189	Alan Renny	249	Doulin	309	Nigel E Smith
190	Norman Broom	250	W Wilford	310	Graham J Budd
191	Brian A Sedgwick	251	Howard A Allen	311	David Robson
192	Ronald Frederick Croot	252	Roger Lord	312	Dennis Cole-Smith
193	J R A Gear	253	Michael Robert Curnow	313	Ken Newbery
194	W R Gear	254	Christopher R Woods	314	Terence John Bright
195	A T Gear	255	Brian Heald	315	S G Brabner
196	Peter Snow	256	Donald James Wilkes	316	B W D Kemp
197	David Barton	257	Mr John G McDermid	317	Colin John Finch
198	Kenneth W Newbury	258	Michael Lawes	318	Tony A Hawkes
199	Andrew Eastwick	259	Philip Rozee	319	Margaret Bedford
200	Steven Wright	260	Martin J Fleetwood	320	Peter Gaston
201	Paul Brice	261	Peter Johnson	321	Peter Gaston
202	John Summerhill	262	Mr E S Melbourne	322	Kevin Watts
203	Brian Denton	263	Adrian J Hayward	323	Ken Rydings
204	Peter Thorn	264	Darren Christopher Hayward	324	Bryan Grimshaw
205	Alan J Galley	265	M Y Jones	325	Charles Timothy Savin
206	Fred Dowry	266	Mr Andrew Merchant	326	E V Acfield
207	F C Smith	267	J A Sibley	327	Steve Kingshott
208	Janet Blackett	268	Collins Family	328	Donald Victor Rice
209	Ken H J Baldwin	269	A I Butcher	329	Ron Price
210	Alan Perry	270	John A Gilmore	330	Andrew Price
211	Richard Jones	271	Paul Mason	331	Kevin Poole
212	Hugh Jolly	272	Richard Bonnington	332	Rowland Clifford George Perry
213	D H Perkins	273	Richard Harris	333	Rowland Clifford George Perry
214	Douglas M Hart	274	Mr Michael John Wright	334	Stuart Jubb
215	Dennis J Curtin	275	Brian M C Evanson	335	Brian Taylor
216	Dennis J Curtin	276	John Brooker	336	P W Edmondson
217	Shirley Doig	277	Graham J Hendry	337	I G Bendall
218	Dr F W B Rilstone	278	Martin Hughes	338	Keith Clough
219	P Roberts	279	Steven C Davidson	339	Brian D Hermon
220	Peter C Vandervord	280	Mervyn Lyndon	340	William H Mitchell
221	Colin H Vince	281	Nigel Lewis Stockwell	341	David Reynolds
222	Mr Gerald Cohen	282	W B Morris	342	Michael W Smith
223	W P Bell	283	J C Reeve	343	Edward J Love
224	M C Sulley	284	Keith Wilfort	344	Terence Bell
225	Alan Bourne	285	Len Norris	345	W G H Tickner
226	Reg Wheeler	286	Stephen J Daniels	346	Donald A L Birrell
227	R A O'Hanrahan	287	Russell Gorringe	347	Robert Miller
228	Bradley Theobald	288	W L Wild	348	Mr Raymond Balcombe

349	Gerry Furner	409	Graham Smith	469	Geoff Davidson
350	Mr Brian Goodwin	410	Andrew R Hogg	470	Harold J Wood
351	K H Edwards	411	C Gilbert Esq	471	Bert Southwell
352	Robert J Gray	412	Christopher N Stokes	472	Derek P Simmons
353	Robert J Gray	413	D P Tilley	473	Mr G E Gostling
354	W J Worth	414	C J Hurd	474	Roger C Wright
355	Mr D H W Frith	415	R J Batchelor	475	Kenneth Merchant
356	Ken Saunders	416	Ruth and Matthew Murray	476	Barry Ennever
357	Liz Murray	417	Roger L Smith	477	David & Jane Slowgrove
358	Brian Little	418	John Langford	478	Mr R S Kendrick
359	H J Sainsbury	419	John Newland	479	John Bassom
360	Janet and Jack Allwright	420	R J Smith	480	John Bassom
361	L J Chandler	421	June Freeman	481	Ralph H H Shelley
362	Derek Chapman	422	June Freeman	482	Bernard Roy Dearlove
363	Nicholas Adam Ward	423	Bernard Phillips	483	Neil J Short
364	P J Wright	424	J A Pugh	484	G R Newman
365	William P O'Connor	425	Peter Moyes	485	David Hudd
366	G D Crysell	426	Jeffrey Fagence	486	D R Avery
367	C W Burgess	427	Michael Graham	487	David George Edney
368	Graham Ritchie	428	David Hughes	488	T F Spurling
369	Mary Bullen	429	Michael Slater	489	Graham John Webster
370	Alan Chapman	430	John M Barrs	490	Mrs Sheila Downing
371	G M Lynch	431	Matthew East	491	Alex Arthurwary
372	Alan Brooker	432	T F Evans	492	David King
373	Brian & Daphne Nurcombe	433	F C Golledge	493	Stuart Arnott
374	Mr R C G Hooper	434	Caroline Doig	494	Barry Corke
375	Trevor John Speed	435	Dr Bob Usherwood	495	C M Perkins
376	Keith Rosewell	436	J N Aves	496	C M Perkins
377	Keith Rosewell	437	Raymond David Merrell	497	S A Hands
378	D F Dunball	438	David G Rowland	498	Edward R Wright
379	Bernard A Salsbury	439	Bryan S Coker	499	J Sargeant
380	Derek Brown	440	Keith Buckley	500	Terence Reginald Biggs
381	Michael John Donges	441	Crolyn Phillips	501	Roy Wood
382	Peter Jones	442	Mr Robert Monk	502	Malcolm Everett
383	Dennis Thomas Walker	443	Mr M Ainsworth	503	Alan Chetwin
384	Michael Oliver	444	Donald W Perkins	504	Miss M J Rayner
385	Robin J H Lee	445	S D Vaughan	505	Neil Fowler
386	Colin R Bush	446	Maurice Kench	506	Leonard F Skinner
387	Robert Michael Cairns	447	Michael L Barton	507	R G Harwood
388	George A Hill	448	Colin J Mayo	508	Miss Carol Scoble
389	Jonathan and Douglas Jacobs	449	Rob Dellar	509	W R Escott
390	Tim Knights	450	David Evans	510	Frank Edwin Haines
391	Barry M Sparrow	451	Ben Gershinson	511	P W Saltmarsh
392	Ronald H Bond	452	Mr M J Tarbun	512	John Leeks
393	John Richard Middleton	453	W H Taylor	513	Mr B M Fearis
394	Gordon Layzell	454	Roger Martin	514	K F Porter
395	Glyn Appleby	455	Roger Martin	515	S T Hart
396	J P Auton	456	Roger Martin	516	P T Rippon
397	Jack Watt	457	Nigel Donald Males	517	L G Menhinick
398	Mrs Vanessa Gardner	458	N E C Shewood	518	Edward A Andrews
399	Fred Battle	459	W J Throp	519	A T Russell
400	Gordon J Hardy	460	Roderick Greig	520	D T Bryant
401	Mr H C Worsfold	461	Mrs P A Payne	521	Mr Brian Wright
402	John Frederick Abraham	462	John White	522	Mr George William Grubb
403	William Long	463	J L Reed	523	Mr Roy A Ludlow
404	C R Jenner	464	Peter J Moore	524	Gweneth E Phillips
405	C R Jenner	465	William Ballance	525	Mr A J Foster
406	Derek Banks	466	Eric Swan	526	Mr S Darkin
407	Ray Cracknell	467	A F Nicholls		
408	Alan Soane	468	R H Baker		